Popular fiction in England, 1914–1918

Harold Orel

THE UNIVERSITY PRESS OF KENTUCKY

Copyright © 1992 by Harold Orel

Published by The University Press of Kentucky, scholarly publisher for the Commonwealth, serving Bellarmine College, Berea College, Centre College of Kentucky, Eastern Kentucky University, The Filson Club, Georgetown College, Kentucky Historical Society, Kentucky State University, Morehead State University, Murray State University, Northern Kentucky University, Transylvania University, University of Kentucky, University of Louisville, and Western Kentucky University.

Editorial and Sales Office: Lexington, Kentucky 40508-4008

Library of Congress Cataloging-in-Publication Data

Orel, Harold, 1926–
  Popular fiction in England, 1914–1918 / Harold Orel.
    p. cm.
  Includes bibliographical references and index.
  ISBN 0-8131-1789-5
  1. English fiction—20th century—History and criticism.
  2. Popular literature—England—History and criticism. 3. Fiction—Appreciation—England—History—20th century. 4. World War. 1914–1918—England—Literature and the war. 5. Literature publishing—England—History—20th century. 6. Books and reading—England—History—20th century. I Title.
  PR888.P68O74   1992
  823'.91209—dc20   91-36651

Printed and bound in Great Britain

Dedicated to Frances Hawkins

Contents

Part I In the beginning

Chapter 1   At the turn of the century   3
Chapter 2   The publishing world in 1914   11
Chapter 3   Authors and the reviewing media   25

Part II Novels that ignored the war

Chapter 4   George Moore's *The Brook Kerith* (1916)   49
Chapter 5   Norman Douglas's *South Wind* (1917)   65
Chapter 6   Frank Swinnerton's *Nocturne* (1917)   79
Chapter 7   Compton Mackenzie's *The Early Life and Adventures
            of Sylvia Scarlett* (1918)   91

Part III Thunder on the horizon

Chapter 8   Mary Webb's *The Golden Arrow* (1915)   107
Chapter 9   Joseph Conrad's *Victory* (1915)   117
Chapter 10 Ford Madox Hueffer's *The Good Soldier* (1915)   125
Chapter 11 Alec Waugh's *The Loom of Youth* (1917)   135
Chapter 12 Wyndham Lewis's *Tarr* (1918)   147

Part IV Novels about the war

Chapter 13 The last year of the war   155
Chapter 14 What the reviewers of the *Times Literary Supplement*
            wrote in 1918   165

Chapter 15	John Buchan's *The Thirty-Nine Steps* (1915) and *Greenmantle* (1916)	177
Chapter 16	H. G. Wells's *Mr. Britling Sees It Through* (1916)	191
Chapter 17	On the home front: Arnold Bennett's *The Pretty Lady* (1918)	203
Chapter 18	In the trenches: (Anonymous), *The Love of an Unknown Soldier: Found in a dug-out* (1918)	215
Notes		223
Bibliography		237
Index		241

Part I

In the beginning

Chapter 1

At the turn of the century

It is not easy, some eight decades after the fact, to measure public attitudes towards the novel as a literary genre at the beginning of the twentieth century. For one thing, the public (then as now) consisted of many interest groups, and did not have a single or uniform response to the thousands of novels published in the years leading up to the Great War. For another, the collapse of the circulating-library control of the three-decker novel, dated by most literary historians as taking place in 1894, meant that novels with more candidly expressed views on pressing social problems, and with stronger links to realistic and naturalistic story-telling conventions on the Continent, could now flourish, insuring a greater variety of subject-matter. And for still another, the genteel tradition of literary criticism exhibited unmistakable signs of weariness; the pose of the man of letters who had read everything and believed that nothing new under the sun should be encouraged was increasingly irritating to intelligent readers and enterprising editors alike.

Nevertheless, an effort to understand how the novel was regarded by literary historians before the Edwardian era dissolved in the crucible of war is worth the trouble, if only to make sense of the fact that most writers of fiction during the war years avoided, as much as possible, confronting either the fact or the implications of the fact that an entire generation was being destroyed on the battlefields of Belgium and France. A literary historian would never gather, from reading most of the novels produced by English publishers between 1914 and 1918, that novelists understood how radically the European scene was being transformed. One did not have to be very prescient then to appreciate how well-nigh impossible it would be to return to pre-war conditions once the German Army had been defeated; but novels were not the place to learn that the old order was passing forever.

Lafcadio Hearn, who occupied the chair of English Literature in the Imperial University of Tokyo from 1896 to 1903, may be accounted one of the more acute critics of his time. Distance certainly sharpened his sense of what might last. His famous lecture on the literature of the second half of the nineteenth century identified three writers who had done so much to put paid to the tradition of the domestic novel, which dealt with 'family life and love and social matters'.[1] (Hearn told his students that until the public became tired of the domestic novel, in the early 1880s, no great literary change could take place.) The writers were Robert Louis Stevenson, Rudyard Kipling and George Du Maurier. Hearn, determined to recommend only writers of talent who might be appreciated by his Japanese students, had been consistent in praising Victorian novelists for their adherence to the probabilities of life. Charlotte Brontë, for example, had written in *Jane Eyre*

> the story of two very plain, very obstinate and very deep natures, alternately attracting and repelling each other, fearing to show love and withdrawing violently when it was shown, yet at last irresistibly drawn together in spite of this long struggle between pride and affection. It was a story of everyday humanity.[2]

Hearn sighed at the remembrance of all the novels that imitated it: 'with ugly women for heroines, and ugly obstinate men for heroes.'

An even better novelist, George Eliot, suffered as a creative artist when she wrote too visibly under the influence of George Henry Lewes; but at her best she depicted 'as faithfully as a great artist can paint it' one of the types of Renaissance man in *Romola*, and a number of characters affected by Jewish standards of morality in *Daniel Deronda*. Hearn did not dare to urge his students to read Charles Kingsley's *Alton Locke* and *Yeast* because they were too closely related to 'particular agitations of English social life',[3] but he obviously entertained a deep affection for them; *Hereward the Wake* illustrated the strengths of an historian ('Only one who has read and studied northern literature and northern history very deeply could have made such pictures for us');[4] and *Hypatia* conveyed truths that 'could not but appeal to the Japanese, imbued with the old Samurai spirit, which was not after all so very different from the northern spirit Kingsley describes, as you might suppose.'[5] These novelists, not to mention

Anthony Trollope, Wilkie Collins and Charles Reade, faithfully reflected 'the manners, customs, thought, and feelings of the English middle classes', though their manipulation of characters, their delight in over-ingenious plotting, and their mutual distaste for learning the necessary lessons that intelligent criticism of their works might provide, scored against them.

Hearn, in the company of a majority of his stay-at-home contemporaries, believed sincerely that the Victorian novel of 1850–80, narrow in its range of subject-matter though it might be, shared a common faith in the power of fact, the virtues of verisimilitude. The death of the domestic novel changed that attitude. Though Stevenson based his novels upon an 'immense amount of research and of exact knowledge'[6] in order to depict the scenes of another century, he knew that his application of realism subserved the Romantic method. Moreover, Stevenson's short stories, written to exploit the rapidly growing periodical market of the 1880s and 1890s, were dreamlike, with a vanishing sense of responsibility, and in them 'the moral sentiment has no existence.' It was perhaps inevitable that, transported to Samoa, Stevenson began to turn out stories 'of the weirdest and strangest description – illustrating the superstitions of a cannibal race whose religious and social customs differed from those of any other race until the time of their semi-civilization by force'.[7]

Kipling – who, Hearn stoutly maintained, was 'without any comparison whatever, the greatest writer of short stories in English', better than Stevenson and comparable only with the French writer Maupassant ('perhaps the greatest short-story writer in the whole history of literature')[8] – differed also from all his predecessors. He was concise, never saying more than he had to. His tales of horror did not rely on the help of the impossible, and succeeded 'by the simple statement of the possible'.[9] Hearn censured his brutality (tenderness in Kipling's stories was rare, and restricted to 'the lips of women', as in the Hindoo Queen's speech on maternity in *The Naulahka*; there was none in *The Light that Failed*). But Kipling was remarkable, above all, for his 'nervous force'. It had no counterpart in earlier Victorian novels.

As for George Du Maurier, Hearn was struck by how much *Peter Ibbetson* and *Trilby* were original works of fiction. The first novel exhibited a style that 'was so queer, so French, free, eccentric, contrary to all English convention, and nevertheless full of poetry and charm'.[10] The second novel, which sold an astonishing half-million copies by the turn of the century, presented readers with an improbable plot based on the powerful effects of hypnotism, yet swept all criticism before it:

> Such work violated all canons, yet there was no denying its power and beauty. Its success could not be called merely vulgar. How could a man who had never studied the art of writing at all, who never had any literary training, who would not submit to any literary rules, perform a feat of this amazing kind?[11]

Lafcadio Hearn, who studied Japanese culture for a substantial part of his life, married a Japanese woman and died in Japan, will always be remembered for the services he rendered in familiarising Western readers with important aspects of Japan's long tradition of story-telling. Yet what he did for his students in Japan deserves to be remembered, too, for he assessed shrewdly the merits of most Victorian novelists. Ryuji Tanabé and Teisaburo Ochiai have written, memorably, that while listening to Hearn 'It often seemed to us as if we were actually leaning out from the bar of Heaven beside the Blessed Damozel, or walking along the corridors of the Palace of Art, till the bell of the fifteen minutes' recess broke the spell.'[12] Hearn's views were mainstream even when he dealt with three critical cruxes. His dismay at George Eliot's tendency to write sermons rather than true novels was echoed in any number of critiques of her art written by other English reviewers. Her novels were readily divided into two or more phases, the first being 'unaffected, genuine and natural' as an 'utterance of her genius' (*Scenes of Clerical Life, The Mill on the Floss, Adam Bede, Silas Marner*); the second being a 'laborious elaboration of her later style' (*Middlemarch, Daniel Deronda*), with novels like *Felix Holt* and *Romola* evoking mixed reactions, because George Eliot worked too hard at achieving her effects.[13] George Saintsbury admired the first phase as being 'the more characteristic and infinitely the more healthy and happy',[14] and detested the second because it was obscured 'by a most portentous jargon borrowed from the not very admirable lingo of the philosophers and men of science of the last half of the nineteenth century'. Her later novels were 'lifeless structures', 'fatally tinged with evanescent "forms in chalk", fancies of the day and hour, not less ephemeral for being grave in subject and seeming, and almost more jejune or even disgusting to posterity on that account'.[15] The general reaction against her didacticism was strong; many censured her later novels as 'ruined' by philosophy, arbitrarily constructed, stylistically flawed; several spoke of her failures as an artist.[16] By the century's end she had become respectable but less than she had been. One literary historian voiced a common view when he wrote, 'Of the idolatry which almost made her a prophetess of a new cult we hear nothing now. She has not maintained her position as Dickens, Thackeray, and Charlotte Brontë have maintained theirs.'[17] He went on to list some of her virtues as a writer, but they amounted to a list of afterthoughts, and it is clear that on this matter of dogma and doctrine in the novel most of his contemporaries shared Lafcadio Hearn's belief that George Eliot had gone beyond permissible limits.

A second critical issue had to do with the standing of Anthony Trollope. Publication of his *Autobiography* seriously damaged his reputation; his fiction apparently had been written on the basis of hard financial calculations, to a set regimen, and as a sideshow to his main work at the Post Office; such, at least, was the ungenerous verdict of the public which was turning away from his kind of novel; he was seen, at last, as 'a mere book-maker'.[18] He was a novelist of ordinary life, to be sure, and a workman of uncommon skills; but he seemed to have written too much, he reflected his time without transcending it, and his accurate observations of the middle class had ensured him a contemporary audience without guaranteeing him aposterity.

The reasons for Trollope's abrupt fall from grace at the end of the century are not easily disentangled, but they were certainly related to a growing sense that the novel as a genre could do more than entertain or be clever, and that a novelist who rested content with character types had failed to explore the full potential of his or her art, and was, as a consequence, to be relegated permanently to the ranks of the second-best. The need for inspiration that Trollope derided as irrelevant, and perhaps even harmful, to his own method of writing books meant that undue emphasis was being placed on so much literature by the word; and out of his own mouth, when he revealed the nature of his method, was he condemned by the critics.

In turning away from Trollope's example (and almost a century was to elapse before some of his novels secured a large audience again), the critics and reviewers of novels hoped to discover something new; but when they came across it – in the writings of Robert Louis Stevenson – they were baffled. Here again a critical problem formed rapidly. Stevenson seemed unclassifiable. He was a Romantic, to be sure, but his stories moved beneath 'clouds of phantasy',[19] his characters were 'less flesh-and-blood persons than the shapes – some gracious, some terrifying – that the Ariel world invoke', and he dealt with 'phantom passions'.[20]

Such a view seriously underestimated the moral element in Stevenson's fiction (both long and short), and, as G. K. Chesterton wrote, Stevenson was consistently misunderstood by his admirers. Chesterton's point – which he documented by examining seriously what Stevenson wrote in his own literary criticism – was that Stevenson insisted that

> we must worship good for its own value and beauty, without any reference whatever to victory or failure in space and time. 'Whatever we are intended to do', Stevenson said, 'we are not intended to succeed.' That the stars in their courses fight against virtue, that humanity is in its nature a forlorn hope, this was the very spirit that through the whole of Stevenson's work sounded a trumpet to all the brave.[21]

Stevenson's fiction may have mystified critics because it had been written in a flowing copy-book hand, but his were not copy-book sentiments.

> He suffered from his versatility, not, as is loosely said, by not doing every department too well. As child, cockney, pirate, or Puritan, his disguises were so good that most people could not see the same man under all. It is an unjust fact that if a man can play the fiddle, give legal opinions, and black boots just tolerably, he is called an Admirable Crichton, but if he does all three thoroughly well, he is apt to be regarded, in the several departments, as a common fiddler, a common lawyer, and a common boot-black. This is what has happened in the case of Stevenson.[22]

The fact that sometimes Stevenson wrote badly was seldom conceded by his admirers, and adulation was bound to produce a counter-reaction; William Ernest Henley's famous tribute to his friend – 'Apparition' in the 'In Hospital' sequence – stressed the versatility that so many critics found unsettling; and Stevenson's reputation as a novelist became equivocal several years before he died.

In reviewing contemporary attitudes towards a substantial fraction of George Eliot's fiction, the whole of Trollope's output and both the novels and short stories of Stevenson, one soon learns to respect the fact that most literary critics were not very far from the prejudices and reading interests of their public; were, indeed, much closer than the editors and reviewers of the great quarterlies in the first half of the century. Briefly summarised, these views amounted to a growing distaste for being preached at (though the roaring success of *Robert Elsmere* in the 1870s must always give one pause); a dislike of being forced to think of the novel as a commercial commodity; and considerable uneasiness at the spectacle of a novelist taking pleasure equally in any number of literary genres. A novel, it seemed, should be a good read, and something more, but at the same time not too much more. It was allowed to explore a wide range of human experience, and it would earn a large audience if it prized action above meditation, stressed narrative values, strove to show character in movement and allowed moral and ethical values to develop as a result of clearly delineated situations involving reasonably (not excessively) realistic men and women. At the heart of every successful novel in the years leading up to the Great War was a human dilemma, not a gorgeously depicted scene of nature or a novelist's bag of tricks, a story rather than a conundrum, an emphasis on what was being dramatised rather than on what the novelist personally believed or wanted the readers to believe.

Chapter 2

The publishing world in 1914

I believe one of the gravest necessities at the present moment is to keep before the commercial community the very old and commonplace phrase, 'Business as usual.'

May I take the opportunity of suggesting that if you have a spare inch of your paper you print:

BRITAIN'S MOTTO:
'BUSINESS AS USUAL'.

For my own part, I am going to do my best to prevail on all our clients to do their advertising as usual, and I think concerted action will prove beneficial to all of us.

(Letter by Mr H. E. Morgan, of Messrs. W. H. Smith & Son, published in several English newspapers in early August 1914)

So far as the book trade is concerned, there is no need to attempt to measure the extent to which it might be affected by such a state of affairs as has been brought within sight by the present appalling development of international events. Yet one cannot but believe that, under the tension of such a harassing strain as we are now called upon to bear, there are multitudes of people who will thankfully turn to books now and again, in order to give their minds 'respite and nepenthe' from the racking excitement so continuously provided by the newspapers.

('Jacob Omnium', *The Bookseller: A weekly newspaper of British and foreign literature* [7 August 1914], p. 1050)

In August 1914 publishers thought only in an unfocused way about what a general war might entail for themselves, or for their authors. They had proceeded placidly, with self-confidence and a faith in the worth of their product, for so long that they financed one of the first posters of the Great War widely distributed throughout the kingdom,

'Business as usual'. For some firms, the war did not destroy the conventions of trade. Charles Morgan, in his history of Macmillan, noted that despite war books and pamphlets written by Winston S. Churchill, Viscount James Bryce, Mabel Dearmer, Edith Wharton, Owen Wister, F. S. Oliver and Rudyard Kipling, the prosperity of Macmillan depended very little on books arising directly from the war. 'Normal publishing was so little deterred by events in Europe that not only were new volumes added to the *Highways and Byways Series* but in 1918 the *Blue Guides* edited by Findlay Muirhead were begun with a guide to London.'[1] At a meeting of the Publishers' Association, in Stationers' Hall (1914), caution was advised so far as 'speculative ventures' were concerned. A brief flurry arose when some publishers announced that contractual obligations between their houses and their authors might have to be cancelled, or at the very least renegotiated, because of what was happening on the Continent. But books of travel and scholarship were largely unaffected, and 'solid books of criticism, politics and sociology showed no signs of falling off'.[2] An audience for poetry expanded. Grant Richards, for example, worked out a most satisfactory arrangement with A. E. Housman: Richards did not have to pay royalty on *A Shropshire Lad* so long as he sold it for sixpence (the book proved extraordinarily popular with soldiers going to the trenches).[3] Novels were read with varying degrees of pleasure by an audience that never contracted during the war years. Over half of what circulated in Smith's, Mudie's and Boot's and of what sold in the bookshops, was fiction in one form or another.

Inevitably, the employees of publishing firms went off to war, like everybody else, and their ranks thinned as a consequence of death and crippling wounds. There were problems with maintaining the flow of books to the new locations of eager readers. Technical books imported from the United States were held up for unconscionable periods of time by the Customs authorities, who regarded books (all books) as luxuries, despite the fact that His Majesty's Stationery Office needed them and government departments recognised their usefulness for the processes of manufacture and for war administration. Air-raids destroyed stocks of some publishers, the vast majority of whom were concentrated around Paternoster Row. Another change, the introduction of women into counting-houses and trade departments, seemed more radical and unnecessary to conservative publishers than (in later years) they were willing to remember.

One of the more striking changes had to do with prices of materials, which (inevitably) rose over the full wartime period.[4] One fairly representative variety of book-paper that cost 2½d. a pound in 1914 gradually advanced to 1s. 1d. in 1918. The rise in price was unimpeded by the usual competing factors of imports and busy papermaking machines – many of the machines went unattended because of a shortage of skilled labour. In 1919, however, the price dropped rapidly to 7½d. a pound before a boom period began, and paper became even more difficult to obtain than during most of the war years. Speculative fevers proved ruinous for many; not until the mid-1920s did the price ease again, all the way down to 3½d. a pound.

As for wages, increases were transmitted directly to the publisher in the form of higher charges for composition and machining. From 1914, when a compositor's minimum rate of pay was 32s. 6d. a week, to 1918, just before the Armistice, when pay had risen to 60s. 6d. a week, the rate of increase was 85 per cent; after the war, and more specifically in the 1920s, the rate kept on spiralling upwards to 70s. 6d., an increase of 120 per cent on pre-war wages. Machine-minders went up 107 per cent and machine-assistants, warehouse workers, and several kinds of unskilled labour were earning in 1920 some 333 per cent more than in 1914. Price increases affected binding as well. Men who bound books improved their wages from 35s. per 48-hour week (1914) to £5 per week (1920), sometimes earning three raises in a year; and women improved from 14s. per 48-hour week (1914) to 17s. 6d. (1916) to 51s. (November 1920), after which the wages fell back 10s. The prices of materials used in the book-binding trade increased at a similarly rapid pace. Good English book-cloth that in 1914 cost 5d. a yard went up to more than 1s. 6d. by the end of 1918. Strawboards soared from less than £5 per ton to £37 per ton. Book-binding machinery more than doubled in price within four years.

In the years before the war, and indeed for most of the war, the published price of a novel was 6s. The retail customer could buy it for 4s. 6d., and the bookseller paid the publisher 4s. 2d. The bookseller had a right to complain that the margin of profit was too narrow, and the printer's staff certainly were not overpaid. But by 1918 the standard price for a novel had risen to 7s. 6d. net, the retail customer had to pay full price and the bookseller paid 5s. 8d. (for a single copy) or 5s. (but only if six assorted novels were taken at the same time, or sometimes the bookseller benefited from a pre-publication bargain).

'In effect', Arthur Waugh concluded his survey of the book trade as seen from Chapman and Hall,

> in order to cover expenses on a novel nowadays [1930], the publisher has to sell at least double the number that he had to sell before the war; and is consequently in a worse position, with the novel priced at 7s. 6d. net than he was when it was issued at 6s., and sold at a discount.[5]

Nothing in all this should imply that by 1919 a large number of publishers had been driven to the wall by inflation, personnel losses, problems with supplies and machinery, or all these factors taken together. The book trade, in fact, was more prosperous in the second decade of this century than it had ever been, and it remained so well into the 1920s. Some historical perspective is needed. Between 1666 and 1756 fewer than 100 new books had been published annually in England; from 1792 to 1802, fewer than 400; up to the mid-nineteenth century, fewer than 600 (and it is likely that these numbers overstate the case). But the doubling of the population in the first fifty years of the nineteenth century, the near-doubling of wages and the halving of the average price of a new book – from 16s. to 8s. 4d. – accounted for the sudden upsurge in the middle of the century, and for the unexpected annual production of 2,600 new books. By the 1860s as many people were engaged in the production of books and periodicals (54,000) as there were bakers. The general trade depression that began in 1879 did not seriously batter the book market. In 1901 6,044 new books appeared, and in 1913, the general time period with which we are most directly concerned, the total had doubled to 12,379. The best-seller phenomenon, which Thomas Hardy (among others) deplored, was responsible for the fact that the monetary value of books tripled between 1907 and 1930, though the number of publications rose only some 50 per cent.[6]

The number of readers interested in books may be measured by any number of indices, including the count kept by public libraries of annual issues, a number that rose to 54 million by 1911. Public library authorities rose from the tiny number of 95 in 1880 to a more substantial total of 352 in 1900, and grew another two hundred in two decades more. Libraries that called themselves 'service points' (because they issued books) numbered 480 in 1896, and these increased to 920 by 1911. During the same period the number of books in their stock more than doubled, and public expenditure on the libraries soared from £286,000 to £805,445.

Moreover, the stability of the book trade, partially ensured by a continuing exploitation of its workers (printers were harder to intimidate), was such that the price of a novel remained in the range of 7s. to 7s. 6d. from 1918 on, for an astonishingly long two decades. Other elements affecting the production and selling of fiction must be considered: the New Book Agreement, inaugurated on 1 January 1900, which produced immediate conflicts because of the determination of some book publishers to end price-cutting (most notably *The Times* Book War that raged between 1905 and 1908); censorship of novels with content that seemed controversial or sexually suggestive (Compton Mackenzie and H. G. Wells were only two of the writers whose novels were banned by Smith's and Mudie's); a hammering-out of terms whereby international copyright had to be respected; the increasing popularity of free public libraries; the astonishing proliferation of cheap editions; and the rise of the literary agent, men like Alexander Pollock Watt, who handled Wilkie Collins, Rudyard Kipling, Bret Harte, Arthur Conan Doyle and Walter Besant, and who died in 1914 worth £60,000, as well as Curtis Brown of the International Publishing Bureau and J. B. Pinker (who worked with the financially lucrative Arnold Bennett).[7] The intensifying interest of newspapers in publicising books through free gifts and cheap editions added a new element to book publishing in the early years of the century. Also, the development of the wholesale bookseller, with attendant economies of operation, improved the profits of the entire book trade.

It is understandable why the publishers of the eleventh edition of the *Encyclopaedia Britannica* (1911), allied as they were with *The Times* Book Club in its effort to contravene the Net Book Agreement, should have defined an author, 'even if he is an immortal genius', as a producer of raw material 'from an economic point of view', and a publisher, 'however eminent', as 'a middleman who works up the author's raw material into a saleable form and places it upon the market' ('from the same point of view'). 'The relationship between the two is one that occurs with great frequency in business, always giving rise to efforts by each party to adjust the division of profits for his own advantage.'

But authors and publishers refused to so consider themselves, despite the frequency with which some authors accepted substantial advances for manuscripts that they never completed, or the blithe behaviour of some publishers in exploiting unwary authors. The heartlessness of H. G. Wells, who fully expected his publishers to bankrupt themselves in his service, was atypical, and Wells's endless negotiations with one publisher after another, in search of higher royalty payments, was noted by more than one publisher as destabilising to the trade. Wells's behaviour was unusual. Over the years the majority of authors built up symbiotic ties of trust and, on occasion, affection with the people who published their books.

One example is Hugh Walpole, who transferred from Secker to Macmillan in 1918. This young man, praised (perhaps beyond his just desert) by Henry James at the beginning of his career, 'wrote too much and too fast', as Charles Morgan said in his semi-official history of Macmillan; 'he entertained too often and was alone too little; he lent his name and his enthusiasm to innumerable enterprises which were outside the devotion of an artist that was properly his.'[8] Walpole's was a strange case, for everyone recognised his generosity of mind, thought well of his encouragement of younger writers and smiled at his enthusiasms. Yet there were signs of strain noticeable at an early stage. He demeaned himself by writing for newspaper readers (he liked the size of the audience), and by writing (with uncertain skills) about the macabre. He did not revise as he should, and he failed to note inconsistencies in his 'continuities' that editors time and again had to straighten out for him. He was a story-teller, and for the sake of his gifts much was forgiven; adverse criticism was held back. It was possible, Morgan thought, that 'only by letting himself go as he did was [Walpole] able to write at all.'[9] Publishers often put up with slovenliness because of their high personal regard for an author, as well as their hope that the author's unsettling behaviour might pay off.

The story of Martin Secker himself, one of the notable success stories during these years, begins with a report by Secker, a reader for Eveleigh Nash in 1909, on Compton Mackenzie's *The Passionate Elopement*, a romance set in the eighteenth century. Secker enjoyed the novel, and thought it well worth publishing. A second reader submitted a negative report. Secker, frustrated by the decision of his publishing firm to reject the manuscript, could not forget the promise shown by Mackenzie's work. When he came into some money shortly thereafter, he set up as a publisher. Remembering Mackenzie, he looked him up, published the story, and began a publishing career filled with novels of distinction: those of Gilbert Cannan, Hugh Walpole (for several years before he transferred to Macmillan) and, of course, Compton Mackenzie. He encouraged Frank Swinnerton to write an important study of George Gissing, and to follow it up with an iconoclastic monograph on Robert Louis Stevenson (which upset many lovers of Stevenson); he persuaded Francis Brett Young to write about Robert Bridges; and later he was to encourage and print work by D. H. Lawrence. He was an extraordinary hunter and gatherer of talents: Norman Douglas (*South Wind*), Lion Feuchtwanger (*Jew Süss*), Thomas Mann (*Buddenbrooks*) and Franz Kafka (*The Castle*), in addition to the popular poems of James Elroy Flecker. He belonged, as Fredric Warburg, the publisher destined to buy out Secker's properties in 1936 for £3,000, wrote, 'with the eccentric, brilliant and adroit publisher–editors of an earlier period – John Lane with his *Yellow Book* and Grant Richards (a personal friend of Secker's), the discoverer of *A Shropshire Lad* and founder of the World's Classics'.[10] Nor did his financial failure mean that his skill in discovering new talents had become uncertain. Among the brand-new, unpublished titles that Secker turned over to Warburg were Erskine Caldwell's *Tobacco Road*, Thomas Mann's *Stories of Three Decades* and Arnold Zweig's *Education Before Verdun*, the second volume in the trilogy that had begun with *The Case of Sergeant Grischa*, the 'biggest' of all books about the Great War until Erich Maria Remarque's *All Quiet on the Western Front* came into print. Secker's formula for the high quality of his list was simple enough: look for quality, and treat authors as human beings who want (and deserve) the best professional and personal treatment possible.

A third example of the friendships binding publishers and authors may be cited. Sir Stanley Unwin, who wrote two splendid books about his trade – *The Truth about Publishing* (1926) and *The Truth about a Publisher* (1960) – built a long and distinguished career on the foundation of his first acquisition, George Allen & Co. Ltd. (George Allen and Unwin Ltd came into existence on 4 August 1914, a day memorable for other reasons.) He pondered gravely the merits of three manuscripts offered to his firm shortly after he began operations. They did not resemble any books on his current list of acquisitions. He did not know how to respond to their availability (he would have swiftly accepted all three eighteen months later, when he became more sure of his own taste). As a consequence, he turned down *The Brook Kerith*, by George Moore, and *My People*, by Caradoc Evans; but the third, *Limehouse Nights*, by Thomas Burke, nagged at him. It possessed exactly the kind of quality he wanted to publish, and he believed that Burke was worth encouraging. Unwin commissioned

Burke to write *Nights in Town*, which became an instant success. He gave Burke a job in his office 'to tide him over temporary financial difficulties', and his philanthropy was twice rewarded: 'He was the fastest typist I have ever known.'[11]

More than shillings and pence were involved. This way of business could sentimentalise itself month after month in the pages of *The Bookman* (founded in 1891 by Robertson Nicoll, this handsome and frequently overstuffed periodical lasted until 1935), the *British Weekly* (a non-Conformist paper important for the literary edicts of Robertson Nicoll, who wrote under the pen-name of 'Claudius Clear'), the *Sphere* (widely read in large part because of Clement Shorter's weekly literary letters) and the *New Age* (a 'Thunderer' in its own right because of Arnold Bennett's reviews, signed with the pseudonym 'Jacob Tonson'). But, in fact, publishing during the years of the Great War was a very special business. It was crazily alive with colourful personalities, many of whom are remembered in the wonderful (and seemingly endless) series of memoirs and reminiscences of Frank Swinnerton. Their foibles, exploits, pranks and whimsical behaviour scarcely prepare us for full appreciation of their success at gauging and satisfactorily catering to popular taste.

This post-Edwardian audience enjoyed reading fiction more than any other category of literature, and novels more than collections of short stories (which for the most part did not sell) or plays (which only slowly became commercial properties). The market kept growing; visions of the future seemed increasingly cheery. John Gross, in *The Rise and Fall of the Man of Letters*, points out that the census returns for 1881 listed some 3,400 'authors, editors and journalists'; a decade later this number had almost doubled (nearly 6,000); another decade, and there were 11,000; and in 1911, nearly 14,000 made the lists. By the turn of the century the London Directory named more than 400 separate publishing houses.[12]

All of which suggests that the literary historian who concentrates on the novels of George Meredith, Joseph Conrad and Henry James as typical pre-war fictions is bound to neglect, or at the very least distort, the truth about the reading tastes of public library patrons and members of the book-buying public. This larger public really liked writers like M. E. Braddon, Mrs Henry Wood, Emma Jane Worboise, Marie Corelli, Mrs M. W. Hungerford and Ouida; and they made life comfortable for scribblers like Guy Boothby, Rita (Mrs Desmond Humphreys), William Le Queux and Florence Marryat, not to mention Fergus Hume, Frank Barrett, E. Phillips Oppenheim and C. J. Cutliffe.

Amy Cruse, in the final chapter (entitled '1914') of *After the Victorians*, sketched briefly the main trends of reading taste in those final months before a long Indian summer evaporated into winter frost and trench warfare. She wrote approvingly of the shrinking public interest in Marie Corelli's works, and the failure of Hall Caine and Mrs Humphry Ward to sustain their audiences from novel to novel. Galsworthy and Conrad, 'serious' writers, secured her approval (she saw in their emergence a maturing of novel-readers, though by 1914 both these novelists were past their prime), as did the spate of fictions dealing with the feminist movement (because they wished to present the question 'dispassionately').[13] The surging popularity of detective stories was noted. *Trent's Last Case*, by E. C. Bentley, appeared in 1913 and inaugurated a vogue for well-crafted narratives focusing on crime and detection. Thesis novels – ridiculed by E. F. Benson in *Dodo the Second* – talked about Home Rule, Soap, Tariff Reform, Christianity, quite in the spirit of 'leaders in the newspapers, full of reliable information'.[14] (Benson may have been thinking of Arnold Bennett's stories about the Five Towns, or H. G. Wells's *The Wife of Sir Isaac Harman*.)

Nevertheless, romance, in one or another of its countless disguises, constituted then (as it has for much of this century) the major fraction of reading matter that the public wanted, paid for either in the bookshop or at the lending library and enjoyed. The wonder is not that escapist novels resolutely denied the power of brute facts and the sheer ugliness of many elements of modern life, but that they continued to do so right through the fifty-two months of the Great War.

One sure way to appreciate the popularity of stories that dealt with the long ago or the far away (and sometimes both) is to recall some of the colourful advertisements placed by book publishers in trade magazines. Werner Laurie proudly described *The Way of the Cardines*, by Stanley Portal Hyatt, as 'a fine and thoughtful novel, gallant with high endeavour', and its hero, though 'prey to the morphia habit', the last of a long race of empire-builders. Before he succumbed to the drug, he wanted to do 'one thing for the Empire'. He planned to rescue the Island of Katu ('the key to the Far East') from the Germans, who were gradually obtaining possession of it through 'the machinations of a gang of scoundrels with supporters in England'.

Everyman's Library, at the beginning of its list of one hundred volumes, to be published at the rate of twelve per month (selling for 1s. net), described 'The Wayfarers' Library' as

> a sincere and purposeful attempt to formulate a collection of books which shall adequately represent the romanticism and imaginativeness of our own time. . . . The odious element which has crept into a large proportion of modern novels will not insinuate itself into the Wayfarers' Library. The iconoclastic 'problem novel' will find no place here, nor will those books whose atmosphere is hopelessly morbid. The trend of the Wayfarers' Library is optimistic, and its sole object is to provide enjoyment for all who love a good wholesome book, whether on a journey or in the warm seclusion of the chimney corner. It is, in short, a resort whither may come the hungry reader secure in the knowledge that here at any rate his literary craving may be appeased without fear of gall within the cup.

John Lane, of the Bodley Head, advertised its 6s. novels with quotations from reviews. Stephen Leacock's *Behind the Beyond* (according to *Punch*) would lead any family member to emit 'sharp, short yelps of laughter' to punctuate 'the decent after-dinner silence'. The *Daily News* praised Frank Harris's *Great Days*: 'Certainly not since Stevenson have we had a story so full of the fun of adventure, the catch in the throat and gleam in the eye, the sharp up-and-doing.' And the *Morning Post* described A. Neil Lyon's *Simple Simon* as 'Genius', adding, 'We used this dangerous word, without apology, of the most incisive of contemporary writers.' Stanley Paul's list included *The Twin-Soul of O'Take San*, by Baroness Albert d'Anethan, and the advertisement for this 'charming Japanese romance' carefully identified its author as 'a sister of Sir Rider Haggard'. Another novel worth pushing was C. Ranger Gull's *When Satan Ruled*:

> The mediaeval orgies and wickedness of the Vatican, and of Italian life in general, in those eventful times, in the hands of a writer who knows how to use them, assure a story of exceptional interest and attraction. The great figures of Michelangelo and Benvenuto Cellini, the famous artists of that artistic age, of Pope Paul III, and the life-like picture of his entourage, all add their quota to the graphic narrative, the romantic scenes and interest which the writer here sets forth.

It is not surprising that the name of a 'reclaimed waif' in *Two's Company*, by Dorothea Mackellar and Ruth Bedford (on the Spring List of Alston Rivers), should be 'Rags', or that the blurb-writer should record thoughtfully that 'his official name, poor boy, was

Ragland'. Heinemann was delighted to announce that William de Morgan's *When Ghost Meets Ghost* (two volumes for 10s., or one volume for 6s.) – 'a wonderland of human sympathy and kindly feeling' – had exhausted its first edition in one week.

Some advertisements, as, for example, the notice by Macmillan that the Wessex Edition of Thomas Hardy's novels had recently added a new title (*A Changed Man, The Waiting Supper and other Tales*, concluding with *The Romantic Adventures of a Milkmaid*, as volume XVIII), were dignified in their type-size and language. Even so, it was difficult to know how to respond to a statement by reviewers, quoted faithfully by Hodder and Stoughton, that Baroness Orczy's *Unto Caesar* was a novel that carried us away 'in spite of ourselves', or that E. F. Benson's *Dodo the Second* was 'exasperatingly clever'. Some of these encomiums are quite marvellous, and fun to read. Gerald O'Donovan's *Waiting*, a novel about an Irish agricultural district, draws the Irish priesthood 'with no hesitating hand'. *The Spectator* benignly nodded on Sir Charles Garvice's *The Woman's Way*:

> If ever there was a novelist on the side of the angels, it is Mr. Garvice.... We rise from the perusal of these pages profoundly reassured as to the soundness of the great heart of the reading public. There can be no decadence in a race which owns the sway of a romancer so kindly in his outlook, so irreproachable in his teaching, so rigorous in applying the laws of physiognomy.

Henry Bordeaux's new novel, *Footprints beneath the Snow*, tells of a wife who is 'swept away from her husband by a mushroom passion', is almost killed with her lover and is reunited with her husband after many 'adventures and misunderstandings' (G. Bell & Sons, Ltd).

Humour redeemed novels that otherwise might have suffered from the mark of Cain (i.e., a gloomy seriousness). 'The red-hot facts of the present year', Smith, Elder & Co. said reassuringly, were treated with the author's 'peculiar gifts of light-hearted fun and half-serious satire' (*The Red Hand of Ulster*, by George A. Birmingham). Love, mystery, adventure! The locale might range from 'the back paddocks of Australia', as in *By Blow and Kiss*, by W. Boyd Cable, to the Chancelleries of Europe (*Her Royal Highness*, by William Le Queux). The appetite for books dealing with remote, exotic, picturesque locales seemed insatiable. Endless columns of reviews were given over to non-fiction books about the Russians in Mongolia, Norwegian fishing-grounds, 'the real Mexico', and sago production in 'far New Guinea'. These might be read in conjunction with novels that brought to English readers the emotional disorder inherent in Japanese romances ('The love of O Fuji San' and 'The wooing of O Sasa San', two stories contained in Clive Holland's *A Madonna of the Poor*), gambling in France ('Paris in May! Paris with my lover!' – unexceptionable sentiments contained in Rachel Hayward's *Letters from Là-Bas*), shipwreck off Sable Island, near Nova Scotia (John Oxenham's *Maid of the Mist*) and the pioneering days of New Zealand under the governorship of Sir George Grey. Even novels about England made the Chiltern Hills, the Yorkshire districts, the Hebrides and 'that sequestered corner where the three counties of Kent, Surrey and Sussex meet' (Sheila Kaye-Smith's *Three against the World*) seem much more isolated than in fact they were in the early years of this century.

Novels about sombre subjects neither sold well nor were expected to sell well. The advertisements I have quoted were typical of both the approach taken by publishers to their intended (or hoped-for) audiences, and by authors who sought to entertain. Books about history were no less determined to succeed: *Remarkable Women of France, 1431 to 1749*, by C. P. Haggard; *A History of Penal Methods: Criminals, witches, lunatics*, by George Ives; *The Tragedy of Two Stuarts*, by Mildred Carnegy; *My Days of Adventure: The fall of France, 1870–71*, by Ernest Alfred Vizetelly; *Morocco the Piquant*, by G. E. Holt; *Royalist Father and Roundhead Son*, edited by the Countess of Denbigh; *Russia from Within*, by Alexander Ular; *Through Madagascar: In quest of the golden bean*, by Walter D. Marcuse; *In Abyssinia: The land of the barefooted king*, by Herbert Schulein; *Napoleon at Bay, 1814*, by F. Loraine Petre; and *Robespierre and the Women He Loved*, by Hector Fleischmann.

English novels published between 1914 and 1918 were not the products of a single school. Definitions or theoretical considerations would play false the impression that a reader gathers from any dozen or so representative examples. But most of the better novels were superior examples of Edwardian fiction, not harbingers of the Modernist movement. And most of them sought to entertain the reading public.

Books of humour, including light-hearted treatments of life in the military, children's stories, patriotic treatments of adventure in Empire possessions and a number of tales of weird and supernatural happenings (the Wellsian tradition proved commercially successful during the 1890s), sold in generous numbers. Late in 1914 other successes included St John G. Irvine's *Mrs. Martin's Man*, Marjorie

Bowen's *Prince and Heretic*, Lady Cromartie's *The Decoy*, Mrs Humphry Ward's *Delia Branchflower*, Edgar Wallace's *Bones* and Mrs Everard Cotes's *His Royal Happiness* (Mrs Cotes being a pseudonym of Sara Jeannette Duncan). In 1915 the indefatigable Hugh Walpole published *The Dark Forest* and Frank Swinnerton brought out *The Chaste Wife*, while Somerset Maugham produced *Of Human Bondage*, Baroness Orczy *The Bronze Eagle*, S. R. Crockett *Hal o' the Ironsides*, Maurice Hewlett *The Little Iliad*, C. M. Matheson *The Generation Between*, Katharine Tynan *Since First I saw Your Face* and Eden Philpotts *Faith Tresilian*. In 1916, publishers were pleased to bring out popular works of fiction by E. F. Benson (*Mike*), Arnold Bennett (*The Lion's Share*), Mrs Humphry Ward (*Lady Connie*), Gilbert Cannan (*Mandel*) and Sax Rohmer (*The Exploits of Captain O'Hagan*). In 1917, in addition to P. G. Wodehouse's *Piccadilly Jim* and Clemence Dane's *Regiment of Women*, we may list as outstanding titles of new fiction the following: A. E. W. Mason's *The Four Corners of the World*, Talbot Munday's *King, of the Khyber Rifles*, E. Phillips Oppenheim's *The Kingdom of the Blind*, R. S. Crockett's *The Azure Hand*, Phyllis Bottome's *A Certain Star*, William Le Queux's *The Rainbow Mystery*, Gilbert Cannan's *The Stucco House*, J. S. Fletcher's *The Rayner-Slade Amalgamation*, and Clive Holland's *The Cinema Star*. The last year of the war brought to market a similar concentration of entertainments: new books by old favourites like Edgar Wallace, William Le Queux, J. S. Fletcher, Katharine Tynan, Baroness Orczy, E. Phillips Oppenheim and Ethel M. Dell, and well-reviewed efforts by Eric Leadbitter (*Perpetual Fires*), Marjorie Bowen (*The Burning Glass*), Frank Swinnerton (*Shops and Houses*), Hugh Walpole (*The Green Mirror*), May Wynne (*Queen Jennie*) and Elizabeth Robins (*Camilla*).

The majority of the English reading public wanted romances, exciting stories of derring-do with courageous men and fascinating women, readable stories about the middle class or the nobility. Novels about disturbing social issues did not interest them. Naturalistic documentation, though familiar in England as a story-telling technique for more than a quarter of a century (crossing the Channel has always meant a serious time delay for any French literary movement), seemed to imply, unappetizingly, a narrative of disillusioned or cynical values, and did not sell well.

Most English authors did not spend much time moralising about progress and civilisation; they took for granted much that came into question during the Great War itself. And it is a nice question, calling for careful judgement, whether the unwillingness of the vast majority of them to treat the war directly, honestly and critically in their fiction constituted an evasion of authorial responsibility. At the time, they did not think so. Neither did their readers.

Chapter 3

Authors and the reviewing media

The explosive growth of educational opportunities following the passage of the Forster Act of 1870 expanded the number of readers interested in literature of all kinds, and of fiction in particular. Though the story of the development of mass-circulation newspapers and periodicals need not be recapitulated here, one point needs to be stressed. The great public schools – the nine 'ancient' ones (Charterhouse, Eton, Harrow, Merchant Taylors, Rugby, St Paul's Shrewsbury, Westminster and Winchester) – and the foundations (Cheltenham, King's College School, Marlborough, and University College School, all founded in the nineteenth century) were losing much of their importance as training grounds for writers that they had enjoyed during the first half of the century. The grammar schools (national and local) and the private-venture schools emerged as cultural authorities in a way that could not have been foreseen before the Taunton Commission investigation of 1864–8 drew up its devastating report on the quality of education in the older schools. One consequence of the change, and perhaps not the least important, was that the pool of authors expanded to include a great many more members of the middle class.

Class distinctions may be difficult to define, but they were real then, and they have not disappeared to this day. Such a generalisation renders imperative some consideration of the result of one survey,[1] which identifies as members of the middle class some 85 per cent of all authors whose names turn up in the nineteenth-century volume of the *Cambridge Bibliography of English Literature*. The authors considered were overwhelmingly male (almost 80 per cent), and the percentage of women writers did not increase substantially from one end of the century to the other. Although one out of five ended education at the secondary level (1900–35), some 72 per cent went on to the university level and more than twice as many preferred Oxford to Cambridge. But the provincial universities were proving themselves equally congenial as homes for literary sensibilities.

The major employment market for writers, editors and publicists was some form of journalism; this proved to be the immediate (and for many the ultimate) destination. Newspapers, magazines and reviews turned out to be most congenial for budding authors. The Church of England offered less support in the way of a subsidised living as the nineteenth century waned; however, various patrons of the arts were beginning to pay serious attention to writing as a craft. Many authors worked part-time at the writing profession, while carrying on as engineers, bankers, military and naval officers and lawyers. They thought of authorship as a lively second career. Sometimes remuneration was paltry. (As one example, Arthur Conan Doyle's income from his medical practice was so negligible that he turned, in desperation, to the writing of stories about Sherlock Holmes and Dr Watson.)

During the Great War a greatly reduced number of members of the nobility and the gentry (less than 10 per cent) and an even smaller number of members of the lower class (some 3 per cent) contributed to the flood of novels published annually. Another way of putting this: while an impressive 97 per cent of all writers belonged to either the upper or the middle class, both classes – taken together – constituted only 25 per cent of the total population. Writers then, much more so than now, belonged to a minority fraction of the public. It is not surprising, therefore, that the subject-matter and tone of most war novels reflected middle-class prejudices and sought to please middle-class tastes. In this, as I hope to show, they were remarkably successful.

Once stated, these truisms seem self-evident. Nevertheless, belonging to the middle class did not guarantee either a happy childhood or a decent formal education. If we consider the lives of several representative writers who had either achieved some measure of fame or were on the threshold of satisfactory literary careers when the war began, we find that their roots were often tangled, and their chances for success in literary careers unclear at the start.

Charles Morgan was born in Bromley, Kent; his father, a civil engineer, encouraged him to enter the Royal Navy as a cadet at the age of thirteen, and he received his education at naval colleges in Osborne and Dartmouth.

Another unconventional education was that of Frank Swinnerton; son of a copperplate engraver, he worked from the age of fourteen as a clerk in a newspaper office on Fleet Street.

(George) Norman Douglas, born in Thüringen in the Austrian Tyrol, despised most of the education that he received in England, and learned what he needed at a *Gymnasium* in Karlsruhe (his linguistic proficiency was to enable him to publish in the German language).

(Enoch) Arnold Bennett, born in one of the six Staffordshire towns that were to amalgamate as Stoke-on-Trent, was the grandson of a potter and the son of a pawnshop owner who laboriously rose in the world to become qualified as a lawyer. Bennett attended middle school at Newcastle-under-Lyme and was a clerk in his father's law practice; though he wanted to attend London University, his father prevented him from doing so.

Henry Major Tomlinson, born into a seafaring family, worked as a clerk in a shipping firm, and laboured there for twenty years before becoming a journalist.

Herbert George Wells was the son of a tradesman and professional cricketer whose unsuccessful business ventures did much to ruin the family's middle-class status; his mother, a former lady's maid, worked as a housekeeper for a Sussex country home. Wells joined the labour force at the age of thirteen; his significant education during adolescent years was at the Normal School of Science in South Kensington (now the Imperial College of London University), and there he was fortunate enough to attend the lectures of T. H. Huxley.

May Sinclair, daughter of a Liverpool shipowner, watched her father decay (he was a heavy drinker) and declare bankruptcy; her education was largely concentrated on books that she discovered for herself, piano lessons and a single year at Cheltenham Ladies' College.

Educated at an advanced curriculum school, Dorothy M. Richardson went to Germany at the age of seventeen, as soon as she could get away from the stifling atmosphere of her family life. Her father sold his inheritance, set himself up as a gentleman and went bankrupt; her mother killed herself shortly afterwards.

It is difficult to decide how much of Mary Webb's dark doctrine developed as an inevitable consequence of her father's Christian mysticism, and how much of it responded to wartime conditions.

Arthur Machen, son of an invalid mother and a clergyman father, was educated at Hereford Cathedral School but failed his surgeon's examination; he would go on to write some of the finest tales of terror of his generation.

William Somerset Maugham, whose father died when he was ten, went to live with his uncle, his father's clergyman brother, at the vicarage in Whitstable; the psychological scars of that experience are described, with appalling fidelity, in *Of Human Bondage*, a bleak novel published in 1915.

On the other hand, some writers grew up in less nerve-racking middle-class surroundings. Hugh Walpole, whose father was a vicar in Parnell, Auckland, New Zealand, received his education at English public schools (Truro, Marlow, King's School in Canterbury and Durham School) and then, as a subsizar who could not pay full fees, at Emmanuel College, Cambridge.

John Galsworthy went to Saugeen preparatory school, Harrow and New College, Oxford, earning a second-class degree. His father, a successful solicitor and manager of real estate, more than made up in tender gentleness for his mother's hypochondria and obsession with cleanliness.

Compton Mackenzie, who would write more than fifty novels (only half his output), was born into a family of famous actors. Their encouragement of his talents led to mastery of Latin at four, of Greek at nine and of 'all' printed versions of plays written or produced before 1830. He attended St Paul's School, and then Magdalen College, Oxford.

Ford Madox Hueffer (later Ford), son of a journalist, author and music critic for *The Times* who had earned his doctorate in philology from Göttingen, and was (on his mother's side) the grandson of the Pre-Raphaelite painter Ford Madox Ford, tried for a university degree, but encountered unexpected opposition (and denigration) from his father.

John Buchan, born in Perth, Scotland, was the son of a minister of the Free Church of Scotland; he attended Hutcheson's Grammar School in Glasgow, and later Glasgow University, before winning a scholarship to Brasenose College, Oxford.

Richard Aldington, like Walpole, Galsworthy, Mackenzie and Buchan, spent a comfortable boyhood enjoying life. He attended University College London, before joining up as an enlisted man in war service; his father, a solicitor's clerk, proudly cheered every manifestation of talent.

Generalisations about the class background of authors may usefully be considered in relation to the major reviewing media.

The great quarterlies of Queen Victoria's reign, with their high-minded and intellectually demanding considerations of political, social and cultural issues, specialised in lengthy essays that required both sustained periods of reading time and a serious response. For the editors of the *Saturday Review*, *Blackwood's Edinburgh Magazine*, the *Quarterly Review*, the *Pall Mall Gazette*, the *Cornhill Magazine*, the *Fortnightly Review* and the *Edinburgh Review*, choices in what to print remained largely the responsibility of editors throughout the century; the audience, consisting primarily of educated members of the middle class, took what was offered – arcane lore, statistical treatments of economic issues, reviews of specialised historical questions, critiques of minor authors long dead and almost forgotten – along with short stories and serialised novels designed to entertain, humorous treatments of family problems and features intended to divert readers. These were magazines in the original sense, i.e. mixtures of miscellaneous matter, and their prices were relatively high; they appealed to a well-defined readership, and often they set the tone of public debate on questions of national policy.

The Victorians, over a period of six decades, had access to well over a thousand periodical titles. A large number (including religious magazines) had serious literary content. Only within recent years has this wealth of material been seriously investigated by scholars, who are now writing histories of individual magazines and assessing the quality of never-reprinted essays and works of fiction.

Why the great quarterlies collapsed is no secret, quite apart from the fact that most periodicals have a well-defined and limited life-span (though some of these quarterlies lasted a very long time indeed). The nature of the reading public changed and fragmented as a consequence of a broadening of the educational base. Innovations in printing technology made possible the cheapening of prices for all kinds of printed matter and the addition of more line illustrations; later, of photographs. Advertising emerged as a powerful force affecting the interests of readers and the format as well as the content of a great deal of published material. Moreover, the specialisation of individual sciences meant that it was becoming increasingly difficult – even for gifted amateurs – to generalise about the contributions made by science in a trustworthy, readable way. New classes of readers, impatient with lengthy treatments of complicated issues, sought out sensation and reading distraction, patronised the periodicals which supplied them with what they wanted and turned away from those which seemed to have outlasted their time.

It was unclear to the Edwardians in what direction the market for literary values was changing, though a sense of something valuable being lost to erosion was expressed frequently in condemnations of the debasing of popular taste and reading habits. A summation of the new periodicals founded between 1900 and 1914 will serve to identify the parameters of the problem inherent in deciding how to accommodate the interests and desires of the new reading public.

In 1900 John Muir and Henry Newbolt established the *Monthly Review*, very much in an old-line tradition of the quarterlies. 1902 marked the beginning of the *Times Literary Supplement* and the liberal *Independent Review*. Ford Madox Hueffer's editorship of the *English Review*, lively though it was, and a congenial home for contributions by D. H. Lawrence and Wyndham Lewis, offered for the most part non-experimental, high-quality selections by such stalwarts as Conrad, James, Hardy and Bennett. All of these were general-interest periodicals.

At the same time the new journals were deliberately seeking to satisfy a coterie, or a more limited audience, than that served by Wilfred Whitten's *T. P.'s Weekly* (Whitten was later to be known as 'John O'London'), founded in 1902, or the *New Statesman and Nation*, which began publication in 1913. There was A. E.'s *Orpheus* (1907), designed to appeal to members of the Theosophical Art Circle, as well as William Butler Yeats's *Samhain* (1901), the journal of the Irish National Theatre Society, which printed plays by Yeats, Douglas Hyde, John Millington Synge and Lady Gregory, and John Eglinton's *Dana* (1904), which aimed at an Irish audience. *The Golden Hynde* (1913), with its emphasis on adventure and light fiction, seemed to have in mind idealistic young people as its major readers. In 1903 *Green Sheaf*, recording 'experiences beyond reality', was launched. Feminists were delighted to see the appearance of *Freewoman*, financed by Harriet Shaw Weaver, and edited by Dora Marsden; this soon turned into the *New Freewoman* and then, more impressively still, *The Egoist* (1914), which would print *A Portrait of the Artist as a Young Man* and sections of *Ulysses*; in 1917 T. S. Eliot would assume the editorship. The Georgian poets and other precursors of Modernism found a small but receptive public in the pages of *Open Window* (1910); *Rhythm* (The 'Yellow Book of Modernism'), edited by John Middleton

Murry and John Fergusson (1911); the *Blue Review* (1913), a supplement to *Rhythm* that assumed a separate though brief existence; and *Poetry and Drama*, edited for all its eight issues by Harold Monro, who printed poems by Robert Frost, D. H. Lawrence, Thomas Hardy and Ezra Pound. There were other 'little' magazines, such as *Commentator* (1908), to which T. E. Hulme contributed, Hilaire Belloc's *Eye Witness* (1911), and T. W. H. Crosland's *Antidote*, nor should one forget the lively and influential *New Age*, edited by A. R. Orage. In such periodicals the battles for Cubism, Imagism and Futurism were fought. Then, in 1914, the first issue of *Blast: The review of the great English vortex* came out with an abrasive championing of Vorticism; its guiding inspiration came from Wyndham Lewis and Ezra Pound. The 150 pages of this extraordinary periodical signalled the onslaught of radically new kinds of literary talent. In 1915 a somewhat smaller second issue, containing some of T. S. Eliot's early poems, appeared. One may argue (it has been so argued) that the cultural landscape was never the same once *Blast* identified what was truly *new* in literature.

The older journals, for the most part, were not noted in 1914 for the services they were rendering to literature, if only because the reviewing and analysis of books occupied only a part (often only a small part) of their pages. On the eve of the Great War the *Academy*, four years past the lively bohemian editorship (1907–10) of Lord Alfred Douglas, had turned into a High Church, High Tory bore. The *Cornhill Magazine* – duly appreciative of John Murray's warning to Leonard Huxley, the editor, that dullness was to be avoided – settled on a mixed diet of adventure fiction and comforting editorial positions. The *Quarterly Review* emphasised history, social themes and politics, while it consistently attacked Modernist tendencies in literature. The *English Review*, under the guidance of Austin Harrison (who replaced Ford Madox Hueffer), tried to become 'adult', and stirred up some minor controversies, though its circulation never exceeded 1,000 copies a month. The *National Review*, with a much larger circulation of 10,000, was edited by Leopold J. Maxse for forty years, but although writers like Austin Dobson and Sir Leslie Stephen contributed critical essays, the audience was narrowly concentrated in the political and social leadership and the space given to reviews was increasingly negligible. *Nineteenth Century and After* (the new name of *Nineteenth Century*, assumed in January 1901) treated science, religion and British imperial policy at great length, literature hardly at all. *Literary Guide*, published in close relationship with the Rationalist Press Association, focused on philosophy and science, and tended to print book reviews that fortified editorial positions. The *Contemporary Review*, at its controversial best between 1890 and 1910, when it really paid attention to literary events, shifted to political themes after Dr George Peabody Gooch assumed the editorship, a post he held from 1911 to 1960; the charge, often made, that it never quite caught up with the times may be documented by reading its often dated analyses of Ireland, war strategy and the Russian Revolution. The *Fortnightly Review*, edited by William Leonard Courtney (1894–1928), stressed politics. Some of the best and most stimulating writing about books was to be found in two newspapers, J. A. Spender's *Westminster Gazette* and J. R. Garvin's *Observer*.[2]

Widely read, and perhaps more influential than all other periodicals as guides to the best in new fiction, were the literary columns and reviews of the *Times Literary Supplement*, the *New Age* (with its popular 'Books and persons', a regular feature contributed by Arnold Bennett), the *Nation* and (later) the *New Statesman and Nation*. None of these journals and periodicals defined their readership as being narrowly elite. Men of letters, no less than novelists, were writing for the common reader. Since the war changed the cultural milieu in ways that were not always well understood at the time, it was not as apparent then as it has become apparent since that the common reader, as defined by Samuel Johnson in his life of Gray, would shortly disappear as the mainstay of the book trade. Dr Johnson thought of the common reader as someone sturdy in common sense, uncorrupted by literary prejudices and indifferent to the refinements of subtlety and the dogmatism of learning. The common reader was not a critic, nor a scholar; indeed, was worse educated than either, as Virginia Woolf was to write in her essay 'How should one read a book?', though her tone was not disapproving at all. The common reader read for his or her own pleasure rather than to impart knowledge or correct the opinion of others. Identifying herself with this reader, Virginia Woolf continued:

> We must remain readers ... we shall not put on the further glory that belongs to those rare being who are also critics. But still we have our responsibilities as readers and even our importance. The standards we raise and the judgments we pass steal into the air and become part of the atmosphere which writers breathe as they work. An influence is created which tells upon them even if it never finds its way into print.

And that influence, if it were well instructed, vigorous and individual and sincere, might be of great value when criticism is necessarily in abeyance; when books pass in review like the procession of animals in a shooting-gallery, and the critic has only one second in which to load and aim and shoot and may well be pardoned if he mistakes rabbits for tigers, eagles for barndoor fowls, or misses altogether and wastes his shot upon some peaceful cow grazing in a further field. If behind the erratic gunfire of the press the author felt that there was another kind of criticism, the opinion of people reading for the love of reading, slowly and unprofessionally, and judging with great sympathy and yet with severity, might this not improve the quality of his work? And if by our means books were to become stronger, richer, and more varied, there would be an end worth reaching.[3]

Virginia Woolf's essay, written more than a decade after the Great War had ended, betrays a wistfulness about, a sense of nostalgia for, an age when bookmen like Andrew Lang, Edmund Gosse and George Saintsbury shared enthusiasms with a large audience of reasonably well-educated and well-read citizens. The war, most literary historians agree, marked a turning-point in the commercialisation of the publishing industry. I will have more to say about this in my final chapter, which concentrates on 1918, but for the moment let me concentrate on what the common reader enjoyed most: the novel which ran on for some three hundred pages (reviewers made a habit of noting when it exceeded this norm), introduced characters not ordinarily met in middle-class society (the most popular novels were not written in the realistic tradition), plotted rapidly-moving adventures and sold for 6s.

In the first week of 1914 *The Bookseller*, most important of the trade journals, printed statistics for three years, 1911, 1912 and 1913, that clearly showed the importance of fiction to the world of publishing. Keeping in mind the fact that some books will always raise questions of classification, one may still be startled to discover that works of fiction outsold the next most prolific category of publication (religion and theology) by a margin of three to one. In 1911, 2,083 books of fiction appeared as opposed to 868 of religion and theology; in 1912, 2,290 of the former as compared to 934 of the latter; in 1913, 2,785 as contrasted with 893. The figures for essays and *belles-lettres*: 796, 895, 876; for children's books: 695, 821, 869; for biography and history: 638, 674, 615; for poetry and drama: 558, 674, 582; for political economy: 520, 621, 394; for works on education: 561, 522, 453; for books with medical and surgical emphases: 325, 367, 303; for music:

244, 300, 329; for annuals and serials: 364, 275, 357; books on law and parliamentary concerns: 234, 249, 139; on art and architecture: 235, 233, 195; on travel and adventure: 222, 213, 188.

Only shortages of paper and necessary printing supplies were to place a limitation on the rapidly expanding interest of common readers in new fiction. Two publishing houses alone, *The Bookseller* reported, had on their lists for 1914 seventy new novels and volumes of short stories. Announcements of new novels were appropriately excited. Ahead of the general reader in 1914 lay more works of fiction by Joseph Conrad (*Chance*), Sir Arthur Quiller-Couch and Maurice Hewlett. This reader could count on the publication of G. K. Chesterton's *The Flying Inn*, Oliver Onions's *A Crooked Mile*, Mr and Mrs C. N. Williamson's *It Happened in Egypt*, Mr and Mrs Egerton Castle's *The Golden Barrier*, William De Morgan's *When Ghost Meets Ghost*, Robert Hugh Benson's *Initiation*, E. F. Benson's sequel to *Dodo the Second*, Lucas Malet's *The Wisdom of Damaris*, Baroness von Huttenn's *Happy House*, Baroness Orczy's *Unto Caesar*, Rose Macaulay's *The Making of a Bigot*, Sir H. Rider Haggard's *The Wanderer's Necklace*, Warwick Deeping's *The King Behind the Throne*, Horace A. Vachell's *Quinneys'*, W. J. Locke's *The Fortunate Youth*, Peter Blundell's *'Oh! Mr. Bigwood': A nautical comedy* (a follow-up to his *The Finger of Mr. Blee*) and Morley Roberts's *Time and Thomas Waring*. The subjects included mid-Victorian romances, historical imaginings *à la* Scott, life along the Baltic shores in the ninth century, the strategies of antique dealers, the heroics of feminist leaders and much more.

Henry James, writing on 'The younger generation' in two essays published in the *Times Literary Supplement* (*TLS*; 19 March and 2 April 1914), complained that the rush of production had exceeded the activity of control; that the reservoir was 'bubblingly and noisily full' of a 'superficial measure of life'. His disdain for practically all modern novelists was severely worded. Their novels were 'swollen by extravagant cheap contribution, the increase of affluents turbid and unstrained'. He offered some kind words about the densely packed details of Arnold Bennett's *The Old Wives' Tale* and Gilbert Cannan's *Round the Corner*, and he saw in Hugh Walpole's *The Duchess of Wrexe* a gift of life 'received direct from nature'; but his praise of Compton Mackenzie's *Carnival* was qualified (the surface was overflooded, it was hard to tell where the story was going, he found the book difficult to judge 'on the whole'), and his dismay at Conrad's *Chance* was scarcely veiled in his acknowledgement that its publication had placed Conrad 'absolutely alone as the votary of the way to do a thing that shall make it undergo most doing'. He patronised D. H. Lawrence as hanging in 'the dusty rear', and he could not resist the temptation to say of H. G. Wells's new novels that they were 'very much more attestations of the presence of material than of an interest in the use of it'. He placed a lion's share of the blame on Leo Tolstoy as the great illustrative master, who had handed on all this ground of disconnection of method from matter and had turned into 'an execrable, pestilential model for younger writers'.[4]

James lamented most of all the absence of literary criticism in England and America, perhaps because too much creative work (i.e. fiction) had overwhelmed the outnumbered forces of criticism. Edith Wharton, responding to James in an essay entitled 'The criticism of fiction' (*TLS*, 14 May), agreed, but pointed out that literary criticism had always been regarded contemptuously in England, unlike France, which had honoured M. M. Sainte-Beuve, Anatole France, Jules Lemaitre and Emile Faguet. Literary criticism in England was in the 'ascidian stage', and should be encouraged. It would help the novelists, who talked about literary methodology but lacked the prerequisite knowledge of history and vocabulary; it would improve good books; it would make mediocre books less bad; and it would contribute to the novelist's intelligent understanding of life.[5]

Criticism, as James and Wharton defined it, was in very short supply in English periodicals during the Edwardian years and throughout the war, but there was no dearth of book reviewers, and plenty of product to consider. The *New Statesman*, a sixpenny weekly with a weekly sale of more than 3,000 copies, second only to *The Spectator* in its class, was destined to review – in its New Novels columns, by no means the most important section of what was primarily a rationalist, socialist, politically oriented publication – some 8,000 works of fiction over the next half-century, and it was not alone in a heroic, and foredoomed, struggle to separate the worthwhile from the dross.

Since the *Times Literary Supplement*, nominally offered for a penny (it came free with the newspaper), offered interested readers as wide a cross-section of notices of new works of fiction as any contemporary newspaper or magazine, it seems appropriate to concentrate on the likes and dislikes of representative reviewers, as expressed in the pages of that publication during the first seven months of 1914. (The official history of *The Times*, which offers no information about the rationale behind the founding or the editing policies of the *Literary Supplement*, implies by its silence that those in charge exercised a free hand in determining the relative value of individual categories of books.)

During this time period, no front-page review considered a new novel, and the usual space provided for reviews of new novels (two to five columns) seriously under-represented the importance of fiction on the contemporary scene. Though a few works of literary criticism were considered for fuller reviews in other sections of the paper, they never dealt with English novels written by living authors. The implications of a report sent back from Russia by a correspondent were never explored: that fiction stood on 'a considerably higher level in Russia than in England', with such active practitioners as Chekhov, Kouprin, Gorky, Adreef, Sologub, Remizof and Bunin making Russia 'the great literary country of the future'. 'The standard set by the public is higher', wrote the correspondent, 'or I suppose it would be truer to say that the general run of conversation in life is more interesting and therefore the literature is more interesting.' In fact, despite some notices of French literature, the *Times Literary Supplement* was astonishingly insular in its interests, and paid little attention to the Continent, patronised Canadian and American literature, and ignored Africa, South America and Asia altogether.

Moreover, its reviews of English novels exhibited all the faults of which Edith Wharton had complained. They debated the question of what subject might be more interesting than the one chosen; they insisted on comparing a new novel with the previous works of the writer (similarities approved, deviations from form and subject-matter sternly chastised); they made random references to the plot, discussed minor episodes at length, emphasised characters whose relationship to the plot remained obscure; and, perhaps as regrettable as any failing in her catalogue of sins, persisted in emphasising an author's view of life as gathered from the conversation of fictional characters rather than from the author's way of dealing with a subject.

Treatment of a major author drew on a long-formed set of attitudes towards the novel considered as entertainment. Thus, Joseph Conrad, long after he had established himself as a knowledgeable observer of land cultures and urban landscapes, was characterised as a novelist of 'the high seas and the deep seas'.[6] The reviewer of *Chance* repeated what to Conrad had long since become a distasteful characterisation of his work: 'We sea-Englishmen . . . owe a debt past all repayment to this stranger who has so nobly and generously made of himself a friend within our gates.' (Conrad did not think of himself as writing for *sea-Englishmen*.) A reviewer who approved of Ford Madox Hueffer's treatment of Henry James as 'the greatest of living writers' and thus 'the greatest of living men', spoke sternly of Hueffer's lack of familiarity with James's books, his tendency to get names wrong, his non-comprehension, his ignorance of history, his slighting of method and content; but a reader who read the review could only be mystified at what the reviewer (as distinct from Hueffer) considered special in James's achievement.[7] Rose Macaulay, in *The Making of a Bigot*, denied the distinction between a novel and life ('that immeasurably important thing that one has to be so sternly approached') as being the privilege, in fiction, of taking as many points of view as one likes all at the same time; to which the reviewer added approvingly, if a little dryly, 'Quite.'[8] And the reviewer of the fourth volume of the annually published *Essays and Studies by Members of the English Association* – containing essays by seven professors writing about drama, Marlowe, Shelley, Galsworthy's plays, place-names and the text of the first edition of *The True-Born Englishman* – complained of the general mediocrity of the analyses (only Spingarn and Elton escaped censure), adding that he favoured 'that unofficial class of writers who, simply as Englishmen and men of letters, keep alive, in books and periodicals, the native and unprofessional appreciation of our literature'.[9]

In a climate where academics were positively discouraged from writing about contemporary fiction (and, indeed, could not require its study as an element in the preparation for set examinations), the tradition of the reviewer speaking up for the common reader went almost completely unchallenged. It was inevitable, in the absence of clearly defined standards, that commercialism should become increasingly significant in the promotion of books. Max Beerbohm, writing a lead article on 'Books within books', conceded that novels were commodities, and that was 'all very well'. But he insisted that serious readers should have no illusion:

> The poulterer who sells strings of sausages does not pretend that every individual sausage is itself remarkable. He does not assure us that 'this is a sausage that gives furiously to think', or 'this is a singularly beautiful and human sausage', 'this is undoubtedly the sausage of the year.' Why are such distinctions drawn by the publisher?[10]

But he knew very well the answer to his own question.

Perhaps no concern seemed more important to reviewers than the question of what was real. This recurring topic was not primarily epistemological, but a catchphrase of considerable power, and had more to do with whether one might recognise on the street or in the drawing room a set of fictional characters than with a novelist's fidelity to fact or the probabilities of an imagined situation. For instance, Mrs Humphreys's *Jill – All-Alone* contained any number of characters, but not one of them was *real*. They dwelt 'in that vast region lying between fact and fiction. They resemble one's neighbours seen in a pageant – dressed up, and unmistakably conscious of it.'[11] Not that being unlike life automatically disqualified a novel from serious consideration. A novel entitled *The Magic Tale of Harvanger and Jolande* was characterised as

> a happy tale told for happiness. And though we occasionally have our doubts of the carles and the ducats and the demi-volts, *Jolande of the Fair Valley* is of romance itself, and remains in memory like a beautiful face seen in a dream of May-Day on the other side of the moon.[12]

The reader of Viola Meynell's *Modern Lovers* reacted to its characters as people whom one might personally like or dislike, and confessed to wanting more information about Effie, whose behaviour had attracted attention.[13] Bernard and Leonore, in Charles Inge's *Square Pegs*, had the distinction of being 'like real people'.[14] In W. Dane Bank's *James*, the main character was selfish and had a mean outlook; could not be considered as other than insincere; and provided unpleasant company.[15] Charles Garvice, in *The Woman's Way*, wrote not 'for the sophisticated who will jeer both at its characters and its situations', but, the reviewer quickly added, the novel had the merit 'that the characters and the situations fit one another'. Mr Garvice took pains to supply what his readers wanted, and he wasted no time on 'subtleties' to which they were indifferent.[16] Alice Herbert's *Garden Oats* was marked down not only because two child-beds and two narrowly escaped perils of a loss of virtue seemed too many in a book of 314 pages (again that emphasis on length!), but because 'in works of fiction presented in autobiographic form liking seems an essential part of the convention', and the reviewer did not like Olive, the heroine.[17] Monsignor Benson's *Initiation* presented its readers with 'one of the most lifelike small boys ever drawn'.[18] Frank Swinnerton, in *On the Staircase*, writing under the influence of George Gissing, depicted 'clever educated people of the lower middle class – clerks, typists, and so forth', characters who talked cleverly, 'but not perhaps too cleverly, and at great length' ('all to the good', the reviewer added).[19] Another reviewer enjoyed Sophie Coles's *Patience Tabernacle*, despite the fact that the story was not very well constructed, because Patience was 'a very attractive and delightful person, not only to the two men, but also to the less fortunate who can only know her in a book. She lives, and it is difficult to detect the trade secret of how she does it.'[20]

A novel had to manifest on every page an author's sympathy with its characters. Miss Broughton, in *Concerning a Vow*, seemed impatient with her people when she had drawn them, and put them to tasks for which they were unsuited. They submitted as well as they could, but it was 'an injustice to people of such vigorous humour'.[21]

Although the majority of these books were escapist fictions, the credibility of fictional characters often sorely tried the patience of reviewers. Often a vigorously imagined story, improbabilities and all, carried the common reader along on an irresistible tide of narrative energy. In the critical vocabulary of 1914 the words 'plot' and 'story' were interchangeable, and the distinction worked out by E. M. Forster in *Aspects of the Novel* (1927) was not yet universally understood or accepted. Thus, Mrs de Vere Stacpoole's *London, 1913* was described as a novel in which everything was 'all a little exaggerated', and in which 'the satire sometimes overshoots the mark', but it remained readable because the plot was 'ingenious enough'.[22] Ella Macmahon's *The Job* was bound to

> rejoice the heart of managers of lending libraries. Never for a moment need they hesitate to insert it in the book-box of the most careful parsonage. For it is 'nice' from cover to cover and very suitable for young persons of the schoolroom age. They will learn from it that, although the course of true love has its awkward places, all comes right in the end for lovers who are really noble and good. Having said so much, we need not consider too closely the details of the plot.[23]

(But, of course, the reviewer went on to do so.) A representative point of view is that of the reviewer who handled William J. Locke's *The Fortunate Youth*. The novel had a preposterous plot, passages of purple prose were everywhere, the presence of English royalty indicated a fundamental lack of seriousness. 'Well', the reviewer sighed, 'this is a grey world, and Ouida writes no more. Mr. Locke is nimble, neat, persuasive, and it is pleasant to meet, outside the realms of reality, with fortune and ability and success which grudging reality denies.'[24]

George Bartram, in *The Last English*, a tale of village vice and virtue in 1840, did not exercise the reader 'with subtle analysis or deep psychology'. The colours of the novel were broad, the characters simple; description was sparingly used, and the action was mainly carried on by the conversations; but it was worth calling attention to because it was an interesting story.[25] A plot did not have to be entirely convincing; although the mainspring of Violet Methley's *The Loadstone* was a scheme to rescue Napoleon from St Helena by a submarine boat propelled by hand, for example, the plot was redeemed by its ingeniousness, and because it was 'not badly written'.[26] Mrs Croker, in *Lismoyle*, described the adventures of a young English heiress who, pretending that she was quite a poor relation, visited relatives she had never seen in County Tipperary, and the result was 'a most refreshing Irish holiday'.[27] R. S. Crockett, in his novel, *Silver Sand*, added to his lengthy list of 'talented, picturesque romances'. With his kindly hand, he created a story 'full of adroitness' and a 'zest for the picturesque'.[28] H. A. Vachell's *Quinneys'* 'could not be considered a serious contribution to contemporary literature', but it remained 'something which novel readers may appreciate more – an engrossing story'.[29] Canon Hannay's *The Lost Tribes* was a novel in which the author enjoyed himself immensely, and the reader was incessantly diverted. 'As for the ten tribes they are once more lost sight of.'[30] H. G. Wells, by these criteria, could not hope to succeed, and in *The World Set Free*, the reviewer argued, he did not. Wells's novel had no singularity as a work of art. 'Considered purely as a story, this novel has the disadvantage of being without a beginning or an end or a central figure.' (*The World Set Free* imagined a world devastated by the dropping of atomic bombs.)[31]

An improbable story might well score heavily when it avoided a factitious verisimilitude. When G. Frederic Turner produced *The Red Virgin*, the reviewer applauded, though he knew well how absurd it all was.

> Mr. Turner has written an exhilarating story in which pistols crack and knives flash unceasingly. . . . There is plenty of blood. . . . The story riots and gallops, the dangers are not surmounted nor is the king out of the woods until the penultimate chapter, when most of the characters are cut or carved, riddled or dead.[32]

George Gibbs, in *Madcap*, was praised for having written a novel in which all comes right in the end. 'It is a gay affair of youth and make-believe, so ingenuously gay that only a churl would refuse the concessions of common sense that the author assumes.'[33] The reviewer (no churl he) may have been the same person who took up Mrs Maud Stepney Rawson's *The Priceless Thing*, and noted, with pleasure, that Mrs Rawson kept one 'urgently' wanting to know what was coming, 'which is, on the whole, a good thing'.[34] Marion Hills's *Sunrise Valley*, a conventional enough story of 'Manhood versus Maidenhood', was filled with stereotyped incidents and characters; the conclusions could be seen coming a mile off; but circulating libraries would love it: 'she has introduced us incidentally to several people whom it has been quite a pleasure to meet.'[35] Herbert Harrison, in *A Lad of Kent*, also told his story along 'well-tried lines', but he had 'a fresh pen, a sense of humour, plenty of invention, and a keen zest for the telling of a stirring tale'. As a consequence, it would appeal 'alike to the manhood in almost any boy and to the spirit of boyhood persistent in most men'.[36] (Many of the books reviewed might well have been treated as children's literature.)

Books dealing seriously with unpleasant topics were relatively rare and elicited strong adverse reactions from reviewers who felt more comfortable with amiable, diverting literary concoctions. Gilbert Cannan, as one example, could not be easily dismissed, but his *Old Mole*, published late in 1913, struck one reviewer as agreeable but somewhat spoiled by bitterness and 'wry-mouthed railing'. He had not gained

> the spiritual level where one can fight on the side of truth with laughter and good will. He must still be railing. And, therefore, while his reader is spurred by his cleverness, warmed by his art, and interested by his wealth of ideas and his keen understanding of the mind's moods and phrases, he will very likely be depressed and discouraged, not heartened, by the time he closes the book.[37]

The reviewer hoped that some day Cannan would write a book filled with the beauty of his vision, and pay only scant attention to sham art, drama, love and life,

> on railing at which he uses up much at present so much of his strength. The vision is there; some day it will absorb him wholly, and he will communicate it to others. In the meantime, all the sham things go on just the same; and it seems to us rather the business of the commentator than of the artist to show them up.

Nor was this an isolated blast at 'thinking on paper'. Darrell Figgis, who had written a fictional biography, *Jacob Elthorne*, was blamed for not having been sufficiently 'above' his material to have mastered it; in later years, the reviewer said firmly, the novel would seem to him 'lacking in the clarity and cleanness of a mature work'.[38] J. MacDougall's *Gillespie* presented an appalled reader with a relentless series of tragedies. 'The reader', complained the reviewers, 'must buckle himself into the armour of fortitude and tolerance – fortitude against a long recital of almost unrelieved sorrow and disaster, and tolerance of the fallacy that excess of detail, even unpleasant detail, constitutes added strength.'[39] Morley Roberts's *Time and Thomas Waring* contained some incidents that were 'needlessly unpleasant'.[40] It was, in fact, highly unusual for a reviewer to praise a novelist for reproducing faithfully the language of working-class men and women. The notice given to Robert Tressall's *The Ragged-Trousered Philanthropists*, a novel describing in detail the manner in which labourers decorated a big house, emphasised that the socialist message, encased in profanities, came across with a 'convincing air of fact', considerable anger at working conditions and a 'living' atmosphere.[41] Reviewers' interests seldom ran that way, and very few novels afforded an opportunity to render such a judgement. Far more common was the reaction to Laurence Housman's *The Royal Runaway, and Jingalo in Revolt*, a novel which resolutely refused to entertain in a conventional way. The book was too long ('400 closely-printed pages'), and too much of a political survey, prophecy and warning. 'One is too constantly listening to startling echoes of ominous contemporary controversies to permit of quite sufficient detachment.'[42]

What was wanted, then?

A clean plot-line. Bernard Capes's *Story of Fifine* dismayed the reviewer who had to report on it: 'when all is said and read, we are little the wiser as to why these things happened or who anybody really was. Perhaps it doesn't matter very much; but perhaps on the other hand it does.'[43]

Likable characters. Kathlyn Rhodes's *The Making of a Soul* was downgraded because it kept insisting that things, places and people were charming, though 'That in which their charm lies we must take on trust.'[44]

Readability, aided by an author's skill in repeating formulas. E. F. Benson's

Dodo the Second, about a 'brilliant girl of the nineties', was 'much more readable than "Locksley Hall sixty years after"', and was (the reviewer was pleased to say) 'extremely readable'. Benson did not 'lash' the new generation. If the new generation was no better than the old, it was at any rate (like Mr Benson) 'much the same.'[45]

A down-to-earth outlook, as in Helen Roberts's *A Free Hand*, a novel that took 'much care', had a 'keen insight', and contributed to its prosaic plot a 'sane' philosophy of life.[46] Or Oliver Onions's *A Crooked Mile*, in which the author could clearly be seen to stand stoutly 'on the side of sanity, marital and political'.[47]

Reading scores of such reviews, one inevitably senses that complaints about writing problems (awkward syntax and diction, clumsy plot construction, weak characterisation) strike tangentially at the failure of most novels to confront life directly and boldly. It is difficult to tell whether the reader of Nesta H. Webster's *The Sheep Track* – a novel about London society within and without the pale – really thought that the pepper of French phrases 'over the English' totally disqualified the book as social criticism.[48] The cudgeling of Mark Allerton for describing, in *The Girl on the Green*, a novice golfer who won a county championship with a score of 75, thus beating the favourite for the male amateur championship, raises the question of what the reviewer thought such a novel should be doing: 'This is surely the most remarkable achievement of its kind since a gentleman in *The Lady of the Lake* cleared eighteen feet with a standing long jump. It is very entertaining, but it really won't do.'[49] The average reviewer detested 'axiomatic whimsies about form and construction and impersonality and restraints' that seemed to be spoiling the common reader's enjoyment of the novel; efforts to develop a critical vocabulary in a few scattered reviews exerted what was perceived as a killjoy effect on 'appreciation'. Thus, William De Morgan's latest novel, *When Ghost Meets Ghost*, reminded one hearty of the ancient golden rule of the English novel: go as you please so long as you please. 'It is a rule that still holds good so far as the great public is concerned', the reviewer wrote, knowing that he spoke for many. 'Not for the sake of critical abstractions do hundreds of thousands of readers devour Mr. De Morgan's millions of words. They read him and love him for himself.'[50]

In 1914, in dozens of periodicals that described and praised novels aiming at entertainment as the highest good, 'critical abstractions' were still both rare and irrelevant to the everyday business of reviewing. Though the vast majority of novels did not constitute a literature of ideas, did not advance the tenets of realism or naturalism and may not be considered as distinguished contributions to the lengthening history of the English novel, the reviews of these novels were evidently written by men and women who identified themselves with ordinary readers. They, in turn, were no abstractions, but warm and living presences, indeed their other selves. Edith Wharton, like James a dedicated student of novelistic form, had conceded that a novel might be almost anything, but stressed that a critic should ask what particular thing was the novel in question trying to be; what had the author tried to present; how far had the author succeeded; and was the subject chosen worth representing? The reviewers, in a more humble way than Edith Wharton, were attempting to answer these very questions, though perhaps they often forgot to ask the last of her questions; their basic assumption was that the liveliness of story and the energy of characterisation were, in themselves, sufficient justification for the choice of subject-matter, however unworthy or trivial the subject-matter might seem to the self-proclaimed high priests of literature.

When the war broke out, and as the guns of August thundered, a leading article, 'Books on the crisis', appeared in the *Times Literary Supplement* of 6 August. Volumes IX to XII of the *Cambridge Modern History* suggested to the reviewer the necessity of taking a longer view than the immediate exigencies of battle might encourage. In the same issue another editor (or perhaps the same one), under 'Notes', refused to be dismayed by the heavy cloud that had been thrown over the prospects of the autumn publishing season. After all, the South African war had not proved as much of a disaster to the book trade as many people had anticipated. In 1899 the number of books published had exceeded by fifty the number published in 1898, and in 1900, 'a year of war and the gravest national anxiety', the number dropped by 418. 'It was only in fiction that the total for 1900 showed a very marked falling off, novels falling from 1,825 to 1,563.' From this statistic the editor drew the comforting conclusion that in times of national peril the reading public showed a tendency to draw away from works of imagination and mere amusement to the literature of thought and history.

That was not to prove the case, for the trends in fiction continued much the same for another four years, satisfying (by and large) reviewers and common readers alike. Anti-war novels were not to be written or published until some years past the Armistice. Experimental novels, fiction illustrating Modernistic principles, unconventional stories that played with time sequence, lay all in the unpredictable future. Yet during the war itself some novels of genuine merit found their way into print, and located their own audience of common readers, who enjoyed them.

The major part of the text that follows concerns itself with novels that barely acknowledge the existence of a war dominating the lives and imaginations of most Englishmen and women (if they do so at all); novels that obliquely and elliptically have something to say about the paramountcy of war; and novels that respond in some direct and immediate way to the fact of war. These divisions are arbitrary, as indeed the choice of novels is selective, based upon this critic's sense of what remains readable after the passage of a full three-quarters of a century, and what still may be recommended to common readers.

There has seemed to be little point in discussing at length trivial or even likable commercial commodities, however much they may have pleased their audiences of the war years. There has seemed to be less point in blaming anybody – publishers, reviewers, booksellers or public – for the high percentage of escapist fictions that came into print; that customers bought and enjoyed; that they swiftly forgot as the following year succeeded the current year's crop of best-sellers. Such books are always staples of the book trade, and less than a half-century after the end of the Second World War one would find it difficult to recall the reasons for the success of most popular novels of that five-and-a-half-year period.

If one point has emerged clearly in my review of the publishing conditions that prevailed at the outbreak of the Great War, it surely must be that literary critics were not obsessed by theoretical considerations of what the novel genre was doing, or ought to be doing. Nevertheless, I hope that I have provided enough information about the widespread interest of reviewers and novelists in satisfying the common reader's desire for a well-told tale of unusual events, involving believable characters in a credible milieu. The pacing of a narrative counted for much, if not all; and overambitiousness in presenting novelties of technique, grimness of detail or negative doctrine of how life's trials may best be endured was usually censured, at times very harshly. Many reviewers concurred with the H. D. Traill, who had written, in a widely quoted essay reprinted in *The New Fiction and Other Essays on Literary Subjects,* that the two most obvious things to be said about the New Realism was that it was 'unreal with the falsity of the half truth, and as old as the habit of exaggeration'.[51]

After a consideration of approximately a dozen novels published between 1915 and 1918 the text concludes with a review of the book trade in 1918. The English novel at that point was about to benefit from a great deal that had been printed before 1920, from a renewed or improved appreciation of the writings of Henry James in his late phase, Joseph Conrad in his early and middle years, D. H. Lawrence's *The Rainbow* and *Women in Love* and James Joyce's *Dubliners* and *A Portrait of the Artist as a Young Man.* Modernism, which had come to England several years before 1920 (Ford Madox Hueffer's *The Good Soldier* was, of course, a Modernist text), was neither well understood nor particularly popular until after the Great War had ended and an inevitable strong reaction against conventional, 'safe' modes of storytelling had set in. But Joyce's *Ulysses,* new novels by Ford, Bennett, Woolf, Isherwood, Waugh, Forster and the almost incredibly complex final stories of Kipling's career constitute the heart of a very different kind of literary history, one that is doubtless better known to most readers of our time than this reconsideration of English novels published during the Great War.

Part II

Novels that ignored the war

Chapter 4

George Moore's *The Brook Kerith* (1916)

Novels published between 1915 and 1918 adopted conflicting attitudes towards the importance of the war as subject-matter, quite apart from the fact that those novels which did treat the war did so with a strong, uniformly patriotic bias. Novelists who wished primarily to prosper needed only to look at the successes of Marie Corelli, who for more than thirty years (and well past the Armistice) was the most popular writer in the world, with each of her successful titles selling more than 100,000 copies. Compare this record with the averages achieved by Hall Caine (45,000), Mrs Humphry Ward (35,000) and H. G. Wells at the height of his career (15,000). Though Marie Corelli wrote her tribute to the Grand Fleet, *With Eyes of the Sea* (1917), and raised the question *Is All Well with England?* (1917), war stories were not her forte. Nor did the war provide a congenial kind of inspiration to a majority of other novelists.

This part considers four well-written, thought-provoking and popular novels that avoided any mention of England's involvement in a war that was to inflict 324,000 casualties during the Battle of Flanders, and that would conclude with even more staggering statistics: more than 900,000 deaths among soldiers of the British Empire, more than 2 million wounded casualties, almost 200,000 prisoners and missing. Casualties were to become three times heavier in proportion among junior officers than among common soldiers. The existence of the new phenomenon of shell-shock, badly understood, was barely acknowledged in the home press. Nor was the devastation caused by venereal diseases (one out of five soldiers was affected) recorded truthfully in contemporary chronicles.

The English novel was not the only literary genre that either ignored or glamorised the cruel realities of what was happening across the Channel, and it should not be singled out as peculiarly irresponsible or indifferent. But it would also be false to the history of the times to ignore the emphasis of countless novels on the 'delightfully humorous' aspects of life in the new army as if war were a continuing lark, or to regard *Zeppelin Nights*, by Violet Hunt and Ford Madox Hueffer (1915), as atypical. These stories, read by a Mr Serapion Hunter to his friends, helped them to escape the boredom of sitting up nights while waiting for German zeppelin raids to pass them by. There were hundreds of such books, prime examples of light reading, even after the Battle of the Somme.

But, as I hope to show, George Moore's *The Brook Kerith*, Norman Douglas's *South Wind*, Frank Swinnerton's *Nocturne* and Compton Mackenzie's *The Early Life and Adventures of Sylvia Scarlett* were substantial achievements as novels – more than light reading, something other than anodynes in a stressful historical period – and their publication signified the continuing good health of England's most popular literary genre.

If ever a novel renounced the techniques or tricks of the Victorian novel, *The Brook Kerith* surely did, with its long blocks of unindented text, its refusal to use quotations marks, and its 'melodic line'. George Moore hated what he considered to be the failures of Charles Dickens and most of his contemporaries (though he excepted George Eliot for having written *The Mill on the Floss*). He whimsically imagined Tolstoy, after having completed *War and Peace*, waking in the middle of the night and remembering that he had not included a yacht race, 'and another night when he awoke screaming: "I forgot high Mass."' Moore believed in the *story*, and rejected ideas as 'worthless' and 'pernicious'. 'Things', he wrote to John Eglinton in 1927, 'are the only good.'[1]

This new style, which began with surprising self-assurance in *The Untilled Field* (1903) and was further developed in the texts of *The Lake*, *Heloise and Abelard* and *Aphrodite in Aulis* as well as *The Brook Kerith*, has evoked a mixed reaction among critics. Janet Egleson Dunleavy likes it: 'In his last works Moore showed that he had learned to combine the perceptions of composer, painter, and writer as he painted with words; he had found ways to make the idea of the interrelationship of the arts serve his own artistic purpose.'[2] A. Norman Jeffares, speaking of *The Brook Kerith* specifically but obviously relishing the late development in Moore's career as a whole, writes:

The Biblical imagery and rhythms add to the epic quality of the story; it is simple and the narrative unfolds effectively, action, description, thought and speech blending in a pattern which provides variation and tension as well as information and reflection. It is easy to read, and it reads aloud superbly; it is spacious, dignified and captivating, an example of the supreme flexibility of the art of a great story-teller whose essential seriousness of artistic purpose is enlivened by the subtle humour and by the inconsequential trivia which give to the novel its feeling of concrete detail.[3]

(Jeffares continues by quoting an excerpt from a single paragraph that runs on for some eight hundred words, an act which seems to be an obligatory exercise for literary critics attempting to convince readers that Moore's prose must be read in bulk before its virtues will fully manifest themselves.)

But Moore's contemporaries expressed reservations, even witheringly negative judgements. George Bernard Shaw complained, 'I read about thirty pages of *The Brook Kerith*. It then began to dawn on me that there was no mortal reason why Moore should not keep going on like that for fifty thousand pages, or fifty million for that matter.'[4] (Shaw may not have reached page 31. Even so, it is unfair to suggest that Moore, or for that matter Tolstoy, had little or no sense of necessity of discriminating between major and inessential data within a fiction.) Shaw, however, was not alone in his disdain. William Butler Yeats believed that Moore, in his later years, misunderstood his powers; that charm and rhythm had been denied him; that Moore had 'pumice-stoned every surface because will had to do the work of nature'.[5] This development, Yeats believed, led to a barren style.

To such charges an explanation of Moore's intentions will not serve as adequate rebuttal, but some consideration of where the melodic line originated seems desirable. Moore identified several originals. He recalled a long sentence that he had written in French in his dedicatory epistle to *The Lake* (1905), describing the Seine and the poplars and the swallows 'flying low over the water', and he admired its suitability (despite its length) for later books: 'And so it was to come about that I was to find an English style in French.' He also acknowledged Wagner's musical pattern, after hearing *Tristan* a third time. Was it possible, he asked himself, to weave a story from start to finish out of one set of ideas, each chapter rising out of the preceding chapter in suspended cadence always, never a full close?[6] There had also been printed praise of Walter Pater in *Avowals* (1903), a critic who became 'the fourth great literary and moral influence that had come into [his] life'. Pater was not interested in telling a 'mere story' in *Marius the Epicurean*, but sought to relate the states of consciousness through which Marius passed. 'It was Pater's wont to include long parentheses and to continue his sentences with the aid of conjunctions, in the hope, and no vain one, of getting his prose to flow to a murmurous melody, rising and disappearing like water mysteriously.'[7] Other influences charmed Moore with the possibilities of reverie: Mallarmé, Dujardin, even Yeats himself. Realism had become increasingly distasteful, though at one time he had written (in *Confessions of a Young Man*, 1883) that upon the rock of Balzac he had built his church. There had also been his visits to Ireland at the turn of the century, which had led him into an admiration of an older oral tradition and intensified his interest in the Literary Renaissance movement there that he had once scorned. He believed that a written story was, by definition, different from a spoken story, which depended on the voice and gestures of the teller; as he wrote to John Eglinton on 6 July 1926, the teller, by his very presence, carried the story along, and he could skip over obstacles without the listener perceiving the skips. It is not surprising, therefore, that Moore's usual style of composition began with dictation of the same segment of a novel, in two-thousand-word installments, over and over again, perhaps as many as twenty times, until the rhythms of the spoken word, improved by his editing of the typescript of each version with a pen, satisfied his sense of what 'imaginative reverie' should offer in the way of delight to an interested reader.[8]

The Brook Kerith is, appropriately, subtitled 'A Syrian story', and all of it is meant to be read aloud. A story bearing this kind of disclaimer is not quite a lie in Plato's sense, but not quite the truth either; it is a version of what may have been the case, it is a plausible simulacrum of history, and it is perhaps not surprising that Moore offers us more than one story-teller here, suggesting the existence of more than one reality in the events recounted. But remarkably, the voices sound similar, and the melodic line – so prized by Moore as a development in the final decades of his life – bears primary responsibility. The more often his 'long, flaccid, structure-less sentences' expanded, as they were joined together by the simple conjunction 'and', the more Yeats's indictment gathered power: Moore was no longer listening (said Yeats) to 'the sentences men murmur again and again', and had armour-plated himself with a style hostile to the living word of the twentieth century. The tripartite structure of the novel was immediately evident to most critics and readers when the book was published: Joseph of Arimathea, Jesus and Paul hold centre-stage at different moments. But Moore, according to Barrett H. Clark, who talked at length with him in Paris in 1921, gave a 'snort' when discussing St John Ervine's remark that *The Brook Kerith* had been conceived from 'three different standpoints'.[9] The important matter of tone was consistent throughout, and that, to Moore, was more important. What the story was about seemed far less significant than how the story was told.

The past quarter of a century has been more respectful of Moore's achievement than Moore's own age ever tried to be. The flexibility of the melodic line has inspired some critical efforts to duplicate its special effects. Janet Egleson Dunleavy, for example, who (as we have seen) is heroically sympathetic to Moore's ambitions even when she admits his failures, writes that the sentences in his late books

> wind back on themselves, then spiral out again in new clauses; characters weave in and out of the narrative; the rooks rise from the nest in ever-widening circles; in the smooth water of the bay, which meets the curve of the beach, the soft, sinuous roll of the hills is reflected. Everywhere the serpentine line is evident.[10]

Anthony Farrow is perhaps less lyrical, but no less respectful of the potentialities of narrative art that this new version of Wagnerian technique empowers:

> in its capacity for capturing the endless flexibility of the human mind as it reflects upon the similarities of diverse experiences compounded and recast into new forms in every stage of life, the style is able, no doubt, to do what Moore hoped for it. Of its nature the technique is more finely attuned to mental, than to physical, events... it unquestionably marks the moment at which George Moore attains a voice which is uniquely and evidently his own.[11]

Jean C. Noël compares, at some length, the ninth chapter of the Book of Samuel to the literary mannerisms of *The Brook Kerith*, and speaks of Moore's simplicity reaching a 'Biblical plainness'. The 'unified level of narration' is achieved through the use of a stripped-down and slightly archaic vocabulary; Moore operates best when he writes within 'the middle of the language'; metaphors are missing here; 'shocks, surprises, and evocative, imitative virtuosity' have been eliminated. (It is hard to decide whether Noël thinks that Moore's artistry equals that of the author of the Book of Samuel, or surpasses it.) 'It seems that Moore in his old age', he writes, 'had really become sensitive to the sweetness and beauty of life's simple form, and this sentiment was transmitted to his prose without disrupting the unity.'[12] And when one adds to the stunned or bemused reactions of critics who experience great difficulty in employing the conventional language of their trade to characterise musical effects our knowledge of the deliberateness with which Moore rejected humour, melodrama, colloquialisms and indeed all the story-telling tricks that had so endeared the novels of the preceding century to readers of all social classes, we can better appreciate the reasons why Moore's modulated rhythms have both overwhelmed and appalled several generations of commentators, and why reactions to the prose style of *The Brook Kerith* have always been, and will remain, equivocal.

Thus, Joseph of Arimathea questioning his father about the appearance of Jesus – 'Tell me, is the Galilean as tall or as heavy as I am, or of slight build, with a forehead broad and high? And does he walk as if he were away and in communion with his Father in Heaven?' – does not use a vocabulary markedly or interestingly different from that of his father Dan. Dan proposes to Joseph that 'he should go there [to Heliopolis] and establish a mart for salt fish as soon as he had mastered all the details of the trade, which would be soon: a very little application in the counting-house would be enough for a clever fellow like Joseph'. Azariah, who teaches Joseph Hebrew and Greek, does not employ a diction or a sentence structure markedly different from that of his pupil, i.e., in Moore's universe all speakers function on the same level plain. Jesus, seen from the outside while Joseph of Arimathea 'tells' the story, is mysterious and eloquent only when his sayings in Scripture are quoted or paraphrased fairly closely; but when we get inside the mind of Jesus, it turns out to be fully as denuded of imagery or striking insight as the mind of Joseph, Dan, Rachel or Azariah. Moore does not bring us too close to Jesus before the crucifixion, so the problem of what Jesus *thinks* does not assume great importance for a very long while; thus, Moore can maintain that Jesus, shocked by the torture and near-death on the cross that he has experienced, is unable for many years to think back on his pre-crucifixion life, or to see the world in other than a shepherd's terms. But this is not really a satisfactory defence of the kind of language that Jesus uses, page after page, and year after year (until he turns fifty-three): the novel even informs us, at excruciating length, how Jesus, the good shepherd, saves a 'poor wee lamb' from death, and we learn much more than we wished to know about what is needed to find milk, to protect a lamb from wolves, to raise it in good health to maturity. These are exasperating commonplaces, but Moore persists in sketching the ordinariness of a shepherd, and doing so in unaccented prose.

The Apostle Paul presumably should be more interesting than Joseph, who cannot assay accurately the relative values of Essene or Christian belief, who performs the one great action of his life (saving Jesus and nursing him back to health) on the basis of an unexamined compassionate impulse, and who disappears suddenly and inexplicably from the novel (he is murdered by a zealot on a Jerusalem street; his death, casually mentioned in a single sentence, disposes of him permanently). Paul should also provide Moore with an opportunity to imagine more explicitly what motives led to one of history's great conversions. Paul, after all, is an egotist ('There did not seem to be on earth a true Christian but myself'), brutal in his willingness to speak frankly to his host or to any possible convert, and insufferable in his sense of rectitude. His unlovableness resembles, in a number of ways, the disagreeable and argumentative aspects of Moore's own personality. But Paul, too, disappears into the smooth-flowing, overlong sentences of the melodic line. Even a recounting of his extraordinary adventures and travels – of a certainty one of the most unusual odysseys of the Mediterranean world in the first century AD – turns into a series of 'And thens'. 'Now, Essenes, this story that I tell of what happened to us at Lystra has been told with some care by me'; 'Myself and Barnabas and Titus returned to Antioch and it was some days after that I said to Barnabas: Let us go again into the cities in which we have preached and see if the brethren abide in our teaching and how they do with it';

> I started with Titus and travelled all over Galatia and Phrygia to Bithynia, along the shores of Pontus, and returned back again, informing the kindly, docile souls, who loved us in their weakness, of Lystra, Derbe and other towns, setting up my loom and preaching every evening the coming of the Lord whither I went in Macedonia, Thessalonica, Iconium, Laodicea, not forgetful of Colossae, for two years or more (I have forgotten).

A reader's objection is not necessarily directed against this bald paraphrasing of Scripture, though the itinerary of cities visited becomes a great weariness to the flesh, and even the Essenes, Paul's audience, welcome the opportunity to rest between segments of Paul's monologue. Rather, the objection is to an insufficiently dramatised sense of what it must have been like to preach to indifferent or hostile Macedonians, Greeks and Syrians. What must it have been like, for example, to preach the word of the risen God to Athenians, with their own long history of faith in and scepticism about a whole pantheon of gods? Paul does not seem to work his miracles of conversion on the basis of either an endearing personality or an interesting mind, and, even worse, the rhythms of his speech are not all that different, are not that clearly differentiated, from those of Joseph or of Jesus.

As a direct result, the dramatic scene towards which the final third of the novel has been inevitably wending, the confrontation between a Jesus who has renounced his faith in himself as the Messiah and a Paul who holds fast to his interpretation of Jesus's teachings before the crucifixion, is drained of intensity; the voices dispute but are heard as if from a distance; the unruffled prose murmurs, and moves on; everything is muted; and Jesus disappears into the east, Paul into his crusade westward, in an astonishing trailing-off. The novel has no true climax. But, as we might have suspected long before the final pages, the melodic line prevents the novelist from either sustaining or benefiting from confrontational scenes. To vary the image, the fact that music is being played is more important than our ability to appreciate the actual melody that is being played.

Nevertheless, *The Brook Kerith* is something more than an experiment in narrative technique. Problems of faith had intermittently worried Moore from the late 1880s on; in particular, the life of Jesus – whose historical existence Moore had more than once doubted – demanded some kind of creative response. 'Ribbons of tooth-paste squeezed out of a tube': thus Yeats described Moore's new style, developed at some cost to Moore's earlier appreciation of the art of the naturalistic novel. But Moore was also determined to work out his own feelings about the Christian faith, and it was perhaps inevitable that his fullest statement should be delayed until the Ebury Street phase of his life.

There had been earlier indications that a work of the order of *The Brook Kerith* was in the offing. In *Mike Fletcher* (1889), an intermittently convincing attempt to modernise the Don Juan legend, Moore found himself torn between suspicion of sensualism and his deep conviction that personal freedom as an ideal transcended conventional morality.

He believed that he had developed a new method (a character sees the world through the prism of personality, and each day remakes his world); but it was clear that Mike Fletcher's libertinism was out of control. It led inevitably to exhaustion and self-disgust. Suicide was the hero's only solution (as one critic noted, 'in the middle of some purple prose').[13] There must be something better, Moore could not help telling himself (he readily admitted, after publication, that undertaking the writing of *Mike Fletcher* had been a mistake). And indeed, Mike Fletcher, in the novel, had contemplated the possibility of writing three plays, to be called *John, Christ* and *Peter*, based on the story of Jesus's life.

Not until the turn of the century, however, did Moore focus on the possibility of writing a novel. Pertinent to any record of his growing concern with this subject-matter is his review of an English translation of Wagner's *Jesus of Nazareth*, posthumously published; Moore's review appeared in *The Musician* (1897). Wagner never finished the opera, but his notes and quotations, taken from the Lutheran Bible, were intended to serve as the basis of a five-act opera. Moore commented on Wagner's interest in the beliefs and psychologies of his characters (Wagner had great difficulty in reconciling this material with his dramatisation of the public life of Jesus), and underscored his theory, in *Mike Fletcher*, that a man's thoughts, taken as a whole, constitute his identity. Edouard Dujardin's *La Source du fleuve chrétien* (1906) caught his attention, and he became deeply interested in John Eglinton's description of a recently published book about the historical Jesus. He wrote a scenario and gave it the title *The Apostle*, sending it for publication to the *English Review*, later he expanded it, and Maunsel published it in 1911. *The Apostle* not only gives us a Jesus who does not die after hanging for three days on the cross (the Romans normally used three days to make sure that a legally condemned man died during the process of being crucified), but invents a scene in which Jesus and Paul meet at Jericho fully a quarter of a century after the crucifixion. (This scene was to be retained as a dramatic confrontation in *The Brook Kerith*.) Paul's discovery that Jesus had died and been resurrected meant that the very basis of Christianity might be undermined, and, to prevent the destruction of his developing religion, an enraged Paul murdered Jesus so that the fact of his having survived could not become public.

Moore corresponded with T. W. Whittaker, an historian of religion (Dujardin had given him Whittaker's name), and mused over the plausibility of the theory that Jesus might not have died on the cross. That suggested, in turn, the existence of a rescuer. Who was more likely than Joseph of Arimathea, who officially requested from his friend Pilate the right to take custody of the crucified body, and to bury it in a tomb that he had prepared in advance? The speculation that Jesus may have been an Essene was plausible. Less so was the notion that Jesus might have lived for another quarter of a century, and gone 'on a preaching mission into India' (Moore talked about this legend in an interview with a correspondent from the *Boston Transcript*). He admitted that such legends were 'vague' and left much unexplained; but historical sources filled in a number of dark shadows, and he fashioned therefrom 'a detailed and coherent tale'.[14] In addition, he felt obligated to visit Jerusalem, towards the end of February 1914, 'in search of a story or drama'. He wanted most to see the place 'where the woman was taken in adultery'. He spent less than a fortnight there, but found time to visit Jericho, Moab and the countryside, 'as naked and as savage as the psalms'.[15] Some (if not the most important part) of his descriptions of the Palestinian terrain derive from this intensely lived, time-compacted visit; Moore, at the age of sixty-two, was understandably reluctant to ride any more horses or donkeys than necessary, especially when the roads wound their way along the edge of precipices.

All of this amounts to a modest amount of personal research and a controlled reading-list of secondary sources. There is no point in claiming for *The Brook Kerith* a greater scholarship than actually served for its footings. Moore remembered cock-fights from what he had seen in western Ireland; the specifics of shepherd life, unchanged in two millennia, could easily be gathered from late Victorian practices on the downs of Sussex. But Moore went to considerable trouble to authenticate the kind of medicines that might have been used, in Jesus's era, to revive a man who had been scourged, nailed to a cross and left to die, and Moore did his best to limn a believable portrait of life among the Essenes. Much of his biographical material about Paul, of course, came directly from Scripture, as already noted. And there is an impressive accretion of his own thought and conviction; the story had been gestating, from beginning to publication in August 1916, for more than two decades. Moore, who outraged his Irish acquaintances with anticlerical statements ('Salve' in *Hail and Farewell* is a truculent announcement of his Protestant beliefs, and that volume came out in 1912), here writes a novel that not only transmits the reports of various witnesses that miracles have been performed, but confirms the credibility of some of their testimony, and liberally allows for the possibility that natural laws of cause and effect have been suspended in order to further Christ's ministry. The fact of a resurrection is not needed for Moore's Jesus to have been what, before his crucifixion, he said he was; he had uttered dark parables, true, but he had also performed miracles. When we recall how little Moore believed in, or understood, the mystical element of religion, this concession becomes all the more remarkable.

His brand of realism was, to adopt the descriptive term used by Frederick W. Seinfelt, 'unconventional',[16] though his attitude towards women in *The Brook Kerith* was, perhaps not unexpectedly, both conservative and somewhat patronising about woman's proper place within the larger scheme of things. The Wagnerian influence pointed in a direction that few beside Moore wished to go, and the melodic line, which is distinctly different from the stream-of-consciousness technique with which some of Moore's admirers have wished to align it, minimises drama by rendering it in language that softens all the rough edges. Nevertheless, the novel became an instant best-seller, selling out three printings within six weeks of publication, and Moore never let go, revising practically every new impression until he settled for the 1927 version that was published in the Uniform Edition. He gave to the dramatisation of a portion of the novel (1923) the old title *The Apostle*, and revised that, again and still again, until in 1930 he was sufficiently satisfied to encourage a production, called *The Passing of the Essenes*, that was staged at the Arts Theatre in London. In brief, he worked hard at making the story come alive, even though he recognised the existence of problems in the narrative line, and admitted with chagrin that the first published version had contained stylistic infelicities, anachronistic words and phrases and structural awkwardnesses.

Joseph of Arimathea dominates most of the novel before the scenes depicting Jesus's long, slow road to recovery from the agonies of the crucifixion. Joseph's incredibly difficult journey carrying the body of Jesus up and down the rocky paths that led from Calvary to his home is so clearly and vividly narrated that he becomes more important than the burden he bears. Moore's intention may be more complex than many readers appreciate: he wants to sketch the childhood of a rich man's son, and to do so in terms that will not make Joseph an unsympathetic prig; he wants to give us a convincing study of a seeker after religious truth; and he is also interested in portraying a good man who, for various reasons, cannot afford to be either boldly or self-consciously heroic. Moore encounters problems in sketching the reasons why Joseph, well on his way to becoming an accountant, a successful merchant of fish and a public-relations expert, should develop anxieties about the true identity of God, and leave home and parents in order to live with the Essenes, a minor, obscure tribe of Jews who have renounced society because of their concern with transcendental matters. The break with Joseph's secular past is too abrupt, the motivation too vague, for a reader to be convinced that this particular Joseph would behave in this particular way. But the multiple objectives of Moore's characterisation are for the most part achieved, and most strikingly so in the dramatising of Joseph's fears for his personal safety if his relationship to Jesus becomes a matter of public record. Moore seems to have felt deeply the naturalness of Joseph's anguish when he learns of the fierce hatred of the priests towards Jesus and all his followers, when he suffers a stormy conflict between the religious duty to obtain the body of Jesus and bury it and when he dreads the possibility that he would thus become a marked man. Joseph bribes a centurion; he allows the centurion to lie to Pilate; he admits his friendship for Jesus to a Pilate who (only hours before) had condemned Jesus to death; he trembles at the knowledge that God did not save Jesus in the end as he expected; he is unconvinced by predictions of the resurrection; he is all too human in his doubts even as he works to save Jesus from the ignominious 'reality of the tomb'. There is something exalted about this Joseph, who recognises the moment when he meets his fate, however much he has tried to obey his father and avoid the troubles that will endanger an untroubled citizenship. In these scenes, as Joseph feverishly oscillates between hope that Jesus can be saved and despair attendant upon his knowledge of how complicated keeping all knowledge of Jesus's existence even from his servants will be, Moore fully justifies his choice of Joseph as a central point of view.

A second strength of the novel lies in its convincing treatment of the community of Essene monks in the arid lands of Jericho. A reader may not find the religious disputations particularly entertaining. Moore's heart is not in this kind of theological speculation, and he obviously has difficulty in understanding how or why prophecies about the end of the world should have so seized upon the imaginations of otherwise intelligent human beings. But he is fair to Hazael, the president of the Order, and he sketches an impressively detailed study of another good man. (When we think back on Dan, Rachel, Mathias, Esora and even the self-important pedagogue Azariah, Moore's recognition of the existence of unselfish goodness grows to be an important element in the novel.) Moreover, Moore prefers a succession of small scenes among the brethren of this community to what could so easily have become a series of 'big scenes' based on Scripture, conveniently developed as models by countless generations of artists (e.g., in the Sanhedrin, at the court of Pilate, on Calvary).

The third and most positive aspect of *The Brook Kerith* is that it attempts to play fair with theological questions that Moore had little sympathy with. Moore did not believe that Jesus was divine, and his adoption of the possibility that Jesus did not die on the cross is essentially a rationalist's approach to the founding of a religious faith that transformed the ancient world. He consistently argued the case that Jesus taught a message inscrutably dark in its details and megalomaniac in its implications, particularly in the final months of his life. Moore suggested any number of reasons why the contemporaries of Jesus should have misunderstood him, and why their misunderstandings, cumulatively considered, led inevitably to the tragedy of the crucifixion; to some extent, Moore quietly suggests, they encouraged Jesus to proclaim himself as the Messiah. Moore's attitude towards Jesus's hubris is very much like that of Pilate, who tells Joseph at one point, 'He seemed to me like a man only conscious of his own thoughts . . . even while speaking he seemed to rouse hardly at all out of his dream, a delirious dream, if I may so speak, of the world redeemed from the powers of evil and given over to the love of God.' Moore, over the full length of his own professional career, regarded this kind of belief as a disordered construct of reality, one verging on hysteria; it could come to no good end.

Moore's conviction that he had done better with Jesus than with Paul, expressed in a letter to John Eglinton (10 May 1916), was well founded. 'Paul is an historical, Jesus a legendary character,' Moore wrote. 'Paul painted his own portrait and did it so thoroughly that he left me very little to add.'[17] Moore might have added that the second half of his novel had struck out boldly – perforce – because he had to imagine what a Jesus recalled to life might remember of his past, and how he might come to terms with that past. In the case of a resurrected Jesus, unlike that of Paul, there were no printed sources to draw on, unless one accepted fully and without question the divinity of

Jesus. Moore thought of Jesus as a human being whose natural instinct, after being saved by Joseph, was to throw up a mental barrier against any remembrance of who he had been before the crucifixion, and what he had done as a preacher carrying the word of God. He simply could not remember (at first), and then he could not speak about it to those who sheltered him, loved him and lived with him. Rather incredibly, he maintained his silence about his past so successfully that they not only agreed not to question him about his antecedents; they failed to identify him with the Jesus of Nazareth who had been crucified not many miles from their cenoby.

The point of Moore's characterisation is that a Jesus who lives on for another quarter of a century after his crucifixion must inevitably change his views, must inevitably grow in some way. Moore presents us, finally, with a Jesus who renounces much, if not most, of his younger self: a Jesus who begins to see God in terms different from those believed in by his forefathers (God is not a man 'who would punish men for doing things they have never promised not to do, or recompense them for denying themselves things they never promised to forgo'), who accepts his humanness (because 'All things are God', which makes Paul neither less nor more human than he) and who ultimately comes to believe that 'God did not design us to know him but through our consciousness of good and evil'. Only to this extent may men know God. Religious faith, though it may begin with love of God, carried to the point of fanaticism leads to persecution. The fictional Jesus thus argues what Moore himself believed, that the value of living for ourselves and allowing others to do likewise is all-important. 'God has not willed us to know him save through our conscience. Each man's conscience is a glimpse.'

It is futile to argue that Moore's Jesus would not inspire a large following or found a religion, for Moore would have cheerfully agreed. The sanctity of one's own conscience – 'God like all the rest is a possession of the mind' – is a singularly modern conception, more Protestant than Catholic, and probably more secular than Protestant. The evolved doctrine of a middle-aged Jesus was bound to baffle and then enrage Paul; there could be no meeting of minds here. 'Whither goest thou? Paul cried, looking back', Moore writes as his novel concludes. 'But Jesus made no answer.' No answer is possible, for Paul, in the last moment of the imagined confrontation, is as Jesus once was. Paul's religious intensity, rising to delirium, will lead to the creation of a formalised, institutionalised Christianity. But Moore's message is stern: Paul's version of Christianity will distort – and perhaps even make invisible – the human side of Jesus's teachings.

One may wish for more emotion in the telling, but the melodic line denies us the primary benefits of drama, and seems to repudiate more than a century of historical development in the novel. A reader may well object to the clumsiness of a novel that stops dead in its tracks twice before picking up the narrative thread, and changes its point of view several times for reasons that do not seem compelling. The casual elimination of Joseph as a character is egregious, and the question of due proportion in assigning meaningful roles to major figures does not seem to have been answered satisfactorily. These would be serious problems inhibiting the readability and the liveliness of any novel.

Still, it was an important book for 1916, and not merely because Moore insisted upon his own version of the New Testament and converted his 53-year-old Jesus into a champion of his own principles. It was, for all its failings, a hugely ambitious and heroically imagined reconstruction of manners and ways of thinking that had long since passed from the world. The prose style is maintained consistently as a stylistic experiment. *The Brook Kerith* cannot help but remind us once again of the limitless capabilities of Scripture to stimulate a creative mind.

Chapter 5

Norman Douglas's *South Wind* (1917)

Miss Wilberforce liked to drink heavily. The death of her fiancé, a sailor, helped to unhinge her; she had since attempted to kill herself more than once; she was no longer responsible, and, because she lived on the island of Nepenthe in Norman Douglas's novel *South Wind*, the reader's assumption must be that her eccentric behaviour was in large measure due to the fact that she had been Mediterraneanised. Since undergoing such a transformation – becoming Mediterraneanised – was Douglas's prescription for a saner and happier existence, Miss Wilberforce's behaviour was intended less to shock than to remind us of the multiplicity of forms uninhibited happiness can assume. She was apt to appear at night, 'a dun phantom of willowy outline, swaying capriciously to and fro, like a black feather tossed by the wind', crooning 'a vulgar song' about a sailor named Billy; it was entirely in character for her to send her hat 'careering across the street', and to undress in the moonlight.

The catalogue of her problems requires time to recite. A thief robbed her house of valuables. Omens of ill portent – for example, the drying-up of the fountain of Saint Elias – pressed heavily upon her, as indeed they did on other residents of Nepenthe. She shocked a policeman 'unaccustomed to her ways' when, naked, she not only sang 'Auld lang syne' but insisted on translating it into Italian for his benefit. Bishop Heard mused quietly, 'Miss Wilberforce apparently can be relied upon to create a diversion of a scandalous nature', but his tone was not censorious; he wanted to 'do something to help such a poor creature', and Mr Keith, the wealthy lover of pleasure to whom he was speaking, responded, 'The dear lady! I don't know what we should do without her.' Who could dislike Miss Wilberforce? Alcohol defeated her shyness, made her 'festive, playful, positively flirtatious'; she sailed splendidly into a 'grand condition'. She loved to declare the occasion for drinking: her birthday. ('Miss Wilberforce had about forty birthdays in the year, each of them due to be worthily celebrated like this one', the narrator informs us.) She was a lady, one who attended Divine Service in the English Church. She was often the only member of the congregation, unless one counted Freddy Parker, the financial commissioner for Nicaragua. (Douglas regarded the historical original – an English picker-up of scholarly trifles – as a rival to himself on the island of Capri.) But she was now 'definitely on the downward grade'. Her unpredictability meant that she became responsible for stricter implementation of the rule that ladies were barred from the Alpha and Omega Club. This 'pathetic local figure' had a ready tongue and wiry limbs, but even these unladylike attributes would not be damning by themselves; her insatiable craving for alcohol meant that ultimately 'she would unavoidably [damage] the reputation of the place, to say nothing of its furniture'. Parker, president of the club, sighed when reminded of her 'problem', and agreed not to pursue the question of admitting ladies.

But the story of her having lost her lover happened to be true, 'for a wonder. She had received a twist for life.' And her habits – her lugubrious remarks to friends who sympathised with her by admitting the loss of their own lovers, her 'noctambulous habits' in which she divested herself of clothes ('a singularity which perturbed even the hardiest of social night-birds who had the misfortune to encounter her'), her nervous breakdowns, her candidacy for a sanatorium (she refused to be talked over 'into doing what was in her own interests'), etc. – suggest how serious a problem she had become. Still, the narrator insists that we appreciate her good points: 'a pretty wit', 'a residue of gentle nurture; tender instincts and a winsomeness of manner that captivated you', and an attractive way of wearing black. Moreover, she was 'old England, through and through'. When Denis Phipps, an idealistic but confused young man, talked to her, she cheered him: 'He might have been sitting with an elder sister just then, eating strawberries and cream and watching a tennis match on some shady green lawn.' She was (in brief) a charming talker, and had a right to her eccentricities.

A minor character in a very large cast, but fully realised: Miss Wilberforce represents wider issues. She was released from prison every time she was sent there. One must think of her with understanding, tolerance and mellow sympathy, and even Signor Malipizzo, the magistrate, ordinarily harsh in his judgements, extended to her the hand of friendship. The novel ends with the problem of Miss Wilberforce unsettled; it may be enough that her scandalous behaviour, now extending to 'broad daylight' hours, was sketched in primarily to inform readers of how the inhabitants of Nepenthe reacted to her; those who condoned her behaviour, or who saw beyond it to the real person (the lady, the star-crossed lover, the still witty Miss Wilberforce), were Douglas's kind of people. For Miss Wilberforce, in casting off her clothes, was 'stripping off, like so many worthless rags, the layers of laboriously acquired civilization', and her symbolic function was fully as important as the attention she drew by her actions. She deserved our compassion, perhaps even our admiration, because she insisted on returning to the real self. She contributed to a reader's startled realisation that here we have 'a community of sophisticated creatures inspirited through release from our polite and respectable society'.[1]

In the Introduction that Douglas contributed to the Modern Library edition of 1925, the question of the factual basis of Miss Wilberforce was addressed directly. She was not a near connection of his own family, Douglas wrote: 'I wish she were!' He claimed that she had been put together as a composite of some twelve women who liked to drink to excess. One of them was 'so passionately addicted to strong waters that it became a doubtful pleasure to sit next to her at a dinner table or anywhere else', though she never threw off her clothes in public. 'I suppose', he added, 'she thought that an Ambassadress should draw the line somewhere. Which was a pity.' He liked the Miss Wilberforce type, and he 'fervently' prayed that the type might never die out.[2]

As Count Caloveglia said to the Bishop, 'In the Mediterranean, Mr. Heard, lies the hope of humanity.' Miss Wilberforce, for all her failings, recognised that fact, and had gravitated to the one area of the world that understood, and forgave, her limitations in exchange for the exuberant contribution she made to the variegated patterns of Nepenthe society. Not that everyone loved an aberrant 'lady'. Signor Malipizzo was almost alone – among the representatives of law and order – in thinking that she deserved a second, and a third, chance. But if Miss Wilberforce's actions did not evoke much sympathy and compassion among most of the officials of Nepenthe, they would evoke even less in the world exemplified (in Douglas's mind) by the preparatory school of Staffordshire that he once attended, and even more strikingly by Uppingham, the educational institution that he so completely detested; both were so *typical* of the frigid and uncaring Northland.

Douglas's comic inventiveness constitutes an important claim to our continuing affection for *South Wind*. The critics who complained about the lack of a well-constructed plot stung Douglas into responding, in *Alone* (1921), that his book suffered from an excess of plot. After all, the novel contained a murder, witnessed by Bishop Heard. The bishop had become so transformed by his experiences on Nepenthe, by the series of challenges hurled at his conventional notions of right and wrong, that he decided to say nothing about the murder to the authorities, or for that matter to anyone else. 'You must unconventionalise him, and instil into his mind the seeds of doubt and revolt', Douglas wrote, attempting to explain the problem that confronted him as a novelist.

> I would defy the critic to point to a single incident or character or conversation in the book which does not further the object in view. The good bishop soon finds himself among new influences; his sensations, his intellect, are assailed from within and without.[3]

Nevertheless, if Bishop Heard came to Nepenthe from Bampopo in the Equatorial Regions (a comparably exotic environment), where the natives were 'Fine, healthy animals; perfect of their kind!', he already knew a good deal about the temptations of indolence; he had already seen (and tolerated) caricatures of Christianity; he could have entertained no guilty conscience about his easy remission of the natives' sins. *South Wind*, in addition, covered so brief a period of time, a little over a week, that it was hardly likely the bishop would have become a sudden convert to the doctrine of *dolce far niente*. The bishop was a convenient puppet-figure, a pretext for Douglas's message about the 'alien influences' that could be set to work on a custom-bound man who had attained episcopal status; but he was not interesting in his own right, and he enjoyed the status of an attendant lord.

Moreover, Douglas's defence of his novel as all plot, or more than enough to spare, seems pegged to an odd proposition: the murder witnessed by the bishop, 'under these particular circumstances', should be seen as not only justifiable and commendable but – insignificant. Quite insignificant! Not worth troubling about. Hundreds of decent and honest folk are being destroyed every day; nobody cares tuppence; 'one dirty blackmailer more or less – what does it matter to anybody?' There are so many more interesting things on earth.[4]

If this was the major message of the novel – and Douglas's assertion that the plot had been deliberately leading up to its annunciation inevitably stressed its importance – then there ought to have been more in the way of character development, more inner turmoil, more agonising by the bishop before he changed his mind. The novel does not dwell on the mental convolutions of the bishop's decision to understand, and to approve, the way in which Mrs Meadows (the murderess) had saved her family. 'Everything was clear as daylight', the bishop decided.

> And he found he had bothered himself long enough about Muhlen [the murdered man]; there were so many other interesting things on earth. A contemptible little episode! He decided to relegate it into the category of unimportant events. He was glad that the whole affair had remained in the background, so to speak, of his Nepenthe experiences. It seemed appropriate.

The change in his opinion of murder, indeed the change in his lifestyle and religious values, was tantamount to a snapping of fingers.

The aesthetic achievement of *South Wind*, however, did not lie in its fidelity to human nature, or in an ordinary citizen's sense of what might be justly rendered either to Christ or to Caesar. The use of the word 'Nepenthe' was intended to denote – specifically – a drug of Egyptian origin (mentioned in *The Odyssey*) that was capable of banishing grief or trouble from the mind. More broadly, it referred to wine, or any potion, which performed a similar function. Miss Wilberforce had evidently discovered its efficacy, and the novel – which praised alcohol as a social gift – ended with several rounds of drinks, an increasingly drunken babble, and the expression of a noble sentiment to the effect that 'We are all at the mercy of youth'. *South Wind* was about something other than the bishop's conversion to more relaxed values; its subject-matter was human personality, and all its permutations. Mark Holloway, whose biography of Douglas offers a well-rounded picture of a surprisingly complicated figure, shewdly noted that 'the motives of Mrs Meadows and the bishop are profoundly unimportant compared with the remaining ninety-five percent of the book'.[5]

All the hedonists portrayed in the novel had their enemies. Of these the most notable was Signor Malipizzo, based on a magistrate whom Douglas detested and feared, Capolozzi the terrible; Douglas more than once believed that he was about to be jailed for real or imagined misdeeds by Signor Capolozzi. Legalistically correct in his usage of judicial forms but willing to manipulate the law to destroy personal enemies, eminently corruptible if approached in a suitably discreet manner, Signor Malipizzo undertook his enquiries into the disappearance of Mr Muhlen (whose murder the bishop, by accident, had seen from a distance) with a singular zest. His motive, however, was sordid: 'Muhlen had practically invited him to stay at his own native town where every kind of amusement was to be had, the female society being of the choicest. Exuberant women – and rich! It would have been a pleasant change after the trim but tedious gardens of Salsomaggiore.' He worked with a Code of Criminal Procedure that could not help but chill the blood of northerners so unfortunate as to be caught in its toils. For example, if any person admitted to having seen Muhlen on the day of his disappearance, he could be imprisoned for an endless length of time while waiting for a trial that might take up to half a century to commence. Caught in Malipizzo's web was a simple and somewhat dim-witted lad who suffered the double misfortune of wearing round his neck a gold coin 'of foreign nationality', and of being related to Malipizzo's arch-enemy, the parish priest. 'This boy', Malipizzo remarked,

> from all accounts, was the pure type of the callous murderer. He stutters. He makes uncalled-for gurglings of a bestial nature. He had pendulous ears, and certain other stigmata of degeneration which are familiar to all conversant with criminal anthropology. Of course he denies everything. But mark my words! After six or seven months, when the prison diet begins to take effect, he will confess.

Malipizzo was a free-thinker. Part of his glee at 'catching' the supposed murderer was that he could thus poke a thumb in the eyes of all the priests on Nepenthe; even as he invented evidence to bolster his case against the youth, he felt appropriately 'enlightened' and 'gloriously free-masonish'. But he had a formidable foe, Don Guistino Morena, the parliamentary representative, who, for a handsome fee, discovered an eagerness welling within him to destroy the magistrate; the case pitted the Vatican against the Quirinal. From Malipizzo's point of view, the issue soon became not one of providing justice in a trial, but of saving himself. Decent obscurity no longer cloaked his official misdemeanours. He had moved into the limelight.

> Don Guistino! He knew him by reputation. A Camorrista of the blackest dye. He took no chances. He never threatened; he performed. Everybody knew that. Signor Malipizzo did not like the prospect of losing his lucrative job. Still less did he fancy the notion of receiving a charge of buck-shot in his liver, one evening from behind a wall. That was Don Guistino's cheerful way with people who annoyed him. Don Guistino. Holy Mother of God! What would to-morrow bring?

Justice on Nepenthe, in other words, was a sometime thing, but when any of its representatives applied the law, they tended to become impatient with calls for compassion. Often enough Malipizzo may have terrorised ordinary people, but Guistino, as 'one of the few representatives of the Black Hand whose word could be implicitly relied on', moved safely through a treacherous world of parliamentary enemies.

> He had a share in everything; commissions and percentages poured in upon him. After making an example of half a dozen tiresome persons by having them quietly stabbed or shot – nothing was ever proved against him though everybody knew it was his work – he experienced no further opposition in his political career.

He was a marvel to behold, a unique mixture of 'vice and intelligence', and an 'implacable enemy of modernism'. Only Don Francesco – a Catholic priest who spoke directly for Douglas's values – held aloof from the 'intimate little dinner' arranged to give the principal clergy and a few favoured laymen of their party 'an opportunity of paying their respects'. 'I know quite well', he said to Torquemada, a God-fearing ascetic related by blood to the unhappy youth,

> that [the Commendatore Guistino Morena] calls himself a good son of the Church. So much the worse for the Church. I understand he was a prominent member of the Government. So much the worse for the Government. And I realize that, but for his intervention, this harmless individual might spend the remainder of his life in prison. So much the worse for all of us, who derive justice from so tainted a source. As to dining at the same table with him – no. Does not the whole world know his history? The animal! He would make me vomit.

Now there was much truth here as well as wit. Douglas was arguing the thesis that human justice, even in Nepenthe, was arbitrary, cruel and worth avoiding, and that those who attempted to live pleasantly (and who did not?) had to devise their own means of striking a balance between virtues and vices. Calling on the resources of the Church, Parliament or the local magistracy for succour in times of emergency was not only foolhardy but unnecessary. Far better to cope unaided by civil or religious authorities with such supposed crimes as the murder of a blackmailer. Far better to push those crimes to the back of one's mind (as the bishop did), if that was at all possible.

Nepenthe never represented pure escapism, and was related to the circumstances of Douglas's departure from England in January 1917. Douglas wrote about his difficulties in *Alone* (the introduction of which was published separately as *The Tribulations of a Patriot*). There he recounted, with some embellishments, his frustrated effort to volunteer for service in the government. He had acquired, after all, an impressive record of foreign travels (principally in the Mediterranean), and honourable duty over a three-year period as a Foreign Service diplomat in St Petersburg; he had published several scientific papers, including 'On the Darwinian hypothesis of sexual selection', which won approval from professionals; and his career as a minor author of short stories, essays and travel sketches (Capri monographs, antiquarian notes, a book entitled *Fountains in the Sand: Rambles among the oases of Tunisia*, 1912, and the graceful and still-loved *Old Calabria*, 1915) had developed promisingly, though sales were always disappointing. It may never be satisfactorily determined why Douglas found his struggle with bureaucracy so disappointing, or what happened to his original desire to serve flag and country; but, overstated though the bitterness in *The Tribulations of a Patriot* may be, there seems to be no question about his decision to give it all up – England, patriotic responsibilities during the Great War and adaptation of his special talents to some altruistic purpose – and to flee to a way of life largely independent of the grim realities of the second and third years of international conflict. He had tried to flourish as literary editor of the *English Review*, but his book reviews (some of which were reprinted in *Experiments*, 1925) did not strike many distinctive notes. After Ford Madox Hueffer left the main editorship, editing had proved wearisome as well. Douglas suffered intermittently from rheumatism. He lacked the funds that would have enabled him to live the good life he felt he deserved. A literary work on which he expended genuine effort as a researcher – *London Street Games*, 1916 – went to half a dozen publishers before his 'breathless catalogue' was accepted and published, with very little immediate result for his finances, or for that matter his literary reputation. (Today it is recognised as a pioneer effort in sociology, one that ranks with the investigations of Iona and Peter Opie.) He sweated on a draft of *South Wind* in Capri and in London (the warm weather of Capri slowed down the pace of his writing). The dreariness of his life was further complicated by the death, in Munich, of his estranged wife and first cousin, Elsa Fitz-Gibbon Douglas, who was burned to death in her sleep. The police never determined whether she had been smoking carelessly. Douglas, who had often spoken of Elsa with a sneer, believed that he had reasons enough to rejoice in their separation and divorce (1903), but one can only puzzle as to why, when he heard the news of Elsa's death (1916), he made some flippant remarks, in excruciatingly bad taste. A well-proven generosity of spirit, operating over a lifetime, renders unlikely any facile judgement that he was indifferent to her appalling form of death.

Beyond all these matters, however, the relentless testing of social proprieties – more bluntly speaking, Douglas's homosexual escapades – was bound to lead sooner or later to a confrontation with the law. This occurred in the same month as Elsa's death (October), and only two weeks after her obituary had been printed in *The Times*. A delicate treatment of how the case developed in Westminster Police Court may be found in Holloway's biography.[6] Douglas fled England before the third hearing, which was scheduled for January 1917, on a charge that he had attempted to seduce a sixteen-year-old boy. His wanderings were to take him to Italy and France. It was the most unpromising time of his life; he might well have disappeared entirely from literary histories if it had not been for *South Wind* and its startling, large-scale success. That novel, published in June 1917, went through seven editions rapidly. Douglas would have become quite wealthy if he had been able to secure legally a royalty on the more than 200,000 copies that were sold in the United States, but a loophole in the copyright laws prevented this.

In *The Tribulations of a Patriot* Douglas wrote, after the Great War had ended (1920), 'What ages ago, it seems, that great war! What enthusiasts we were!'[7] The remark was vinegarish; but for most English men and women, a full three years after the Great War had begun, the vision of a better, saner world seemed brown-edged and tired, and the continuing sacrifices demanded seemed excessive. *South Wind*, with its zest for living, or more precisely speaking, for living well, with its high valuation of civilised accomplishment, and its creation of a consistent world society on a small island somewhere 'away', struck exactly the needed note of light-heartedness.

Yet it remains difficult to define exactly what makes *South Wind* a pleasure to read. H. M. Tomlinson has remarked, 'In spite of its subtropical gaiety, I should call it a sorrowful book',[8] and seventy-five years later we understand his reaction. The hot-house culture of Nepenthe was fragile, and the febrility of several lengthy passages of dialogue provides a hint that Douglas, master of all he surveyed and creator of this demi-paradise, was less than confident that Nepenthe would endure much longer. The plot, such as it was, did not have much texture. Despite Douglas's spirited defence of the way he made the bishop a party to innumerable revelations calculated to shock him out of complacency, the pallid quality of the bishop's mind, conjoined with the implausibility of a bishop who had soldiered in Africa among the heathen being startled by Nepenthean culture, offered neither sufficient intrinsic interest nor narrative suspense to sustain a long narrative. Much space was provided for the regeneration of the English student Denis Phipps, but he too turned out to be no more than a pretext for owlish wisdom supplied by the narrator: the 'relentless paganism' of Nepenthe unsettled and finally uplifted him to a better sense of self-identity; but in behaving as a second dull dog, Denis simply repeated, in his stupefied innocence and his slow-witted responses to provocative remarks, the pattern set by the bishop.

One would be hard put to identify a single action that mattered much. Count Caloveglia sold fake antiques, but van Koppen, the American millionaire who bought from him, knew that he was purchasing, in the Locri Faun, a masterpiece with a sham ancestry; that his consultant, Sir Herbert Street, who vouched for its authenticity, had been bamboozled by the count; that he himself, through his acquisition of something he did not need, and in the provenance of which he did not believe, had played 'yet one more trick upon that great Republic whose fathomless gullibility no one had ever exploited to better purpose than himself'. Bazhakuloff, a Russian mystic and fake (patterned on Rasputin), leader on Nepenthe of a motley group of Russians, preached doctrine that fooled nobody of sense (and the elders of the island were all pragmatists who possessed sense). Edgar Marten, 'bright but dogmatic, a slovenly little plebeian but a man who after all had a determined, definite point of view', was introduced deliberately to demonstrate coarse language and an inability to grapple with genuine ideas. 'When I'm not actually at work', he told Denis, 'I'm always thinking about girls. I wish I could talk better Latin, or Italian. Not that I should be running after them all day long. I've got other fish to fry. I've got to catalogue my minerals, and I'm only half-way through.' He berated Denis for worrying about his soul: 'Get rid of it. The soul! That unhappy word had been the refuge of empty minds ever since the world began.' The bibliographer Ernest Eames – about whom scandalous and untrue stories were propagated by a lady who sat at home weaving lies 'and other bright tapestries' about *all* the inhabitants of Nepenthe – was 'the ideal annotator', with 'an ant-like hiving faculty', whose great ambition in life was to bring Monsignor Perrelli's *Antiquities* (of Nepenthe) up to date.

A babel, therefore. Perhaps all the speakers were Douglas, the ventriloquist in charge. Douglas denied that the real Mrs Snow who inspired the character of the duchess had contributed very much to his portrait. Other ladies were important, and imagination played its part.

> I have never tried to draw a figure from life, as they say. My creed is that a human character, however engrossing, however convincing and true to itself, must be modelled anew before it can become material for fiction. It must be licked into shape, otherwise its reactions, in a world of fictitious characters, would be out of focus. No authentic child of man will fit into a novel.[9]

That statement undercuts Ralph D. Lindeman's list of the historical sources for Douglas's cast (John Ellington Brooks for Mr Eames, a man named Martin for Count Caloveglia, Freddy Parker and his lady for Mr and Mrs Harold Trower and the Baron Fritz Von Meltheim for the blackmailer Muhlen),[10] though Lindeman is justified in stressing the grounding of *South Wind* in factual and biographical detail, and correct in seeing Mr Keith, called an 'angel' by the duchess, as more like Douglas than any other personality in the novel. Douglas wrote:

> Mr. Keith was older than he looked – incredibly old, in fact, though nobody could bring himself to believe it; he was well preserved by means of a complicated system of life, the details of which, he used to declare, were not fit for publication. That was only his way of talking. He exaggerated so dreadfully.

Mr Keith believed that one must be a stylist to run an island properly (a characteristic way of praising the despotic duke who built the fountains on Nepenthe), and, by extension, to live on it properly. He talked at length, and proffered freely his ideas on education, the relationship between the sexes, the secret of happiness, the distressing truth about those who patronised the Alpha and Omega Club and the art of obscenity.

> He could tell you how many public baths existed in Geneva in pre-Reformation days, what was the colour of Mehemet Ali's whiskers, why the manuscript of Virgil's friend Gallius had not been handed down to posterity, and what month the decimal system was introduced into Finland. Such aimless incursions into knowledge were a puzzle to his friends, but not to himself. They helped him to build up a harmonious scheme of life – to round himself off.

He attacked (no other word seems appropriate) different fields of knowledge, assimilating what was useful or interesting to himself, discarding the rest. When he swam, he looked like 'a rosy Silenus'. He prided himself on doing the right thing, was punctual to the minute ('it was one of the many virtues he possessed in common with Her Majesty Queen Victoria') and detested death. Behind the hedonist's laughter lay the fear of dying. Mr Keith frequently ruminated to this effect:

> It is with Death as it is with God – we call them good because we are afraid of what they can do to us. That accounts for our politeness. Death, universal and inevitable, is none the less a villainous institution. Every other antagonist can be ignored or bribed or circumvented or crushed outright. But here is a damnable spectre who knocks at the door and does not wait to hear you say 'Come in'. Hateful!

Douglas encountered serious problems when, in constructing his philosophy of Mediterranean hedonism, he avoided abstract thought, deriding mathematics, for example.[11] Mr Keith may be thought of as an irrepressible (and perhaps self-deluded) amateur. And there was something artificial, something created by patient pushing, poking and patting into shape, about the learned disquisitions on the life and martyrdom of Saint Dodekanus, patron of Nepenthe, the 'five clearly marked periods' of Bazhakuloff's career ('the probationary, dialectical, political, illuminated, and expiatory'), the Saint Elias Fountain (the only one of twelve streams of 'pestilential odour' that continued to flow), penitential processions, funeral rites and much else. They seem worked up for the occasion; every time we come to such an essay, the narrative slows.

We would not want to do without them, however. Play adaptors have staged ferociously edited versions, and Graham Greene once considered how to write a film-script based on *South Wind*. Eliminating purple passages, extended soliloquies and speculations on the 'right way' of looking at life may be no less a sacrilege than trimming a supposedly superfluous character from a play by Chekhov; the missing passages of text will immediately become noticeable. Nancy Cunard reminds us how difficult it is to locate the excellence of *South Wind* (even after we record all its failings as a conventional novel) in theme or plot, the 'beautiful writing' and the characterisations. But she finally gives full credit to its 'indications and implication, shrewd remarks and scintillating epigrams. . . . How rich it all is, how beautifully *made*.'[12]

It is not surprising that Norman Douglas should have been an atheist and a hater of Christian doctrine; but it surely was unexpected that his most likeable character in *South Wind* should turn out to be Don Francesco. Douglas appreciated the fact of his mortality. 'When a man reaches my age', he once remarked to Constantine FitzGibbon, who was fifty years younger than himself, 'he thinks about death *all the time*.'[13] He did not attempt to commit suicide, though he was very much afraid of becoming 'senile and helpless, an object of compassion', and he was more than a survivor. He was a wit, a Johnsonian personality and a hater of humbug. 'He had the rare and delightful quality of being able to understand without any desire to interfere', FitzGibbon has written. 'Luckily, perhaps more even than most great writers, his talent was such that some part at least of his personality lives on in his books.'[14] That fair statement serves as an eloquent obituary notice.

Chapter 6

Frank Swinnerton's *Nocturne* (1917)

Nocturne, a wonderfully representative example of a popular novel that appealed to common readers of all social classes, began life under another name. Frank Swinnerton really would have liked to call his novel *Night-piece*, after one of Herrick's poems that he admired, but Arnold Bennett 'wouldn't hear of it',[1] and Martin Secker, the publisher, thought that *Night-piece* was 'orally ambiguous'.[2] Rafael Sabatini, the historical novelist who served at the time (early April 1917) as Martin Secker's partner, looked wise when Bennett's suggested new title, *In the Night*, was put to him; he preferred the name he himself had suggested – *Nocturne* – but did not protest too strenuously when the book went to press with the name *In the Night*. Bennett, after all, was enthusiastically arguing that it would sell 'in thousands', and Secker, delighted at the prospect, wanted a commercial success. But Lord Gorell's book, *In the Night*, unexpectedly made an appearance before Swinnerton's novel went to press, and the latter underwent a metamorphosis, to Sabatini's recommended *Nocturne*.

Swinnerton's career up to that point had not amounted to very much. Born in 1884, Swinnerton had seen much of the worst of London life, though it did not ruin a naturally optimistic and amiable temper. A friend's interest led him to J. M. Dent and Company, which had earned a reputation among publishers and general readers for its publication of the Temple Classics and the Everyman Library. He wrote his first novel at the age of eighteen, and then another two that also were never published; that period was followed by the publication of three novels that failed to win an audience of even moderate size. Only after this dreary start did he catch the attention of critics, who began to look on him as one of the better young novelists. Philip Lee Warner asked him to be proof manager at Chatto and Windus (Warner was a partner there), and that house, after securing an outside reading, published his first book, notifying him of its acceptance on his twenty-fourth birthday. By then it was obvious to Swinnerton that he had been serving a priceless apprenticeship in a lively world of publishers and literary figures; that it was time to write in order to watch himself say something fine, or at least something worth listening to. Though much of this early material was consigned to the flames, his easy-going, discursive, companionable prose style was finding its place in Georgian society, and securing the respect of men and women whom Swinnerton admired for their wit and their accomplishments.

Not that the path to success could be travelled without stumbling. His critically acclaimed study of George Gissing was followed by an unpleasant controversy about his mild strictures on the literary values of what Robert Louis Stevenson had accomplished. No review of Swinnerton's career should minimise the miseries accompanying the illness that struck him shortly after the Great War began. He lost 'extravagant quantities of blood and albumen', and took to his bed for more than three months.[3] Eventually he rallied, and found on all sides old and new friends, clubs, social engagements, professional commitments that he scrupulously observed, and in himself an intensifying *cacoëthes scribendi*.

Nocturne, 'P.M.' tells us, was written in 'a period of the greatest domestic stress, illness, anxiety and loneliness'.[4] Its seeds could be traced back to a conversation with Nigel de Grey, who was working in 1916 for Heinemann's and about to leave for military service. De Grey had expressed his curiosity about a novel, yet to be written, that might concentrate on the doings of a single night. Secker's desire that Swinnerton should write a short novel 'under the Methuen contract length' fitted neatly with Swinnerton's own wish to focus his attention on an evening's activity. His weekly wage of £5 was (up to this time) not markedly increased by the money paid for reviewing assignments or arranging small press-runs of books that never seemed to excite anybody. His water-pipes required hot-water bottles lest they freeze in a particularly severe winter. He was obliged to spend most of his time reading manuscripts, reviewing books and writing reports on them. His primary energies (when these duties had been taken care of) were spent in taking care of his invalid mother. Only in the evening, beginning at about eight o'clock, could he concentrate on the rash promise he had made to Secker, and he felt some empathy with the novelist who once had told de Grey that he had run out of subject-matter. For Swinnerton was out to create characters for whom he could not remember models, or real-life prototypes; to describe the social habits of Kennington Park and environs, when he had only taken casual walks there; and to spin a thread of narrative line when he had the greatest difficulty in imagining even a single scene.

Fortunately, he had been aboard Arnold Bennett's yacht, the *Velsa*, for a weekend in April or May of 1914. Bennett's kindly concern for the younger man had been stimulated by the publication of *The Young Idea*, and he had issued an invitation to Swinnerton: 'There is something in your new novel that makes me want to see you again.'[5] For a full description of how much Swinnerton relished his 'most expensive of yachting caps', how he was supplied with tea by a real steward and how much he enjoyed seeing 'eight colossal British battleships' that saluted Bennett's blue ensign by running their own white ensigns down and then up again, a reader may be referred to Swinnerton's autobiography; surely there have been few landlubbers so overwhelmed by so brief a seagoing expedition. 'And after dark Bennett took me for a terrifying row over sinister water in the dinghy, which he managed with a kind of impressive slow thoroughness. I – a non-swimmer – was secretly frantic with fear.'[6] This nocturnal trip, which took place near Holehaven, was put to good use when Swinnerton needed to describe, in the novel he was now writing, a trip that the heroine took from the south side of Westminster Bridge to a yacht on which her lover lived as a sailor.

That adventure supplied several needed touches of authenticity. But, as Bennett pointed out at a later time, Swinnerton 'ennobled, magnified, decorated, enriched and bejewelled it' till the owner of the *Velsa* could not recognise his 'wretched vessel'. Bennett added:

> The yacht in *Nocturne* is the yacht I want, ought to have, and never shall have. I envy him the yacht in *Nocturne*, and my envy takes a malicious pleasure in pointing out a mistake in the glowing scene. He anchors his yacht in the middle of the Thames – as if the tyrannic authorities of the Port of London would ever allow a yacht, or any other craft, to anchor in midstream![7]

To be sure, Swinnerton wrote 'anchored' when he should have used the word 'moored', and he misinterpreted the Scottish Law of

Inheritance, and he should not have allowed his heroine to wear on the same evening a hat which she had 'just' steamed 'into freshness'. 'These errors', he confessed with some rue, 'were duly recorded against me.'[8]

Yet, even if his mother fell asleep when he read aloud pages of the manuscript to her, and even if some reviewers thought it a comedown from his previous work, Secker's faith that it was a masterpiece never wavered. H. G. Wells, incensed by a too-brief notice in the *Daily News*, wrote to that paper with high praise for the realism of *Nocturne*. Moreover, he wrote a preface for the American edition that started a small boom. Ten thousand copies sold within a few weeks of publication. The news of enthusiastic notices in American publications crossed the Atlantic; and though the English edition, after selling out its original press run of 1,500 copies, went out of print for eleven months (mostly because Secker was away from the office), it came back into print to sell 1,000 copies a year until 1933, when it sank to 500 copies; a sixpenny edition sold 30,000 copies; and in the United States the sales soared to 50,000. It was translated into half a dozen languages, and more than one dramatist tried to adapt it for the stage.

Swinnerton confessed himself a little dazed by his transformation, for five minutes, into 'the pet of the intelligentsia',[9] but his knowledge of how rapidly reading tastes shifted saved him from becoming conceited over his fashionableness, and he never raised his low rating of the novel as a stunt, one that began with artificiality. His normal procedure, before and after the writing of *Nocturne*, was to begin with a situation or with characters; the method might have defects, but it was 'at least imaginatively pure'.[10] *Nocturne*, he knew, had been conceived as a timetable. Later novels 'of concentrated time and fortuitous assembly' were to become, from his perspective, a nuisance, and the authors who wrote them exploiters of the ingenuity of *Nocturne* at the expense of everything else. 'The lessons of culture superseded everything old-style and humane', he sombrely reflected. '*Nocturne* thus amusingly indicates the point at which the new fiction parted company with the old'.[11]

This overstatement of the case ignored the independent development of the rigid time-frame of James Joyce's *Ulysses* (to cite the most famous example), well under way before the publication of *Nocturne*, and the inevitability of experiments with time as the novel genre moved away from the conventional narrative mode of story-telling. It would have been safest, perhaps, not to claim too much for *Nocturne*, which took only a month to write (beating the accelerated schedule of Alec Waugh's *The Loom of Youth*). But it must be listed as one of the more popular novels of the Great War. (Swinnerton did almost as well with *The Elder Sister* and *Young Felix*, but *Nocturne* made his reputation, and he was best remembered for it. Because of it, he was treated for much of the 1920s as a major novelist.)

In the late 1920s and early 1930s the development of radio programmes about books proved a mixed blessing for publishers, and book clubs pushing a few books at the expense of all the others often operated at the expense of booksellers. Swinnerton, in an excellent position to judge, had a consistent point of view about the need to encourage the development of popular literature. He wanted more good talk about books that entertained, that gave pleasure to readers. If critics, reviewers, radio commentators, book societies, etc., increased the availability of such pleasure, they were to be commended.[12] His fiction provided a yardstick whereby the more praiseworthy qualities of most best-sellers of the time might be measured.

Swinnerton often thought and wrote about this matter. Late in his life (1963) he denied that all best-sellers were alike. He dismissed Mrs F. R. Leavis's attack on popular writers in her influential study, *Fiction and the Reading Public* (1932), because it assumed that Gilbert Frankau, Philip Gibbs, Edgar Rice Burroughs, A. S. M. Hutchinson and Ethel M. Dell were automatically inferior to Virginia Woolf, E. M. Forster, D. H. Lawrence and T. F. Powys. The task of a critic, Swinnerton implied, was to take a close look at comparative sales rather than to compile (as Mrs Leavis had done) a 'ghastly accumulation of trivia known as "research".'[13] Some best-sellers never went beyond 5,000 copies, and 20,000 copies were 'exceptional'. Only a very few books, and not always the ones publishers believed would succeed, became best-sellers. Mrs Leavis, in other words, was wrong in believing a writer's inferiority was the prime reason for his or her inflated sales. Illiteracy and bad taste in the reading public were not to be blamed automatically for the commercial success of any writer. 'What sells books is talk; personal recommendations.'[14]

The secret of the best-seller was simple (though writing one on the basis of a formula was tricky): 'each person who reads it feels himself or herself to be "in" it. Not "the swim", although that does influence a few; but the actual scene.'[15] Swinnerton's explanation accounted for the vogue for romances (Stevenson, Anthony Hope, Stanley Weyman and Henry Seton Merriman) at a time when nineteenth-century life had become too prosaic. Middle-class portraits (by Galsworthy, Bennett, Wells) provided countless readers with a gratifying opportunity for self-identification in this century. Swinnerton, who tried to paint normal people as he saw them, counted himself lucky that in his more than thirty novels, written over a half century, many of his readers saw themselves moving through interesting events. 'I have been for nearly eighty years a lucky and a happy man.'[16] He added that even if he were to be forgotten as soon as he was dead, he doubted 'if any other octogenarian will meet his inevitable doom with greater equanimity'.[17]

All of which is disarming, because Swinnerton, who sought deliberately to write as many best-sellers as he could, found himself sufficiently satisfied when he satisfied his readers. His sales were less important than his respect for the desire of the reading public to be entertained by his fictions, a desire that he never underestimated or denigrated. He appreciated the fact that certain kinds of fiction remained forever beyond his ken. The pride that he took in his own good humour, which prevented him from becoming conceited, prevented him also from understanding fully the reasons why other writers could legitimately consider themselves as something more than entertainers. But Swinnerton's modesty was engaging, too. 'This is why I write novels', he said. 'Sympathy with the shortcomings, the failures, and the sufferings (but also the triumphs) of his fellows does, I think, enrich a man's mind more than bookknowledge, of which I have plenty.'[18]

H. G. Wells agreed with Swinnerton's self-assessment, when he wrote his introduction to the American edition of *Nocturne*. He praised Swinnerton for seeing life and rendering it 'with a steadiness and detachment and patience quite foreign' to his own disposition.[19] Swinnerton, Wells wrote, was interested in 'exquisite presentation'. He was not trying to persuade the reader to do anything; rather, he wanted to create characters as 'realities inside and out'.[20] He concluded, '[*Nocturne*] is perfect, authentic, and alive.'[21]

The novel had a limited cast, only five characters: two men, two women, and 'Pa', the father of the two sisters, Emmy and Jenny, whose 'dates' constituted the main story. All belonged to the working class. Their inarticulateness had less to do with the limitations of their vocabulary than with the inchoate condition of their emotions. Swinnerton was seeking to make credible the existence of complex states of minds in people almost completely out of touch with books, art and all semblances of high culture. Pa, who even in his youth could not have been eloquent of speech, had declined into senility and helplessness as the direct consequence of a paralytic stroke. Once 'a strong man, a runner and cricketer' and 'rather obstreperously disposed', he now resembled, as he peered out from beneath his bushy grey eyebrows, 'a worn and dilapidated perversion of Whistler's portrait of Carlyle'. As he looked at his two daughters, it was as though 'he were trying to remember something buried in ancient neglect; and his eyes would thereafter, perhaps at the mere sense of helplessness, fill slowly with tears'. Everything had to be done for him, save his final struggling out of daytime clothes into his 'extraordinary faded scarlet nightgown', a ritual in which cunning replaced competence; he had learned to cope; he knew how 'the braces may be made to do their own work, how the shirt may with one hand be so manipulated as to be drawn swiftly over the head'. But he was helpless otherwise. He needed to have his food divided into eatable portions. Even the bread pudding, a dish that Jenny detested, had to be called 'bready butter pudding' for Pa's sake, so that he would recognise and eat it. He liked to smoke, but was incapable either of loading or setting light to his own pipe; his two girls had to do that for him. He loved his beer, but his allowance was carefully controlled; he was (we suspect from the cautious way in which the sisters speak of his craving) incontinent. And though he asked everyone what was the day's 'noos', he could not remember what he was told from one minute to the next, and repeated his question endlessly, whiningly. Left alone in the house for a few hours, he struggled from his bed, searched for beer, got up on a chair and fell from it to sprawl full length across the kitchen floor. (Emmy, returning from an evening out with her new 'boy friend' Alf, was to discover him there.)

Pa Blanchard, in brief, was the most unpromising kind of literary material. He could not speak for himself; he was a ruin of a man locked by mental and physical problems into an animal-like existence. A novelist who placed him dead-centre ran a considerable risk: such a character might repulse readers; it was ruinously easy to sentimentalise or patronise him; in most novels Pa might be used less as a person than as a force impactive upon other characters. Probably this is what Wells had in mind when he pointed out that, though every reader could appreciate the truth and humour of such a creation, it was more difficult for the reader 'without technical experience' to realise 'how the atmosphere is made and completed and rounded off by Pa's beer, Pa's needs, and Pa's accident, how he binds the bundle and makes the whole thing one, and what an enviable triumph his achievement is.'[22] Pa's realisation of his own helplessness, vivified by several moments in which flashing stabs of his old intelligence and awareness of what was happening around him startled his daughters, had links to the invalidism of Swinnerton's own mother. When she died at the age of seventy-six,

> she was exasperated with herself for being helpless, exasperated with others for having power over her because of this helplessness, constantly planning ways of recovering the use of her legs and never quite succeeding by determination in giving back to old wasted muscles an old strength.[23]

Swinnerton's achievement was in transmitting a sense of the *humanity* of such a man.

Emotional storminess hid behind the seemingly bland and uninteresting exterior of Emmy, the older sister, whose primary duty was taking care of Pa. As a consequence, she had been deprived of normal social contacts and any opportunity for finding and securing a lover. The difficulty involved in making Emmy something other than humdrum, other than resentfully understanding of her blighted role in life, should not be underestimated. A long-suffering woman, almost by definition, had long brooding silences. Emmy resented strongly – 'passionately' would be a more accurate word – the relative freedom of Jenny in her milliner's shop. (Jenny, quite rightly, protested that hers was not an idyllic existence.) What Swinnerton did was get right into her head. Emmy had the moral dimensions of a true heroine. She could feel in her bones the full bitterness of her father's soul.

> She was not born a fighter. She was harder on the surface, but weaker in powers below the surface. Her long solitudes had made her build up grievances, and devastating thoughts, had given her a thousand bitter things to fling into the conflict; but they had not strengthened her character, and she could not stand the strain of prolonged argument.

But she was no less intense than Jenny, who mistreated Alf, the man she secretly loved; Jenny could not see Alf's worth, but Emmy knew that she would be better for him than her younger sister; and in her outburst of jealousy she fought for the right to be noticed, not only by Alf but by Jenny herself – as a person, a *woman*, as Emmy.

The source of Emmy's feelings of inadequacy traced back to the mother, dead for a full decade. Jenny had always been Mrs Blanchard's favourite (thus the rivalry between the sisters). During Mrs Blanchard's lifetime Emmy's need for love had always been greeted by a series of rebuffs and chagrins. After the mother's passing from the scene, Emmy had been frustrated by Jenny and her freer ways, the fact that she could live her life outside the cramped and gloomy house. Emmy saw herself as a sacrifice, which in truth she was. Swinnerton made the point effectively: Emmy was older, and 'the love she needed was under her eyes being wasted upon Jenny'.

Emmy was something more than a querulous crank, though Swinnerton could easily have made her into one. She loved Jenny, and she embraced her younger sister after a fit of rage. She took stock of herself objectively, and measured accurately her limitations as a candidate for marriage; and she possessed a mordant sense of humour which kept half-smothered ideals and hopes in proper perspective. Swinnerton, while describing the meanest of London homes, transformed Emmy, an all-too-typical product of this kind of environment, into a woman who felt and thought in a way that was completely credible; she became a woman for whom the common reader inevitably felt sympathy. Alf's judgement of her, at first cool, became positive on closer acquaintance: 'She was intelligent: that was it. Intelligent was the word. Not lively, but restful . . . . Rather a nice girl, Emmy'.

More space was given to Jenny. Perhaps Jenny had an even keener sense of humour than Emmy: 'more power to laugh, to be detached, to be indifferent'. She had more poetry in her soul. Even at the moment that the tramcar turned the corner from the Embankment to cross Westminster Bridge, 'The glistening of reflected lights which spotted the surface of the Thames gave its rapid current an air of such mysterious and especially sinister power that she was for an instant aware of almost uncontrollable terror.' (Emmy would never have had a similar reaction to 'darkness and the sense of moving water'.) Jenny tried continually to shine up the dull fabric of her existence ('no danger threatened Jenny but the danger of uneventful life', as the narrator said) by recalling the bright shards of other people's lives.

> What was it the girl in *One of the Best* said? 'You may command an army of soldiers; but you cannot still the beating of a woman's heart!' Silly fool, she was. Jenny had felt the tears in her eyes, burning, and her throat very dry, when the words had been spoken in the play; but Jenny here and now were different persons. Different? Why, there were fifty Jennys. But the shrewd, romantic, honest, true Jenny was behind them

all, not stupid, not sentimental, bold as a lion, destructively experienced in hardship and endurance, very quick indeed to single out and wither humbug that was within her range of knowledge, but innocent as a child before any other sort of humbug whatsoever.

Jenny, whose 'care-free, happy-go-lucky' temperament closely resembled that of her father, was apt to say exactly what she thought, even if it were 'perfectly outrageous', though she never meant to hurt anybody seriously by her uninhibited candour. Jenny had 'innumerable insights and emotions' that Emmy could not share, or even know. Swinnerton provided several examples, but of them all perhaps the most startling (and unexpected) was Jenny's sudden image of herself as a cream bun, and Emmy as a scone. 'Jenny did not like scones. She thought them stodgy. She had also that astounding feminine love of cream buns which no true man could ever acknowledge or understand. So Emmy became a scone, with not too many currants in it.'

On the yacht, vulnerable to the blandishments of a sailor named Keith, Jenny might well respond to the moon silvering the river, the stars that shone 'like swarmed throbbing points of silver', the 'chequer of contrast, beautiful to the eye, and haunting in the spirit'; but her struggle – the heart combatting 'the tumult of merciless self-judgment' in her mind – was always credible. She was twenty-five, old enough to appreciate the dangers of surrendering to a momentary passion on board a deserted yacht. Keith (who had confessed to a term in prison and various escapades with women, available to him because he was 'a sailor-man') lived by a double standard that might well be hostile to her own best welfare. '"What I'm wondering," she said to him in a slow and rather puzzled way, "is, what you'd think of me if I'd lived with three different men"'. 'For her real freedom was her innocence and her desire to do right'. She might belong to Keith, she might be his forever, 'but he did not belong to her'. After she allowed him to seduce her, she could not forgive herself. It was impossible for her to get back to 'the old way of looking at everything'. Her life had changed, and she could not even be sure that it was for the worse. Nor can we, as readers, dislike Keith. His troubled past, his sincere efforts to reform, his genuine affection for Jenny, spoke on his behalf; and there was no telling what the future would bring, or whether he would some day make of Jenny an honest woman.

But Swinnerton did not write a soap opera. The novel has three sections: 'Evening', grim in detail and naturalistic in technique, about the dreary home life of two sisters and their invalid father; 'Night', about Jenny's romantic adventure aboard a yacht (the final chapter of which is entitled 'Cinderella'); and 'Morning', which returns us to the Blanchard home and to the inevitable 'consequences' of a night of pleasure. In painting, the term 'nocturne' denotes a night scene, but Swinnerton may have had in mind the musical meaning, in which 'nocturne' connotes a 'dreamy character'. Swinnerton encouraged no illusion about a sudden improvement in the lot of either Emmy or Jenny, though for each woman an alteration in world-view took place by evening's end. Pa Blanchard would require nursing care for his remaining years (none knew how many), and Alf, though he would rather cut free from this particular entangling alliance, would have to put up with Emmy's father if he intended to enjoy Emmy's company.

There was a factual world, named Kennington Park, and a fictitious world, represented by the theatrical performance to which Alf and Emmy went on their night out. Swinnerton knew a good deal about the latter, and rendered, in this novel at least, an unfavourable verdict on its values. The theatre was ablaze with 'the staring vehemence' of electric lights (Emmy was 'alarmed at the disclosures which the brilliance might devastatingly make', presumably about herself). The gilded mirrors – 'gilding' in its older meaning, as a fair but deceptive outward appearance – threw their reflections backwards and forwards 'until the stairs seemed peopled with hosts of Emmys and Alfs'. Because they missed the first five minutes of the play, they did not fully appreciate the fact that an actor was 'only pretending to be an American'. Emmy did not understand why, having spoken twenty words, 'he must take six paces farther from the footlights until he had spoken thirteen more'. The 'crook' play that they were watching dealt with the planning of a robbery; by intermission the heroine had already received 'wild-eyed the advances of a fur-coated millionaire'. When Alf bought chocolates from an attendant for Emmy, the box (they discovered) contained 'much imitation-lace paper and a few sweets'. The plot of the play, traced in general terms, seemed to be a mess of improbabilities, and Emmy's practical-minded judgement was that 'It's only a play.' Alf agreed: 'Of course.' Something was happening every moment on the stage. Members of the gallery, 'not wholly absorbed by the play', generously augmented the kisses of the players; the speeches were 'of irreproachable moral tone'; 'sudden wild appeals' were addressed to 'the delighted occupants of the gallery'. The play moved to its predestined and long-foreseen ending:

> The fur coat was much used, cigarettes were lighted and flung away with prodigal recklessness, pistols were revealed – one of them was even fired into the air; – and jumping, trickling music heightened the effects of a number of strong speeches about love, and incorruptibility and womanhood . . . . The climax was reached. In the middle of the climax, while yet the lover wooed and the villain died, the audience began to rustle, preparatory to going home. Even Emmy was influenced to the extent of discovering and beginning to adjust her hat. It was while she was pinning it, with her elbows raised, that the curtain fell.

This witty attack on a typical melodrama was simultaneously a critique of Art, in this case the art of the theatre, and its arrogant claims on the audience's imagination. Swinnerton's characters were well aware of the differences between Art and Life. Neither Alf nor Emmy discussed the play they had just seen as they walked away from the theatre. They spoke of more immediate, and significant, matters: namely their relationship to each other, their sacred obligation to take care of Pa, the possibility of love and even of marriage, and Jenny's future prospects.

Ultimately, the value of *Nocturne* was the strength of its plea for recognition of the value of believable characters in a novel. Swinnerton, though he gave full marks to Henry James's faithfulness to his own artistic standards, and to his championing of form and development, detested virtuosity of the extreme kind that James developed at the expense of character. James, he wrote, was inferior 'at the very core of the novelist's art' because of it.[24] In some of Swinnerton's novels character creation was more successful than in others, but the achievement of *Nocturne* was genuine. Swinnerton was wrong to undervalue *Nocturne* simply because it demonstrated his mastery of a trick in structuring events to last no longer than a single night. It was (many readers believe) his best documentation of the truth: that imagination at its best was the power to 'instantly and sympathetically comprehend the thoughts and feelings of other people'.[25]

Chapter 7

Compton Mackenzie's *The Early Life and Adventures of Sylvia Scarlett* (1918)

Edward Montague Compton Mackenzie, born on 17 January 1883, died at a venerable age, on 30 November 1972. His parents were theatrical people: his father an actor–manager in charge of the Compton Comedy Company, and his mother an American actress. The grandfather on the paternal side had also been a well-known actor, and his grandparents on the maternal side had run the Lyceum Theatre in London, where Henry Irving had appeared; and by blood the family was related to the Siddons, the Kembles and a number of other distinguished acting families. Fay Compton, Compton Mackenzie's sister, enjoyed a long list of theatrical successes, and indeed Compton, alone of the two sons and three daughters of Edward and Virginia Compton, decided not to try the stage as a career. (Nevertheless, he wrote several novels about actors, actresses and the theatre. Sylvia Scarlett, the heroine of the novel we are considering, is continually involved with footlights and theatrical fancies.)

Compton Mackenzie's life was singularly crowded with incident, and it is very difficult to credit the assertion contained in a foreword to a later edition of *Sylvia Scarlett*, that his heroine was not biographically based. Compton Mackenzie was always writing about real people. Two of his major literary heroes were Balzac and Stendhal, novelists who balanced 'the claims of the heroic with the admission of the commonplace through the medium of contemporary manners'.[1] The world (Mackenzie believed) had become a far more interesting place because of its hurly-burly of stress and incident:

the rush of education, the multiplicity of newspapers, the increasing publicity, the helter-skelter criticism, the swift veering of popular ideals, the racking fatigue, and all the ills of democracy many times magnified beyond the gloom of the great pessimists of the past, flung at our heads together with virtues and triumphs undreamed of before they were beheld.[2]

Mackenzie was pleased by the information that Mrs Browning had been so overcome by her first sight of Paddington Station that she had been forced to take to her bed 'for some days' in order to recover from her impressions. He believed that modern novelists were still trying to discover if there were any poetry in the chaos of sense impressions created by the conditions of modern living. In a characteristically splendid conceit, tossed off almost casually, Mackenzie mused that the Tube might well be 'almost the finest adventure of travel which the world has known'. Jaded urban dwellers often missed the point of their own existence:

> For me, certainly, every journey is an Odyssey from the moment I enter the lift, with its subtle variation of mood – the subdued gaiety of expectation about half-past seven in contrast with the lassitude of the afternoon – the personalities of the liftmen, and the curious intimacy and relaxation of by-laws late at night. There is the waiting on the tempestuous platform, the Cyclopean eye of the advancing train, the adventure of boarding, the fastidiousness in the choice of a neighbour, the sense of equality, the mysterious and flattering reflection of oneself in the opposite windows, and even the colours of the various stations – from the orange and lemon of Covent Garden to the bistre melancholy of Caledonian Road, or Camden Town faintly cerulean like an autumnal sky. Surely the poetic novelist should never be called upon to defend his instinct for decoration when the stark realities are so full of suggestive colour.[3]

Mackenzie was precocious, reading before he was two, acquiring foreign languages at a rapid and startling pace and attending, with some distinction, Colet Court (his preparatory school), St Paul's public school in London and Magdalen College in Oxford, earning there a second-class BA degree in history (1904). Though he joined the Inner Temple, he was not called to the Bar, and he found much more congenial the calling of a professional writer. His first novel, *The Passionate Elopement* (1911), followed a volume of poems printed largely on the basis of his father's contribution of £40. Though Mackenzie wrote that he had tried to place *The Passionate Elopement* seventeen times over a two-year period, Martin Secker, the publisher who finally accepted it, could not help being pleased by its modest success, and a number of reprintings were called for. *Carnival* (1912) was an unexpected hit, indeed his greatest commercial success. David Arthur Thomas and Joyce Thomas, in their splendid bibliographical study, record five reprintings in the year of issuance, new and cheaper editions and a grand total of 500,000 copies in all editions. It became the subject of two stage plays, three films, six radio performances (including the BBC's first full-length radio play), the libretto for a BBC radio opera and a BBC 'Book at Bedtime' reading. *Sinister Street* (published in two volumes in 1913 and 1914) sold more than 35,000 copies of the first volume within four months, and its companion volume, also published at 6s., was similarly successful; a one-volume edition inevitably followed, in 1923.[4] Two-volume novels were not much liked by booksellers, and the high quotient of scandalous material in Mackenzie's treatment of Oxford undergraduate life made it a natural target for censorship; Boot's and W. H. Smith at first refused to stock it. Ford Madox Hueffer (soon to become Ford Madox Ford) proclaimed Mackenzie, Lawrence and Ezra Pound as the young hopes of literature, while André Maurois and Max Beerbohm thought of *Sinister Street* as both a faithful record of Oxford ambiance and a book that would endure. Perhaps the most striking evidence of Mackenzie's appeal to a younger generation — not that Mackenzie was all that old, at the age of thirty-one — was to be found in F. Scott Fitzgerald's effort to evoke, in his description of Princeton in *This Side of Paradise*, a world of fully imagined detail that might be compared to the world of Oxford as described in *Sinister Street*.

Guy and Pauline (1915) was begun on Capri, and finished in three and a half months; it was to remain Mackenzie's favourite novel, one he did not wish to rewrite or tinker with. An author as prolific as Mackenzie could not afford to linger long on any single work, and before he had finished his amazing career he was to write 116 books wholly by himself, and to contribute a foreword, introduction, epilogue or chapter to another twenty-three, as well as some 2,000 additional items in the form of contributions to the press and periodicals (not to mention some twenty plays).[5] Converted to Roman Catholicism, and married to Faith Stone (the marriage would last more than half a century, despite affairs on both sides), Mackenzie sought and received a commission as lieutenant, accompanying the Royal Marines to Gallipoli, after which he became a captain and the Military Control

Officer in Athens from the end of 1915 on. Later, he was to become the director of the Aegean Intelligence Service on the island of Syra in the Cyclades. His passionate attachment to Greece, its culture and its people, lasted a lifetime.

Sylvia Scarlett ran to some 300,000 words. Mackenzie, who liked to shuffle and reshuffle his fictional characters in the manner of a Trollope, and whose interest in trilogies reminded contemporary critics of the ill-fated triple-decker tradition, wrote a very long novel indeed: he planned it as three books, *Sylvia and Philip*, *Sylvia and Arthur* and *Sylvia and Michael*, and each book was to consist of seven chapters. He wrote and revised for twelve hours a day, and completed 280,000 words in eighty days; then, on 17 January 1918, he broke down with a fierce attack of sciatica. His recovery was hampered by knowledge of his wife's affair with an Italian boy some nineteen years younger than herself, as well as by the heavy stresses of war. Indeed, he had been trying to complete the manuscript during a three-month period of official leave, and the gargantuan effort exceeded his powers. Martin Secker, anxious to get into print what was already available (as in the case of *Sinister Street*, the first volume of which had to be printed earlier than Mackenzie liked in order to keep up with a publication schedule), could not delay the printing of the first half until the remaining 20,000 words were written. Sylvia Scarlett, first introduced in *Sinister Street* as the cheerfully hedonistic companion of Michael Fane's girlfriend, here became the heroine of a narrative that Mackenzie maintained he had not planned originally as a two-volume work.

The novel began in France, where Sylvia was born, and moved to England, home of Sylvia's father. The restless wanderings of Sylvia took her to France and Belgium, across the South Atlantic to Brazil, back to France and on to Spain and Morocco, with expeditions to New York City and 'Sulphurville, Indiana', before moving on to Toronto and eastern Canada and winding up in England again.

Fortunately, the sciatica let up as the psychological problems of Mackenzie's household lightened, and by May Mackenzie finished the wordage that he had set for himself. The second large instalment built on the success of the first volume, which had sold 12,000 copies within two weeks of publication. *Sylvia and Michael: The later adventures of Sylvia Scarlett* appeared in 1919, and described Sylvia's adventures in Paris, Petrograd, Kieff, Odessa, Warsaw, Bucharest and Samothrace. Since the second odyssey of Sylvia's wanderings did not appear while the Great War was still under way, I will not discuss it here among other novels published before the end of 1918. But there seems no reason to contradict the statement made by Mackenzie in his foreword to the reissue of 1950, '[*Sylvia and Michael*] was the first novel affected by weariness and disgust of war', or by his fuller statement in *Octave Five* of his autobiography, 'in 1919 most of the critics had been left behind by the march of time; they still thought war should inspire lofty and romantic notions in the mind of a novelist'.[6]

Mackenzie became keenly aware of how military service, with its emphasis on crisp statement, was directing his story-telling skills towards an increased emphasis on conversation as a means of advancing plot. Stendhal became an important model, too. The countless telegrams that he sent at nearly 2s. a word was a critical factor in emptying the honey from what the *Encyclopaedia Britannica* called his 'mellifluous style'. Because his supply of paper was inadequate, he turned upside-down the manuscript of *Guy and Pauline* and tried to avoid as much as possible rewriting sentences; some of the revised sentences of *Guy and Pauline* were on the pages on which he was writing *Sylvia Scarlett*, 'and an infernal nuisance they were'.[7] Mackenzie had now identified for himself the kind of fiction he found most congenial, and his fifth novel set him on a long road that would have no turning. He was to disappoint the critics, but he did not worry too much about their disapproval, since he scoffed at their 'lack of any width of experience'. He went on:

> Relying as I do so much on dialogue, I fancy that only readers with a dramatic sense enjoy my novels; they must be able as it were to play all the parts themselves, and so grasp their life. I am not interested in creating characters of such psychological complicacy that pages of patient analysis of human motive are required to present them on the printed page. The writer who does this [Mackenzie was thinking of Henry James] seldom convinces me that his characters ever existed outside his own imagination and I am not interested in reading about abstractions to which my own imagination is unable to give flesh and blood.[8]

Mackenzie smarted for years over having been patronised by Henry James, and he surely suspected that even the high praise that James had lavished on him as a rising star had been qualified. James had detected (fairly early) a possible change in Mackenzie's narrative technique, as evidenced by the first volume of *Sinister Street*: a shift from 'a controlling and a pointed intention' holding all the details together, to an 'episodic form' that might be compared to pearls loosely strung together. James was willing to accept saturation, the slice of life, only if a writer had answered for himself the key question about his ultimate goal: 'Yes, but is this *all*? Where is the interest?' He confessed himself puzzled by Mackenzie's developing career. Although Andro Linklater, author of the best biography thus far published on Mackenzie's life, complains of James's 'opaque' language in this critique,[9] it seems evident that James was reconsidering his initial enthusiasm for Mackenzie's fictions, and wondering with some concern what might come next. Though he died before the first volume of Sylvia Scarlett's adventures appeared, and for that matter before he could read the second volume of *Sinister Street*, James was expressing a hope that Mackenzie did have in mind more than a self-satisfied saturation in his portrayal of Oxford youth; he wanted a selective sense to take charge, even though he admitted the merits of a saturationist's technique (if well done).

James preferred Mackenzie's equivocal art to that of Arnold Bennett, Gilbert Cannan, Hugh Walpole and H. G. Wells, all of whom settled for an endlessly on-going narrative about 'things', but eventually he would have found it necessary to lament the lack of control in *Sylvia Scarlett*. Not many other critics ever regarded Mackenzie as a 'saturationist' in James's sense, but the mild stir of discontent with unfocused story-telling cleverness in *Sinister Street*, expressed in a number of reviews, became a rumbling when *Sylvia Scarlett* appeared. 'After every volume by Mr. Compton Mackenzie since his first', one reviewer wrote in the *New Statesman* issue of 7 September 1918, 'one has looked up and asked perplexedly: what is wrong with this distinguished, graceful and entertaining writer? He has knowledge, he has charm, he knows how to write, but the reader is not quite convinced.' The new book, about a quarter of a century in the life of a young woman named Sylvia Scarlett, reinforced the reviewers' 'perplexity'. There may have been some dissatisfaction with Mackenzie's sketchy characterisations, many of which were indistinguishable one from another, and critics frequently voiced their suspicion that Sylvia's adventures neither changed nor broadened her understanding of life. The scenes of wartime desolation in *Sylvia and Michael* seemed to be taking place in locales remote from the central areas known to most English soldiers. Mackenzie's disgust with small-minded manipulators who lengthened the war – 'Foreign Offices and War Offices and bureaucrats and shoddy kings and lawyers and politicians', as Sylvia put it – carried force, but did not constitute a convincing analysis of the major causes of what had happened to Europe, or of what was happening on the Western Front, though some excellent passages of description of refugee-clogged roads enlivened the text. Bulgaria, Rumania and Serbia were very far from England, but even their remoteness was not a sufficient excuse for the far-fetched plot twists and outrageous coincidences to which Mackenzie, more frequently than in his earlier novels, seemed to be growing addicted.

Mackenzie claimed that he did not pay much attention to critics, and thought their strictures unjustified anyhow. He resented having been pigeonholed so early as a certain kind of novelist, and he was willing to argue that his wartime cynicism – as expressed in *Sylvia and Michael* – irritated critics unaccustomed to frank treatment of the motives underlying military conduct. But the casual recounting of Sylvia's religious conversion (to Catholicism, the faith of her childhood, which she had long since abandoned) in a Bucharest church was of a piece with all her earlier sexual and personal crises. The evenness of the narration ultimately counted against any single adventure becoming crucial to Sylvia's understanding of motivation or behaviour. A reader might sigh wearily, after reading seven hundred pages of the combined double novel that constituted a whole, that the child born in Lille in the 1880s frequently expressed – before the age of fifteen – insights shrewder and more telling than most of what she had to say more than twenty-five years later in central Europe. Perhaps the critics whom he detested for writing on the basis of inadequate information about the wider world than he had himself experienced did not get their major point across to Mackenzie: growth in a major character's perspective was vital if that character was intended to dominate a very long novel, and to be present in almost every scene.

The strengths of *Sylvia Scarlett* were not to be located in the rattle-trap locomotion of sentences that ran on, filled with unsorted types of information:

> At six o'clock on the morning of Ash Wednesday in the year 1847, the Honourable Charles Cunningham sat sipping his coffee in the restaurant of the Vendanges de Bourgogne . . . Charles Cunningham had arrived at the Vendanges de Bourgogne to watch that rowdy climax of Carnival, the *descente de la Courtille* . . . . Presently the road outside was thronged for the aristocrats of the Faubourg St.-Germain to alight from their carriages and mix with the mob. This was the traditional climax of Carnival for Parisian society.

Nor were they to be found in the casual couplings which might or might not have long-lasting consequences, as when Charles Cunningham met 'a poke-bonnet garlanded with yellow rosebuds', learned (with some astonishment) that she loved him because he talked so well, and went to bed with her in an 'adventure'. This was only one of several such arrangements. Sylvia resisted Jimmy Monkley, who attempted to rape her – the botched attempt amounting to Mackenzie's satirisation of a conventional scene in Victorian melodrama – but she married Philip Iredale, a graduate of Balliol who inevitably reminded readers of Angel Clare because of his hypocritical fastidiousness, and later became the mistress of Arthur Madden, an uninteresting young man given over to sieges of self-pity, without thinking once of the possibility that Jimmy might be superior as a human being (because he suffered from fewer illusions) to both her choices. She hardly ever looked back.

Not that Sylvia had much opportunity to choose between acceptable alternatives. She moved for much of her early life in raffish company, and when her social circumstances improved, she cast herself adrift among narcissists and failed artists. Love never became more than a brightly coloured word for Sylvia. Readers were not reassured when, in the final pages of *Sylvia and Michael*, Michael asked Sylvia to marry him: her happiness was not likely to be found in his direction. Michael, like Sylvia, searched for certainties, and thought that religion would illuminate his path. D. H. Lawrence noted, in a letter to Mackenzie, that Sylvia's adventures amounted to a 'rolling stone business', and that Sylvia seemed to be busily hunting 'something *permanent*'. 'Don't like the Christ hankering – sign of defeat', he continued, but even so, he allied himself with Mackenzie; they were two writers who had failed to find a way out of the labyrinth. 'How we hang on to the marriage clue! Doubt if it's really a way out.... Whither poor Sylvia? The ideal? I loathe the ideal with an increasing volume of detestation – *all* ideal.'[10]

The traces of Mackenzie's earlier conception of Sylvia – she had been characterised as a lesbian in *Sinister Street* – were not wholly effaced in this new effort to imagine her milieu. One of the brighter moments of comic invention described how Sylvia, leaning over the parapet of Waterloo Bridge while she munched hot chestnuts, was picked up by a middle-aged man 'in a dark-grey coat with collars and cuffs of chinchilla', and taken to a party in the vicinity of Radcliffe Gardens. Here the servants dressed like gondoliers ('So much more picturesque than a horrible housemaid', her host said), and the house smelled strongly of incense and watered flowers. One guest smoked Russian cigarettes, and informed Sylvia that his cigarette case was made of Chinese jade: 'I've even got a jade toilet-set.' He added that it was 'dreadfully expensive'. Raymond, one of the guests, leaped into the middle of the room 'with a wild scream', and threw himself into 'all sorts of extraordinary attitudes'. The host expressed pleasure: 'Oh, Raymond, you're too wonderful! You make me feel quite Bacchic.' But Sylvia was not surprised that anybody should feel 'backache' – 'she had thus understood her host' – in the presence of 'such contortions'. A second 'lightly clad and equally shrill youth called Sydney' joined Raymond in a choric frenzy. The two chased each other 'round and round, sawing the air with their legs, and tearing roses from their hair to fling at the guests, who flung them back at the dancers'. The 'adventure' continued with Sylvia drinking four glasses of crème de menthe (her first taste of the liqueur) and becoming rather drowsy; the outbreak of a ferocious quarrel when Sylvia was recognised as the perpetrator of an earlier scam on a newly arrived guest; pinching, stepping on Sydney's bare toes, face-slapping, kicking; and Sylvia's being hastily ejected into the street by two gondoliers. Sylvia returned to Waterloo Bridge and bought fifty more chestnuts; returned home; and pondered 'the whole extraordinary business'.

The episode was characteristic of Mackenzie's story-telling art, partly because its interest in a rather good-natured raunchiness ran through any number of Mackenzie's novels: the 'Theatre of Youth' series – his 'complete survey of contemporary society in which the personages of a large and complicated series of books were to be shown in youth'[11] – as well as Count Marsac in *Vestal Fire*, Rosalba Donsante and her female victims in *Extraordinary Women*, Geoffrey Noel in *The Four Winds of Love* and Henry Fortescue in *Thin Ice*. The party scene was particularised; its details were so densely recorded that they precluded all abstraction and moralising. The would-be orgy was comically alive; an aspiring author could hardly do worse than study the way in which Mackenzie briskly summarised the alcoholic effects of what to Sylvia was a novel drink: 'a green mist of crème de menthe'. The description of the effect that each of her four glasses produced, one on top of the other, was professionally brisk. The episode was also typical in that whatever Sylvia thought about that afternoon's adventure, her meditation led to no better insight than she had before she participated in it; she 'vainly' tried to understand it; and the upshot of the whole affair was her decision to change from her boy's disguise (she had been wearing a boy's clothes for several years) to more appropriate dresses.[12] She did not respond directly to Jimmy Monkley's warning, 'Shows how careful you ought to be.' It was not even clear whether she agreed with Jimmy.

The inventiveness of *Sylvia Scarlett* deserved commendation, though readers inevitably wished that more might be made of individual adventures, or that Mackenzie indicated more plainly why he wrote so many extended anecdotes about Sylvia's passage through life. Mackenzie wrote to better effect when he dramatised a reception at the Emperor of Byzantium's home in Stanmore Crescent; the confidence schemes of Jimmy Monkley and Henry Scarlett (in which Sylvia frequently participated, though without much sensitivity to moral and ethical problems); the scene in which Sylvia managed to drive a cab with an unruly horse; the lurid moment in which Danny Lewis threatened to kill Sylvia with his clasp-knife, and Sylvia, reacting instantly, emptied a water-bottle over him; Sylvia's play-acting as an odalisque in the Hall of a Thousand and One Marvels at the Exhibition ('from eleven in the morning till eleven at night on a salary of fourteen shillings a week, all extras to be shared with seven other young ladies similarly engaged'); the pattern of education at Miss Ashley's school for young ladies on Campden Hill (Mackenzie was, perhaps surprisingly, respectful of both what it intended to do for young ladies and what it actually accomplished); the boredom (a 'multitude of insignificant little threads') and ultimately the intolerable frustration of life in Green Lanes, when Sylvia attempted to live up to Philip Iredale's moony expectations about an ideal wife (Mackenzie compressed months of increasingly restive domestic relations into a relatively small number of pages); the knockabout farce of the visit of the anti-papist Treacherites ('two young men with pimply faces who swaggered into church and talked to one another loudly before the service began, commenting upon the ornaments with cockney facetiousness'); Mrs Gainsborough's eloquent memories of General Dashwood, stirred to the surface by his recent funeral ('You should have seen him lay out two roughs who tried to snatch me watch and chain once at the Epsom Derby'); Sylvia's life as a music-hall singer, a natural enough development resulting from her continuing ties with continental mountebanks; the passion that Lily (Sylvia's friend) developed for gambling and diamond-encrusted ornaments in Brazil, and her fear of, and fascination for, the ruffian Camacho;

Sylvia's truly astonishing night out at the toughest dancing-saloon in Buenos Aires with the fantastically rich (and reckless) Carlos Morera; the encounter with the despairing Italian dancer Concetta at the Alhambra (by moonlight, naturally); the melodramatic death of Rodrigo, a Spanish urchin to whom Sylvia took a sudden fancy; the crowded street-scenes in Morocco; the flaring egos of the personalities involved in the touring production of the play *A Honeymoon in Europe* ('"Damn it, Miss Tremayne, didn't I ask you not to go on talking?" the producer shouted'); the unspeakable dreariness of the Plutonian Hotel, Sulphurville, where nasty-tasting water was sold in bottles 'as a panacea to the great encouragement of lonely dyspeptics with nothing else to read at dinner'; and Sylvia's evening of triumph – the beginning of a successful run – as a monologist, working with 'improvisations' based on her own adventure-stuffed life.

The number of characters who made distinct impressions by virtue of their turns of speech was truly generous. Though the Mrs Gainsborough type turned up in several other novels by Mackenzie, the genuine article, the original Mrs Gainsborough, was overwhelming in her vulgarity, ignorance, cheerfulness and quintessential Englishness. As a travelling companion of Sylvia, she played an important role in the last third of the novel. On being invited by Sylvia to accompany her to Spain, Mrs Gainsborough exclaimed,

> Spain! Upon my word I never heard anything like it. We'd better take plenty with us to eat. I knew it reminded me of something. The Spanish Armada! I once heard a clergyman recite the Spanish Armada, though what it was all about I've completely forgotten.

She regarded as disgusting the Spanish habit of 'carrying wine inside of goats', and no better than a scheme to force travellers to buy water. She objected to the childish way the Spanish had for starting a train – 'blowing a toy horn like that. More like a school treat than a railway journey.' As for the Spanish diet:

> I don't feel like chocolate in the morning. I'd just as lieve have a slice of plum-pudding in a cup. Why, if you try to put a lump of sugar in, it won't sink; it keeps bobbing up like a kitten. And another thing I can't seem to get used to is having the fish after the meat. Every time it comes in like that it seems a kind of carelessness. What fish it is, too, when it does come. Well, they say a donkey can eat thistles, but it would take him all his time to get through one of those fish. No wonder they serve them after the meat. I should think they were afraid of the amount of

meat any one might eat, trying to get the bones out of one's throat. I've felt like a pincushion ever since I got to Madrid.

There were fine rows, too, as when Danny Lewis and Jay Cohen tangled at Mrs Gonner's boarding-house:

> The confusion in the shop became general: Mr. Gonner cut his thumb, and the sight of the blood caused a woman who was eating a sausage to choke; another customer took advantage of the row to snatch a side of bacon and try to escape, but another customer with a finer moral sense prevented him; a dog, who was sniffing in the entrance, saw the bacon on the floor and tried to seize it, but getting his tail trodden upon by somebody, it took fright and bit into a small boy who was waiting to change a shilling into coppers.

Mackenzie's technique was only intermittently realistic. Leo Robertson, a personal friend of Mackenzie, once wrote that the 'excess in situation and characterisation' in *Syvia Scarlett* should not be censured as an unreasonable 'heightening of effects beyond what is discernible in reality'.[13] He justified it by saying that Mackenzie was here adapting the picaresque novel – which sought to depict life 'merely in its external and mechanic motions' – to a modern mode, even though he remained true to the picaresque tradition by minimising introspection. Mackenzie's real intention was to show us 'how the sources of loving-kindness and sympathy, congealed in his heroine by the frosts of circumstance, so that none would suspect their existence from the hard and cynical exterior she presented to the world, came to flow again'. Well, perhaps, though Sylvia's dislike of most of the men who attempted to establish serious relationships with her, and her greater ease with a number of women, particularly her actress-friend Lily, suggested the existence of a troubled sexual identity, the full implications of which Mackenzie would not, or could not, develop during the late months of the Great War.[14] D. J. Dooley, in a judiciously balanced critique, noted that if Sylvia's religious awakening were the novel's major theme, 'it is often lost sight of', and 'her conversion is not prepared for'.[15] It may be that Mackenzie's primary interest in writing *Sylvia Scarlett* will remain impossible to identify. D. H. Lawrence's remark about Sylvia's unsatisfied search for meaning in her life implied that Lawrence believed Mackenzie had not settled on either marriage or a 'Christ hankering' as that meaning.

Both the incidental pleasures and the overall readability of *Sylvia*

Scarlett remain fully evident to this day. Mackenzie's reputation suffered grievously with the passage of time, perhaps because a prolific writer raised in many readers' minds the suspicion of careless repetition of themes and character-types. But Edmund Wilson, in 1962, objected to the critics who refused to give Mackenzie credit 'for being the fine artist that at his best he [was]',[16] and Wilson's insistence that we look beyond Mackenzie's description of himself as an 'entertainer' was a point well worth making. There exists in *Sylvia Scarlett*, and perhaps to a lesser degree in *Sylvia and Michael*, an enthusiasm for living and observation that ran counter to Mackenzie's own sense that he had written a novel of 'weariness and disgust'. Despite its length, it may best be regarded as a truly important novel still in the making.

Part III

Thunder on the horizon

Chapter 8

Mary Webb's *The Golden Arrow* (1915)

Novelists no less than any other citizens (and doubtless more than many of them) were well posted on current events. They read newspapers; they wrote for the periodical press on issues related to the English commitment on the Continent; they responded patriotically to Charles Frederick Gurney Masterman's request, made on behalf of the Cabinet, 'to consider what role eminent authors might play in formulating and publicizing British principles and war aims';[1] and many of them donned uniforms. But, as we have seen, fictions oblivious to the existence of current wartime conditions could be written, and were, throughout the war years, and indeed constituted a majority of the novels published.

Yet some novels could not avoid referring to the fact that England was engaged in a conflict that seemed to worsen with each passing season. In my consideration of the following five novels – Mary Webb's *The Golden Arrow*, Joseph Conrad's *Victory*, Ford Madox Hueffer's *The Good Soldier*, Alec Waugh's *The Loom of Youth* and Wyndham Lewis's *Tarr* – I will have something to say about the way in which each author described the possibility that something had gone hugely, monstrously, and permanently wrong in the lives of fictional characters living in England, and the conditions of life across the Channel. It was not as if these authors spoke directly of the problem. Rather, theirs was an awareness of, a sensitivity to, rumblings of thunder at a distance. And the novels frequently attempted to deal with anticipations of disaster by oblique, indirect, and often symbolic techniques. In some cases doing so enriched the potential significance of the dramatic situations being explored. In other cases the exploitation of a reader's awareness of a world war being waged beyond the confines of a study seemed pretentious or unwarranted, and did not improve the artistic merit of the story. Nevertheless, such novels exhibited a sense of responsibility to history, if not to the writer's craft.

Mary Webb wrote the first draft of *The Golden Arrow*, her first novel, within a three-week period in the spring of 1915. Her voice was immediately recognised as distinctive. Her setting, in all her novels save *Precious Bane*, was the hill country of south-west Shropshire; but even in *Precious Bane*, as Stanley Baldwin noted, the dialect spoken by residents of the Ellesmere district of north Shropshire was that of south Shropshire.

Overemphasising her regional concerns, however, may do her an injustice, since Baldwin was not the only reader to be carried away by her 'blending of human passion with the fields and skies'.[2] Her background had prepared her for romantic fiction. Her mother was the daughter of an Edinburgh physician who took pride in belonging to the clan of Sir Walter Scott. Her father, George Edward Meredith, read Scott's novels over and over; he wrote poetry, painted, cultivated a garden; he was a much-loved schoolmaster who prepared students for Sandhurst and the universities. The household was altogether congenial for the cultivating of Mary's imagination, and as her biographer Thomas Moult pointed out, she paid her father high tribute in *The Golden Arrow*. 'He is old John Arden, who keeps the lamp shining.' Since half a dozen years separated her from the next-born in what was to become a family of six children, she had time to develop a quiet, contemplative character wrapped inside a child's outer garment; she often held back from children's games; she communed with nature; and she observed, with editorial judgements that she was not always able to keep to herself, the cruelty of blood sports, the hypocrisy of her peers and the injustice of adults.

A large part of *The Golden Arrow* was based on Mary Webb's memories of her home at Weston-super-Mare, in which she had lived with her husband, Henry Bertram Law Webb, for a dismal two years prior to their removal to Rose Cottage, Pontesbury, near Shrewsbury, Shropshire. Fortunately, her marriage turned out to be happy, and remained so. (She dedicated both *The Golden Arrow* and *Precious Bane* to him.) Within four years of her meeting him, she was to complete her first draft of *The Golden Arrow*.

G. K. Chesterton, in his introduction to the Uniform Edition, enthusiastically compared her 'prose poems of a Shropshire Lass' to A. E. Housman's songs of a Shropshire lad, and singled out for praise the 'very heroic heroine' of *The Golden Arrow*, a novel which dealt with 'that western county which lies, romantic and rather mysterious, upon the marches of Wales' (as, indeed, did all her other novels: *Gone to Earth, Seven for a Secret, The House in Dormer Forest* and the unfinished novel upon which she was working at the time of her death, *Armour Wherein He Trusted*). Others who contributed introductions to the Uniform Edition included Robert Lynd, John Buchan and Walter de la Mare, as well as the Rt Hon. Stanley Baldwin, who had written to her in 1927 from 10 Downing Street:

> My people lived in Shropshire for centuries before they migrated to Worcestershire, and I spent my earliest years in Bewdley, which is on the border. In your book I seem to hear again the speech and turns of phrase which surrounded me in the nursery. I think it is a really first-class piece of work and I have not enjoyed a book so much for years. It was given to me by one of my secretaries and I read it at Christmas within sight of the Clee Hills, at home. Thank you a thousand times for it.[3]

Others recognised her unusualness as a writer of novels about a remote corner of England. Rebecca West, for example, proclaimed *Gone to Earth*, Mary Webb's second novel, the novel of the year (1917), and used the epithet 'genius' to describe its author. Thomas Hardy was sufficiently impressed by the manuscript of *Seven for a Secret* that he allowed Mary Webb to dedicate the novel to him. In the spring of 1925 the 'Femina Vie Heureuse' Committee decided that *Precious Bane* was the best imaginative work in prose or verse descriptive of English life by an author who had not gained sufficient recognition (1924–5). And publishers' records indicate that cash advances sent to her were consistently generous.

Yet Mary Webb, though she relished every kind word written to her or spoken on her behalf, struggled in obscurity all her life until she died of pernicious anaemia and Graves's disease (8 October 1927, at the age of forty-six). Only *Precious Bane* sold more than a thousand copies during her lifetime, and not many more than that. The reviewers 'noticed' her novels only as items in a list of widely disparate fictions, or not at all. Sir James Barrie, in a conversation with the Prime Minister Stanley Baldwin, at the Royal Literary Fund annual dinner (1928), praised her highly, while expressing some puzzlement at the fact that 'no one buys her books'. If posthumous fame can compensate for this kind of neglect (in a real sense, it cannot), she has achieved some recognition as a less accomplished regional writer in the Hardy vein; her novels have been compared to *Under the Greenwood Tree*, but never with much conviction that death cut off a talent that may have been on the verge of writing a novel on the scale of *The Return of the Native*.

The reason why readers in 1915 did not respond more enthusiastically to *The Golden Arrow* is not hard to identify. The characters were uniformly unpleasant. Moreover, despite its (approximate) length of 100,000 words, the book was underpopulated, and Mary Webb seemed unwilling to invent much in the way of dramatic incident. The plot can all too easily be summarised.

The focus of attention was the Arden family, living in a stone cottage 'in the midst of the hill plateau, higher than the streams began, shelterless to the four winds'. John Arden, a quiet and dignified farmer, and his wife Patty (usually called Mrs Arden) were the parents of two children who married the wrong people. Joe, the son, was stolid, fairly unimaginative and hopelessly smitten; the woman he loved was Lily Huntbatch, a pretty but exasperatingly self-centred young woman. The major strand of the narrative dealt with Deborah, the daughter. She was overwhelmed by her passion for a sometime preacher of the gospel and mine-foreman named Stephen Southernwood. Stephen refused to marry Deborah for many months after he began 'living in sin' with her; changed his mind unexpectedly; wed her; and then abandoned her – she was pregnant – and sailed off to America aboard a cattle-boat. Deborah, overwhelmed by the discovery that her husband did not love her, burned the furniture of her home and then collapsed. Her parents took her home and nursed her through a long illness. At the novel's end, with June flowers blooming ('The Seynty tree's gold over!', Mrs Arden cried, after the christening of Deborah's baby), an exhausted Stephen – ill from the after-effects of typhoid – returned to the village of Slepe and to Deborah. He asked to be forgiven. Deborah, unforgiving, rejected him, and he left. But the 'primaeval, ungovernable passion for the reassurance of touch' swept over her, and she called out for her wayward husband. Nighttime came, and Stephen returned. Mary Webb assured us that this 'cut love' would mend. To agree with her required, from most readers, an unusual amount of sympathy for people they had never been persuaded to like.

Nevertheless, two elements of the novel – Mary Webb's heightened language and an increasingly powerful sense that the larger world had gone awry – deserve attention.

The idiom of her characters has been censured as improbable, coming from ill-educated folk whose only reading was the Bible. The problem may lie in a failure to differentiate sharply enough between what the characters say and what the novelist, in setting the scene or analysing the motivation, said about the Shropshire world within which they functioned. Some of the language was very striking, beginning with the author's poem which prefaced the novel:

> We have sought it, we have sought the golden arrow!
>   (Bright the sally-willows sway)
> Two and two by paths low and narrow,
>   Arm-in-crook along the mountain way.
>   Break o' frost and break o' day!
> Some were sobbing through the gloom
> When we found it, when we found the golden arrow –
> Wand of willow in the secret cwm.

These lines versified an ancient custom of hunting for a golden arrow at Easter-time. 'And it was said', John Arden explained, 'that if two as were walking out found the arrow they'd cling to it fast though it met wound them sore.' Finding the arrow, in other words, was not necessarily a cause for rejoicing, for it cast a spell on lovers that could not be broken either 'in the flower of life' or 'in the brown winrow'. 'And the tale goes', Deborah's father continued,

> that once long ago two found it in the sally-thickets down yonder. And they came through Slepe singing, and with such a scent of appleblow about 'em as never was – though appleblow time was a full month off; and such a power of honeybees about 'em as you only see in summertime. And they went like folks that want nought of any man, walking fast and looking far. And never a soul saw them after.

Though the cynical comments of one farmer serve to anchor this flight of poetic fancy – 'Apple-blow as met have set into good cooking apples at seven shilling the pot' – the intention of the allegory was fully accessible to ordinary readers. The allegory, meant to describe the relationship of Deborah and Stephen, who have sought the arrow and found it to their sorrow, *works*. The ghosts who had not been pierced by the golden arrow (John Arden was insistent that 'there's allus some finds the arrow in the worst years') gathered to sing their melancholy song: 'We lived 'ard; we supped sorrow; we died respected; but we'm lonely.' They set up a cry 'like a yew-tree on a windy night: "Out o' mind! Out o' mind!" Then the ghosses stir like poplars, all grey and misty-like in a ring round the Chair, and there's no sound but sobbing.' ('The Devil's Chair,' a mass of quartzite, 'blackened and hardened by uncountable ages', and the major topographical feature of this rural community, was the most important symbol in the novel.) But it hardly mattered whether the search for the golden arrow was successful or not; John Arden's explanation of the legend seemed to suggest that one was compelled to search, and that the outcome was bound to be an awareness of how transitory all happiness could be.

John Arden's speeches were perhaps more elevated in diction than those of any other character. He cherished his simple faith in Cariad, the name in singing Welsh of 'the Flockmaster, the won'erful one', who went westering even as he called 'all the white sinners and the stained mighty ones, and even the little blue fishes in the hill streams'. His quotations of Scripture were always pertinent, as when he comforted the sick and forlorn Deborah: 'I sought him whom my soul loveth, I sought him and I found him not. It was but a little time . . . but I found him whom my soul loveth: I held him and would not let him go.' The words, Mary Webb informs us, 'fell like April rain on her seared heart'.

Deborah, despite her implausible behaviour at crucial moments, was often as eloquent as her father. If Stephen woke her after only two hours of sleep, she was apt to respond, 'It's mortal early.' She denied that her father talked in the language of chapel or church Christianity; rather it was 'just home brewed'. Her father's discussion of religious matters was 'like cowslips in your hand. Keys of heaven, cowslips be called.' When she spoke of her love for Stephen (before the great betrayal and abandonment), her words vibrated with a sincerity that went beyond language: 'I be ready, Stephen, ready for all. I'll go with you gladsome in wet weather or in shiny; and lie quiet in the daisies knowing we loved true.'

The tension between this cadenced, supernal diction and Mary Webb's bleak assessment of life's possibilities never lets up. In fact, it grew stronger as the novel moved to its conclusion; when Stephen, completely disillusioned by what had happened to himself, and unconvinced that he was fully responsible, came to believe that there was 'no court of appeal', no one 'to defy, curse, be tortured by; just vacancy and the insect-like lives of himself and the other millions in the world, all going nowhere for no purpose except extinction'.

In several uncanny respects Stephen resembled Conrad's Heyst in *Victory*. He had sought to renounce the world, but the world insisted on his knowing that it was there. He had tried to live an idyllic existence, but life must be lived on its own terms. And he was cursed by his consciousness of himself as an English gentleman, which prevented him from confiding in Deborah, whom he regarded as a social inferior, less educated in book-knowledge than himself.

The Devil's Chair was thus a material representation of the inner self. It was described, at various times, as 'a fist flourished in the face', 'inviolable, taciturn, evil', 'like some black altar when curtains are drawn for an unholy rite'. Or it was characterised as a chair from which the occupant had just risen, to which he would shortly return. 'Whenever rain or driving sleet or mist made a grey shechinah there people said, "There's harm brewing." "He's in his chair."' The *he*, of course, was the Devil.

The only time we hear of Stephen's preaching, his sermon (we are told) was not based on personal experience. Stephen spoke of death 'as a child does – quite unable to believe in his own skeleton, coolly sorry for those who were weak enough to suffer such indignity'. His 'eloquent comfort', bestowed on those who have truly suffered, came from one 'who has never seen the blank wall that rises between the last tremor and the eternal stillness on the beloved's face'. Stephen was 'sure of himself, God, and the small shell that was his creed'. He could not arm himself with such a shield against the blows of an unrelenting fate.

We learned little or nothing about Stephen's background or religious faith. His loss of belief seemed implausible; it was, at any rate, inadequately prepared for. It was hard to tell why Stephen insisted so strenuously that he was not the marrying kind; or why, later on, he agreed to marry; or why marriage so depressed him that he refused to accept responsibility for the child he had fathered. His irritation at being where he was baffled Deborah.

When Stephen attempted to dynamite the Devil's Chair – an effort that failed miserably – Mary Webb tells us that 'it was the Chair's emptiness, the impersonal element in the world, that overcame him'. He had rejected 'the safe and rather misty glass of ready-made dogmas or legends', but had found nothing to take their place. Explanations of why this sudden belief (or loss of belief) overtook him were given ('partially the outcome of the dark doctrines he had been taught as a child', 'partly inherited from a race that had come of the soil', and 'the primaeval instinct of the poet and the savage, who find in rock and flower a fearful alphabet'), but these were inadequate, and never convincing. A door to all the unanswerable questions had been opened:

> What if there had never been a grain of truth in any creed, and everything – all the beauty, the goodness, the effort, the achievement – were purposeless as dust in the wind, fortuitous, annihilated now, tomorrow or in an aeon? What if he were no more than the moth, flickering for a moment in imbecile activity on the bleak mountain in the cold night wind?

It was not far from such questions to convictions that religion was filled with frauds and that there was '*no* God', no anything, no immortality. 'It was the horror of emptiness, utter negation – that modern ghost, more ghastly than medieval devils or the ancient gods of slaughter.' Hence, the Devil's Chair, an empty throne, became for Stephen the perfect symbol:

> no devil, no angel, no god ever was there, ever would be there, nothing. There was no court of appeal, there was not even any one to defy, curse, be tortured by; just vacancy and the insect-like lives of himself and the other millions in the world, all going nowhere for no purpose except extinction.

Deborah, too, had been devastated by Stephen's desertion to the point where she believed in nothing. Her despair was akin to 'the emotions of a Teresa confronted with incontrovertible proof that Christ never lived, or of a mother, not yet free from the pains of childbirth, told that her baby is dead'. Just before she put a match to her furniture, she cried, 'The longest night is come!' At the heart of her emotional turmoil was a perception of the hopelessness of love: 'She had no purpose left – either to live or die.' Later: 'She was like one asphyxiated.'

This anomie was not cancelled by the 'happy' ending. It was completely inexplicable if we think only of Mary Webb's romantically satisfying marriage, her affectionate ties with family, friends and neighbours and the enormous pleasure that she took in the physical act of writing. It makes a good deal more sense, however, if we regard

The Golden Arrow as a novel that reflected a growing awareness in 1915, among all sensitive men and women, that values of decency, kinship and love were daily being damaged, and were ultimately to be radically changed, by the horrible war raging on the Continent.

Chapter 9

Joseph Conrad's *Victory* (1915)

Joseph Conrad hated publishers who attempted to edit his work. He found it difficult to tell his literary agent, J. B. Pinker, exactly what he was doing, or to be realistic about deadlines. 'Writer's block' crippled him for lengthy periods. He certainly did not need the stimuli of newspaper headlines to confirm his dark reading of human nature.

Nevertheless, he was fully aware of strains created by the Conservative opposition in the House of Commons in the three years that preceded the assassination of Archduke Ferdinand, and he would have had to be deaf and dumb to ignore the tumult caused by the Women's Movement and the numerous examples of labour unrest. The years between 1911 and mid-1914 constituted a chronicle of troubles and widespread malaise. For only a few men and women could they be called 'the last great Garden Party'.[1]

In 1912, while writing a number of short stories and polishing the text of *Chance*, Conrad interrupted his labours to comment on the sinking of the *Titanic*, and did so in the form of two vigorous articles for the *English Review*. The construction of this ship, he believed, had been a mistake from the beginning. He described the sinking as an event likely to exert a chastening influence on the self-confidence of mankind. Its passengers had, 'to the last moment', trusted 'mere bigness',[2] and their misplaced confidence had been bolstered by 'the reckless affirmations of commercial men and mere technicians and in the irresponsible paragraphs of the newspapers' which overpraised the construction of such ships.[3] As a captain of long experience, Conrad did not believe in the concept 'unsinkable', and had known, from the beginning of its use as a refrain accompanying publicity about the

117

building of the *Titanic*, that the ship had undertaken needlessly a burden too heavy for its good health. 'I ask myself', wrote Conrad bemusedly,

> whether the Marine Department of the Board of Trade did really believe, when they decided to shelve the report on equipment for a time, that a ship of 45,000 tons, that *any* ship, could be made practically indestructible by means of watertight bulkheads? It seems incredible to anybody who had ever reflected upon the properties of material, such as wood or steel.[4]

The *Titanic* had been decorated 'in the style of the Pharaohs or in the Louis Quinze style – I don't know which', to please a couple of thousand rich people 'who have more money than they know what to do with', despite the demonstrable fact that at sea 'size is to a certain extent an element of weakness'.[5] A ship must be even more delicately handled when it exceeds conventional dimensions of bulk and length. The *Titanic*, in brief, was

> a sort of marine Ritz, proclaimed unsinkable and sent adrift with its casual population upon the sea, without enough boats, without enough seamen (but with a Parisian café and four hundred of poor devils of waiters) to meet dangers which, let the engineers say what they like, lurk always amongst the waves, sent with a blind trust in mere material, light-heartedly, to a most miserable, most fatuous disaster.[6]

Conrad's anger was directed primarily against the technicians, 'the high priests of the modern cult of perfected material and of mechanical appliances', those who prohibited the profane from enquiring into their mysteries. 'We are the masters of progress, they say, and you should remain silent. And they take refuge behind their mathematics.'[7] The modern world, however, committed an unforgivable sin when it bowed down in homage before the technicians:

> But mere calculations, of which these men make so much, when unassisted by imagination and when they have gained mastery over common sense, are the most deceptive exercises of intellect. Two and two are four, and two are six. That is immutable; you may trust your soul to that; but you must be certain first of your quantities.[8]

The *Titanic* had sailed into danger with too few boats, but its sinking was not traceable to a problem of boats at all.

It is the problem of decent behaviour. If you can't carry or handle so many boats, then don't cram quite so many people on board. It is as simple as that – this problem of right feeling and right conduct, the real nature of which seems beyond the comprehension of ticket-providers.[9]

The loss of the *Titanic* signalled an end to easy faith in technical solutions; for many it was the ringing down of the curtain on innocence itself. Conrad interpreted it as a repudiation of the common sense of marine traditions, developed over countless centuries, and a portent of dire events.

The year 1912, though Conrad did not appreciate it at the time, marked the end of his long years of disappointment in trying to find a larger audience of interested readers. *Lord Jim*, published in 1900, had not sold 5,000 copies by 1912, and his short stories had earned less than 10 guineas apiece when published in *Pall Mall*. (The German publisher B. Tauchnitz paid him 10 guineas for the continental rights of one of his books and thought the sum generous.)

After the publication of *Chance*, however, the world changed for Conrad. A poll conducted by *The New Age* – 'What did readers think was the best book of fiction published within recent years?' – resulted in the majority of votes being cast for *Chance*, which sold over 5,000 copies within twelve months.

In April 1912 (the month that the *Titanic* sank), Conrad began a short story that he entitled 'Dollars'. At first he may have meant it to run no longer than 'Heart of darkness'. His major character, an idealistic man named Berg, was far more concerned about the happiness of members of the human race than he was about dollars. But by the end of the year Conrad decided that his hero had to be more sharply differentiated from any of his previous heroes, and that this short story really called for the full length of a novel. Writing it proved more arduous than he had anticipated, however. His comments about it during the full two and a half years of its gestation were almost uniformly dispirited, and on occasion depressed. Even so, its appearance – first in *Munsey's Magazine*, in New York, beginning in February 1915, and then in the *London Star*, beginning in August 1915 – created a considerable stir. As a book it quickly sold 10,000 copies. The reviewers compared Conrad to Robert Louis Stevenson, Henry James, Gustave Flaubert; they praised either its atmospherics ('texture') or its Hamlet-like hero, Heyst, as a nobly-conceived characterisation.[10]

Though not a word of *Victory* was written before the war broke out, the novel is remarkably prophetic in its study of a humane man's despair in a world that lacks meaning and direction. In his note to the first edition, Conrad admitted that he had debated with himself on the advisability of changing still one more time the title of his novel. 'The word Victory, the shining and tragic goal of noble effort, appeared too great, too august, to stand at the head of a mere novel.' But he was also concerned that such a word, printed in the midst of a great war, might deceive the public into believing that he had written a novel dealing, in some way, with the events of that war. He decided to retain the title:

> Victory was the last word I had written in peace time. It was the last literary thought which had occurred to me before the doors of the Temple of Janus flying open with a crash shook the minds, the hearts, the consciences of men all over the world.

Though Conrad called the outbreak of the war a 'coincidence', he could not treat the coincidence lightly. The word 'victory' was worth saving, but the complexities of Heyst's fully shaded characterisation made Heyst's 'victory' at the novel's end a far more equivocal and uncertain resolution than perhaps Conrad had intended. Nor does it require much critical acuity to see that, in this particular novel, any total, soul-satisfying victory was impossible.

An open ending – one in which the narrative ends indeterminately – reflects our modern understanding of experience, which does not conveniently conclude when we read the final chapter of a novel, but continues. We encourage mimetic art because it enables us to appreciate better the world which mimesis attempts to reproduce. However, no mimetic artists can rest content with a fidelity to fact, but must impose a pattern upon their novels. Contradictory impulses in the narrative became most evident in the last few pages. Because the finality of the last chapters in any novel was authorially imposed, the novel had to lie.[11] And Conrad, in the conclusion of each of his five major novels (*Lord Jim*, *Nostromo*, *The Secret Agent*, *Under Western Eyes* and *Victory*), delineated clearly 'the very impossibility of conclusion that necessarily compromises the task of writing an ending or of writing definitively about one'.[12]

A few comments about Heyst are in order before the peculiar nature of the victory that settled the affairs of all the major characters is evaluated. Heyst, so Conrad tells us, began with some illusions. At one time he thought it possible that his employers, the Tropical Belt

Coal Company, might become the means of a 'stride forward'. He loved the islands. In a fit of enthusiasm, he even told the manager of the branch of the Oriental Banking Corporation in Malacca that they enchanted him. He was, therefore, a utopist (which, Conrad believed, was a dangerous stage in the evolution of a man's character). It is unnecessary to review plot details, but Conrad's scepticism about the inscrutable and heartless workings of capitalism gave the novel its first strong push. Heyst, named as a manager of TBC Co., flourished only so long as the bankers and government in London believed in it (not very long, in other words), and lost his place when they abandoned it.

It would be a mistake to interpret this story of a ruined entreprencurial scheme as the most important cause of Heyst's disillusionment. Conrad disposed of it briskly during the relatively straightforward, conventionally narrated section of *Victory* before his major allegory began. Heyst's problems with life traced back to the heavy and destructive influence of his father, which pressed down long before Heyst announced to an interested, sympathetic narrator that he was done with facts. The elder Heyst was a philosopher who wrote books (always a mark of parched emotions, from Conrad's perspective), and who, for vague reasons, had quarrelled with his family in Sweden: 'Just the sort of father you would expect Heyst to have', as Davidson, who replaces the cynical and omniscient narrator, told his curious audience. The father had claimed for mankind 'that right to absolute moral and intellectual liberty of which he no longer believed them worthy' (what changed his mind?).

> For more than sixty years he had dragged on this painful earth of ours the most weary, the most uneasy soul that civilization had ever fashioned to its ends of disillusion and regret. One could not refuse him a measure of greatness, for he was unhappy in a way unknown to mediocre souls.

That, in turn, created in Heyst 'a profound mistrust of life'. In a key passage of the novel,

> The young man learned to reflect, which is a destructive process, a reckoning of the cost. It is not the clear-sighted who lead the world. Great achievements are accomplished in a blessed, warm mental fog, which the pitiless cold blasts of the father's analysis had blown away from the son.

Heyst's decision to 'drift', taken deliberately as a defence against life, was the inevitable consequence of his father's teaching.

Heyst reviewed the conviction of his father that the wages paid to all mankind – workers in a universe which his father likened to a factory – was counterfeit money. He must have re-examined, however timorously, the notion that 'Man on this earth is an unforeseen accident which does not stand close investigation.' He must also have found in himself some fatal flaw which prevented him from becoming more than a drifter, an independent spectator.

Because Conrad could not resolve Heyst's moral and intellectual difficulties at the level of mere sex, Heyst's passion for Lena, the stray waif whom he rescued from a brutal Teuton, hardly seemed credible. Lena was too inarticulate, her conversation too monosyllabic, to give Heyst 'a greater sense of his own reality than he had ever known in all his life'. Despite Conrad's insistence on the redemptive powers of love, Heyst had travelled too far down the road disbelieving in life's possibilities. His final words, spoken to his only genuine friend, the ship's captain Davidson, are, 'Ah, Davidson, woe to the man whose heart has not learned while young to hope, to love – and to put its trust in life!' But for a long time Heyst had not been young. It was fitting that the last world of *Victory* should be Davidson's sigh, 'Nothing!'

The logic of the plot will suggest to most readers that what Conrad intended to show was the saving of Heyst's soul. Heyst, after all, had helped a bankrupt trader, rescued Lena and learned about himself. Even in death, and despite death, there was always the possibility of victory, for he could learn how to hope, love and put his trust in life, before dying.

But Heyst consistently misunderstood Lena's actions and motivations, and quarrelled with her tiresomely, unnecessarily, right to the very end. (Lena and the three villains, Ricardo, Mr Jones and Pedro, also behaved as they did on the basis of similarly mistaken perceptions. Yet Heyst was, or should have been, the major figure, and his angle of vision should have counted most.) At the end Heyst, incapable of understanding Lena, seemed to be incapable of acting, even if he possessed a needed weapon – Ricardo's knife – and he caused Lena's death inadvertently. Lena died believing that Heyst 'was ready to lift her up in his firm arms and take her into the sanctuary of his innermost heart – for ever!' If Heyst had indeed reached that state of readiness, he had put his trust in life. Instead, he committed suicide by burning himself in the bungalow where Lena's corpse was lying.

Later, Davidson came to believe that Heyst could not stand his thoughts before her dead body – 'and fire purifies everything'. Heyst, understanding fully the horrors and the emptiness of the modern world, chose to end his life. Lena did not redeem Heyst. Heyst did not even understand that she sacrificed herself for him. The 'victory' lacked salvatory content.

All the while a storm was gathering:

> Beyond the headland of Diamond Bay, lying black on a purple sea, great masses of cloud stood piled up and bathed in a mist of blood. A crimson crack like an open wound zigzagged between them, with a piece of dark red sun showing at the bottom.

The world was tumbling into chaos: 'Everything – the bungalow, the forest, the open ground – trembled incessantly; the earth, the sky itself, shivered all the time.'

The sinking of the *Titanic* had been a sign (among many others) that prudence, the hard-won prize of centuries of human effort and custom, had become insufficient to ensure the continuance of healthy civilisation in the face of what Thomas Hardy called the new barbarism. In *Victory*, ill-defined good intentions did not survive in a universe of hardness and motiveless malignity. Nor will it do to respond that Jones, Ricardo and Pedro did not triumph either, as if the totality of the debacle in the final chapters suggests some room for hope, some possibility of emerging purified from the wreckage. It is true that Davidson piously mumbled, 'Let Heaven look after what has been purified. The wind and rain will take care of the ashes.' But that was not Conrad's message. *Victory*, despite serious flaws in the plot, remains to this day starkly honest in its refusal to define the terms whereby a victory for men of good will might be obtained on the eve of Armageddon.

Chapter 10

Ford Madox Hueffer's
The Good Soldier (1915)

In December 1913, Ford Madox Hueffer was forty years old. His bibliography, still growing, had become impressive. He was the author of eighteen novels, six books of poems, five books of literary essays and art commentaries, a memoir and a biography, as well as four books of children's stories and a large number of periodical pieces. He had, in addition, served as the energetic and brilliant first editor of the *English Review*.

He began to write *The Good Soldier* on 17 December. The first instalment of the novel ran under the title *The Saddest Story* in the first number of *Blast* (20 June 1914); and the retitled novel was published in England in 1915. Hueffer himself did not think of it as a commentary on either the European crisis or the war itself. His subtitle, after all, was *A tale of passion*, and the epigraph *Beati Immaculati* commented on its protagonist's unreformable innocence (and perhaps that of other characters).

By 1915 the prospect of an easily winnable war had faded, even if Hueffer overstated the case in calling the first half-year of the conflict 'the darkest days of the war'. The publisher, John Lane, wanted another title. 'The Saddest Story', he said, 'would at that date render the book unsaleable.' Ford telegraphed a reply: 'Dear Lane, Why not *The Good Soldier?*' Lane accepted the suggestion (to Hueffer's 'horror'), and the novel appeared under that title six months later. Though the title had nothing to do with war, some readers read the novel in the expectation that it might offer some insights on the military mind. Edward Ashburnham, a major character, was described early on as 'the cleanest-looking sort of chap; an excellent magistrate, a

125

first-rate soldier, one of the best landlords, so they said, in Hampshire, England'.

Still, the novel was not about him only, and the world was not seen from his point of view. In important ways this story commemorated the end of the Edwardian era. Asa Briggs has justly described these years – roughly between the conclusion of the Boer War and the onset of the Great War – as a period of enormous tensions. He writes:

> Edwardian society was picturesquely but perilously divided, and the greatest of the many contrasts of the age was not that with what had gone before but that between the divergent outlooks and fortunes of different groups within the same community. The implications of the clash of outlooks, fortunes, and tactics could seldom be completely evaded, and during certain years of the Edwardian period, if more particularly during the four years after the king's death in 1910, there was open and violent internal conflict. Will transcended both law and convention. The greater international violence of 1914 was a culmination as well as an historical divide.[1]

But to the majority of the leisure classes the happiness of the few was not tempered by the misery of the many (a necessary codicil to Professor Briggs's incontrovertible assertion that the misery of the few was better documented, more vocal and more active than it had ever been). In 1913 nobody envisaged as inevitable the ending of *Pax Britannica*, the Edwardian years to be referred to later as an Indian summer.

Hueffer believed that his main concern had been with matters of style. He wanted to do for the English novel what Maupassant had done for the French in *Fort comme la mort*, and he quoted with some complaisance, in a letter to Stella Ford, his friend John Rodker's judgement that *The Good Soldier* was 'the finest French novel in the English language'. Nevertheless, Hueffer's interest in making his fiction's disaster total went far beyond Maupassant's intention. Whereas Maupassant dealt with a single tangled and increasingly impossible relationship between an older man and a younger woman, Hueffer doubled the number of tragic loves, changed the mistress to a wife, and destroyed her in the process of working out her fate.

The relationships of the Dowells and the Ashburnhams – John, Florence, Edward and Leonora – were intended from the beginning to have a larger significance. 'Someone has said that the death of a mouse from cancer', John Dowell wrote very early in Part One, 'is the whole sack of Rome by the Goths, and I swear to you that the breaking up of our little four-square coterie was such another unthinkable event.' (Hueffer was probably paraphrasing Hugo von Hofmannsthal's 'Lord Chandos letter' of 1902.) John Dowell, who traced his lineage back to one of William Penn's colleagues, owned title deeds of wampum, giving him the rights of possession to a farm 'which once covered several blocks between Chestnut and Walnut Streets' in Philadelphia; but (more to the point in turn-of-the-century Europe), he enjoyed an income of $50,000 that released him from any obligation to work for the rest of his life.

To emphasise the horrific dimension of what went wrong, Hueffer first had to depict the world of these rootless expatriates as idyllic.

> Supposing that you should come upon us sitting together at one of the little tables in front of the club house, let us say, at Homburg, taking tea of an afternoon and watching the miniature golf, you would have said that, as human affairs go, we were an extraordinarily safe castle. We were, if you will, one of those tall ships with the white sails upon a blue sea, one of those things that seem the proudest and the safest of all the beautiful and safe things that God has permitted the mind of men to frame. Where better could one take refuge? Where better?

The relationships of John, Florence, Edward and Leonora made up, altogether, a 'long, tranquil life, which was just stepping a minuet'. These two couples always knew where to go or sit; they chose a single table unanimously; without a signal they could rise and go, 'always to the music of the Kur orchestra, always in the temperate sunshine, or, if it rained, in discreet shelters'. John Dowell repeated to himself, 'It was true sunshine; the true music; the true splash of the fountains from the mouth of stone dolphins.'

Later, he remembered what sort of life he led with Florence:

> Well, she was bright; and she danced. She seemed to dance over the floors of castles and over seas and over and over the salons of modistes and over the *plages* of the Riviera – like a gay tremulous beam, reflected from water upon a ceiling. And my function in life was to keep that bright thing in existence.

Though he spoke of the difficulty he experienced in doing so, comparing it to trying to catch with one's hand a 'dancing reflection', and of the length of time that he was set at the task ('years'), he did not decry either the difficulty or the investment of time; he did not regret the fact that happiness had been an illusion.

In 1904, when the main narrative commenced, John Dowell came out on 'the carefully swept steps of the Englischer Hof' in Nauheim, and looked at 'the carefully arranged trees in tubs upon the carefully arranged gravel whilst carefully arranged people walked past in carefully calculated gaiety, at the carefully calculated hour'. It was all so reassuring. He took to counting the steps he walked, the exact distances between places, as a pleasant way of passing time. It was not accidental that the details of the dining room were so lovingly recreated – Hueffer, who had published a study of Henry James in 1913, was impressed by James's insistence on being precise – or that they were elevated to a paean of praise for a bygone era:

> Whole castles have vanished from my memory, whole cities that I have never visited again, but that white room, festooned with papier-maché fruits and flowers; the tall windows; the many tables; the black screen round the door with three golden cranes flying upward on each panel; the palm tree in the centre of the room; the swish of the waiter's feet; the cold expensive elegance; the mien of the diners as they came in every evening – their air of earnestness as if they must go through a meal prescribed by the Kur authorities and their air of sobriety as if they must seek not by any means to enjoy their meals – those things I shall not easily forget.

John Dowell insisted on what these good people took for granted: 'beef underdone but not too underdone'; a good liqueur brandy for the men after lunch; 'a very light Rhine wine qualified with Fachingen water' for the women.

> It was also taken for granted that we were both sufficiently well off to afford anything that we could reasonably want in the way of amusements fitting to our station – that we could take motor cars and carriages by the day; that we could give each other dinners and dine our friends and we could indulge if we liked in economy.

Surely there was a price to be paid for such smugness, though for the longest time, for a full nine years in fact, John Dowell could not remember anything happening. He spoke of this period as one of 'uninterrupted tranquillity'. Taking everything for granted because one had sufficient money to indulge whims, to satsify needs as soon as they materialise, meant that it soon became difficult to know how one passed time, or to remember time that has passed; one had 'nothing whatever to show for it'. Moreover, 'as for experience, as for knowledge of one's fellow beings – nothing either'.

A pattern of images differentiating true hearts from false ran through the novel. Florence carried on a major deception about the 'perilous' condition of her heart, to prevent John from having unwanted sexual relations with her (and to enable herself to carry on adulterous relationships). John neglected all other serious responsibilities in order to take care of his wife's 'invalid' condition. Old Mr Hurlbird, Florence's father, worried about his heart condition until he died at the age of eighty-four. But 'he died of bronchitis, there was found to be absolutely nothing the matter with the organ. It had certainly jumped or squeaked or something just sufficiently to take in the doctors, but it appears that that was because of an odd formation of the lungs.' John Dowell, who ultimately proved to be the most unreliable kind of narrator, was perhaps most truthful when he recorded a characteristically baffled comment, 'I don't understand much about these matters.' Maisie Maidan, the object briefly of Edward's affections, died grotesquely; though John Dowell came to the conclusion that she did not commit suicide, a real heart failed in this case. (If the reader is a romantic, her heart broke because she discovered that Edward did not truly love her.) And Edward – who was rumoured, falsely, to be suffering from a heart problem – soon got over Maisie's death: 'Indeed, it was the one affair of his about which he never felt much remorse.'

But even these images, which impelled the narrative forward with demonic energy, did not constitute a satisfactory explanation of why the Edwardian faith in the stability of institutional values came a cropper. 'Isn't there any Nirvana pervaded by the faint thrilling of instruments that have fallen into the dust of wormwood but that yet had frail, tremulous, and everlasting souls?', John Dowell asked. He answered his own question, with some vehemence:

> No, by God, it is false! It wasn't a minuet that we stepped; it was a prison – a prison full of screaming hysterics, tied down so that they might not outsound the rolling of our carriage wheels as we went along the shaded avenues of the Taunus Wald.

In sophistication, mastery of technique and complex characterisation *The Good Soldier* exceeded by a light-year everything Hueffer had written prior to the war. In his dedicatory letter to Stella Ford, dated 9 January 1927, he went beyond a statement that this was his best book up to 1913, and called it his 'great auk's egg' because he knew even at the time he completed it that it was 'something of a race that will have no successors'.[2] 'And I will permit myself to say that I was astounded at the work I must have put into the construction of the book, at the intricate tangle of references and cross-references.'[3]

Taking their cue from statements like these, generations of critics have concentrated on the art of *The Good Soldier*: the rightness of the images, the tautness of the chronological scheme, the skill with which Florence's suicide served to conclude a major movement (at which point a second major movement began and rushed on to an even more astonishing climax), the sheer limpidity of the language. Perhaps the most influential single essay on *The Good Soldier* stressed the comic elements and comic devices. '*The Good Soldier* is a comedy of humor', Mark Schorer wrote, 'and the humor is phlegm.' Comedy was the means whereby Hueffer displayed his art, and as an author, he had 'comic genius'. Schorer's critique emphasised 'comic metaphors', 'comic events' and an 'incessant wit, of style and statement, the wittier for its deceptive clothing of pathos'.[4] But a reader will never absorb the full meaning of Ford's opening sentence, 'This is the saddest story I have ever heard', if such an interpretation is used as the primary guide to Ford's intentions.

The Good Soldier may be read and admired for its narrative skills, as Schorer recommended, but it was not in any major sense a comedy, however disenchanted the brand. Hueffer's story was, rather, a tragedy of misunderstandings and wasted lives. Though the major point of view – that of John Dowell, a wealthy American who had failed to discover a worthy goal for a life's work – was unreliable, even deluded, we as readers may not take comfort from an easy assumption that we could have known more than he, given the circumstances, or would have done better in choosing between options. All the characters made wrong choices. Hueffer suggested no reason why they should do so time and again. Comedy as technique, yes, but not as basic theme.

Far more important was the fact that *The Good Soldier* employed narrative skills of the highest order to deliver an editorial judgement on the collapse of a social order. The novel never mentioned war. It did not prophesy the coming war. But it had much to say about the increasing meaninglessness of life at a time when human relationships were being subverted by false values.

Most of *The Good Soldier* took place on the Continent of Europe, not in America (where hope was still possible). In the second decade of the twentieth century, personal relationships encapsulated the fates of larger populations. John Dowell, as he contemplated the significance of what he knew or only half-guessed at, became, in John A. Meixner's telling phrase, 'an individual who brilliantly objectifies this lamed modern spirit', just as much as his wife Florence goes through life 'cheerfully doing evil'. The one thing we know about John Dowell is that he protested, over and over, his ignorance about the nature of things: the truth behind human relationships, the reasons why given speeches were made or specific actions were taken, the kind of interest taken by God in our doings. When Leonora referred cryptically to a previous affair – 'Once I tried to have a lover but I was so sick at the heart, so utterly worn out, that I had to send him away' – very early in his acquaintance with her, John Dowell was astonished that Leonora should have cried over her deception of Edward. He wondered whether her confession, ending with the question, 'It certainly wasn't playing the game, was it, now?', was the remark of a harlot or 'what every decent woman, county family or not county family, thinks at the bottom of her heart'. He did not know; but the way he phrased the problem universalised it. 'Who knows?' He was certain that his own thoughts had been clean, that his own life had been chaste.

> At what, then, does it all work out? Is the whole thing a folly and a mockery? . . . I don't know. And there is nothing to guide us. And if everything is so nebulous about a matter so elementary as the morals of sex, what is there to guide us in the more subtle morality of all other personal contacts, associations, and activities? Or are we meant to act on impulse alone? It is all a darkness.

His professions of ignorance should not be taken at face value; there were moments when he should have been more aware (of, for example, the fact that Florence committed suicide), and his obtuseness was consistent to a degree that damaged his reliability as a point of view. John Dowell, a man less knowing than he should have been, was indeed the least knowing of the several main figures in this sad, sad story. (Not a tragedy, John Dowell insisted, but a story of drift and disintegration.)

Nevertheless, John Dowell was saying something more than that he was deceived by all concerned. He was describing a 'blind and inscrutable destiny' that tormented everybody. His specific questions about the problems confronting his narrow range of acquaintances were, invariably, generalisations about the state of the world. 'You ask how it feels to be a deceived husband', he wrote at one point. 'Just heavens, I do not know. It feels just nothing at all.' But he was soon commenting on a problem larger than his dawning consciousness that Leonora was 'pimping for Edward' so that Edward could sleep with Florence; he and she and all of them 'were only poor wretches creeping over this earth in the shadow of an eternal wrath. It is very terrible.' John Dowell recalled seeing a picture of an immense plain, and, suspended in mid-air, three figures, 'two of them clasped close in an intense embrace, and one intolerably solitary'. 'And the immense plain is the hand of God', he allegorised, 'stretching out for miles and miles, with great spaces above it and below it'.

Love, for one who had been betrayed as often and as completely as John Dowell has been, did not count for much. 'I have come to be very much of a cynic in these matters; I mean that it is impossible to believe in the permanence of man's or women's love. Or, at any rate, it is impossible to believe in the permanence of any early passion.' This passage suggested a mockery inherent in the very term 'romance' (a word that served as the title of Hueffer's third novel, written in collaboration with Joseph Conrad). John Dowell continued: 'We are all so afraid, we are all so alone, we all so need from the outside the assurance of our own worthiness to exist.'

John Dowell, no less than Edward Ashburnham, suffered from sentimentality, a too-willing readiness to feel compassion for the unworthy and the suffering. He had been maltreated by those who he thought had every obligation to treat him as kindly as he had behaved towards them, but he continued to think of Edward and Leonora as 'two noble natures, drifting down life, like fireships afloat on a lagoon and causing miseries, heartaches, agony of the mind, and death. And they themselves steadily deteriorated. And why? For what purpose? To point what lesson? It is all a darkness.' John Dowell, in his grim, self-scrutinising honesty, could not even identify a villain in his story. His refrain, repeated many times, was that the human heart was a very mysterious thing. As he moved towards the astonishing events that concluded Part Four – the saddest part of the story – John Dowell asked himself 'unceasingly', 'What should these people have done? What, in the name of God, should they have done?' He did not know. His mind went 'round and round in a weary, baffled space of pain'. Nancy Rufford repeated endlessly, '*Credo in unum Deum Omnipotentem. . . . Credo in unum Deum Omnipotentem*', and these were reasonable words for her to say; but they were 'the only reasonable words she uttered', and she was certifiably mad.

'It's a queer and fantastic world,' John Dowell said still again, and we recall that he often emphasised his wealth as alms stored up against oblivion. 'Why can't people have what they want? The things were all there to content everybody; yet everybody has the wrong thing. Perhaps you can make head or tail of it; it is beyond me.' He continued:

> Is there then any terrestrial paradise where, amidst the whispering of the olive-trees, people can be with whom they like and take their ease in shadows and in coolness? Or are all men's lives like the lives of us good people – like the lives of the Ashburnhams, of the Dowells, of the Ruffords – broken, tumultuous, agonized, and unromantic lives, periods punctuated by screams, by imbecilities, by deaths, by agonies?

Even if he concluded these rhetorical questions with the old (and by this time shopworn) 'Who the devil knows?' the answer was implicit in the very fact of repetition. The answer was that no one knew. Nowhere could one be at ease in Zion.

The destabilisation of all civilised and humane values was exemplified in terms of tangled sexual affairs, but Hueffer was talking primarily about an unworthy world. In Carol Ohmann's biting judgement, 'Ford sympathizes with his characters in *The Good Soldier*, but he has learned to judge them for their immaturity, their egoism, their foolish rejection of things as they are, and their head-long pursuit of an impossible conception of themselves.'[5] They were not presented as unusual, or talented, or especially sensitive people; their ordinariness was what made them recognisable; the world in which they functioned unworthily was unworthy itself (Carol Ohmann admits this). If Ford's indictment suggested a larger moral – that the world was meaningless, and that as a consequence human happiness was a chimera – the on-rushing events of the first year of the Great War documented his case.

Chapter 11

Alec Waugh's *The Loom of Youth* (1917)

Alec Waugh's first novel, *The Loom of Youth*, remained his biggest success for forty years, until at the age of fifty-seven he produced *Island in the Sun*. As his brother Evelyn wrote, in a sentence of affectionate dismissal, Alec passed the time 'continuously writing, earning a fair subsistence but not in general very highly regarded', enjoying his love affairs 'with ladies of a great variety of age, race and appearance'.[1]

The fact that success came so easily and early had an unsettling effect. Born in 1898, Alec Waugh had grown to manhood in comfortable, book-lined surroundings. His father, Arthur Waugh, managed the affairs of Chapman and Hall; he was an intelligent, likeable and benevolent literary critic who exemplified several aspects of Victorian and Edwardian life at their idealistic best. Alec Waugh followed his father's example in attending Sherborne, a public school, and took naturally to its sports, its learning opportunities and its beautiful surroundings. Many of these elements are reproduced in the first of his three autobiographies, *The Early Years of Alec Waugh* (1962). My primary concern is with the novel written after he left the congenial ambience of, first, Sherborne (renamed Fernhurst in *The Loom of Youth*), and then Sandhurst.

The Loom of Youth was written in six and a half weeks after he joined the army and, at the age of seventeen and a half (young men often count the halves), gone to a camp at Berkhamsted with the Inns of Court Battalion. He detested everything he knew about the military up to that point in his life: 'the impersonal military machine, the monotonous routine of drills and musketry, the endless foot-slogging, the perpetual petty fault-finding'.[2] He rose at 4.30 each morning, and sent typescripts to his father for correction and typing (he *never* revised); in the evening, after the day's duties, he would return to the chore of writing. From September 1915, when he enlisted, to July 1917, when *The Loom of Youth* was published, a reasonably straight arc was traversed, even though a few rejection slips preceded Grant Richards's acceptance of the manuscript. The book appeared in the bookstores the same week that he was posted to France as a second lieutenant attached to the Machine Gun Corps.

A number of factors contributed to its success: the fact that it was written by a soldier ('and in his teens', as Alec wrote in 1954 for a new edition); a relatively quiet moment on the fiction scene, when interesting novels were at a premium; the rebelliousness of the mood raging behind the story (though he did not write about the army, his picture of maladroit administration in a public school fitted in with public unease about the blundering direction of public policy); and Arthur Waugh's reputation as a kindly man of letters (his son seemed to deserve a break). Moreover, Thomas Seccombe, the history professor at Sandhurst, contributed a helpful preface that swore to the truth of the book. He confessed that he had had to overcome serious misgivings about reading still another novel of school life. 'I was agreeably disillusioned', he admitted. Waugh's picture of the public school in the years leading up to the Great War was notable as a 'realistic effort', one written out of full knowledge, 'the result of close proximity to the subjects'.[3] Seccombe was impressed by the honesty with which the novel treated the 'Tyranny of the Bloods', schoolboys who believed that games were all-important and that would-be scholars were contemptible. 'The old stupidity of splendid isolation' – the ignorance of young English patriots who believed that Ladysmith was a siege in the Indian Mutiny, 'or a town in which Lord Kitchener was surrounded by the enemy during the whole of the Boer war',[4] and who did not care to correct their knowledge of what was not so – could hardly be believed by those unfamiliar with the system. The faith of the public-school boy, Seccombe wrote with withering sarcasm, 'has fairly helped, you may say, to get us out of the mess of August, 1914. Yes, but it contributed heavily to get us into it!'[5] He concluded: 'The Athletic god is a fine and a clean and in the main a necessary one, but its monopoly makes Patriotism far too small a thing. This book shows how.'[6]

In addition, the novel alluded to the existence of homosexual relationships, even if so discreetly many readers missed the references.

Not all parents, however. Several wrote to housemasters all over England demanding reassurance that what happened at Fernhurst could never taint 'their Bobbie'. Angry reviews and articles in *The Contemporary*, *The Spectator* and *The Nation* fed the flames, as did Grant Richards's gossip column about his books and authors, published each week in the *Times Literary Supplement*. Printed in very dark type, it 'caught the eye'.[7] Richards even used unfavourable publicity about *The Loom of Youth* to help boost its sales.

Alec Waugh derived a considerable amount of pleasure from the success of his first novel. He did not believe he had libelled his school, and he was unhappy that some of his masters had been distressed by his candour. It was an understandable shock that his name should be removed from the Old Shirburnian Society (and his father's name, too). But France kept him busy. After fighting at Passchendaele and Cambrai, he became a prisoner at Arras in March 1918. He had other problems to contemplate in the heat of warfare besides yelps of outrage that the public-school system had been criticised, or that the link between schools such as Fernhurst and imperial destiny was being questioned.

The Loom of Youth was a story of values in an average English public school. It had serious limitations as a structured novel, nor was it easy to tell which targets of abuse Alec Waugh disliked most, or which ones he thought could be tolerated. The educational novel, the public-school novel if one is to narrow the focus, had been around a long time. *Tom Brown's School Days* (1857) – written by Thomas Hughes as 'an Old Boy' – was not the first such work of fiction, though its transformation of the headmaster into a demigod was a lesson absorbed with ingenuity and skill by Rudyard Kipling in *Stalky & Co.* (1899). And since *The Loom of Youth* inescapably reminded a common reader of Kipling more than Hughes, comparison and contrast seemed appropriate then, and still does.

For one thing, Kipling's United Services College at Westward Ho!, Devon, was in the business of preparing most of its students for the Indian Civil Service and for the military, just as Sherborne sent many of its graduates on to Sandhurst. H. G. Wells, in *The Outline of History*, identified the ties between the schoolboy jokes of Stalky, M'Turk and Beetle and British imperialism; in Waugh's novel, the Empire was what British soldiers going into Sandhurst were expected to defend. Wells overstated his case in censuring the brutality of a public-school education, and assuming that Kipling himself did not entertain serious reservations about various aspects of public-school life. (The head's recommendation of Beetle for a job on a newspaper must be considered unusual; USC was not primarily in the business of training intellectuals or artists.)

For another, Kipling and Waugh both stressed punishment by the masters as a means of licking bear cubs into shape: punishment in the form not only of canings but of extra assignments, the completion of which was essential if even more assignments were not to be imposed. These penalties were not laid on heavily because of the masters' irresponsible sadism, but because the pranks and peccadilloes of the students could not be ignored, and demanded some sort of disciplinary recognition. Corporal punishment was accepted as a necessary ingredient of school life.

Moreover, the intention lying behind both books was deliberately, unashamedly didactic. Kipling began his sketches with the aim of writing 'some tracts or parables on the education of the young'. When Cormell Price, his 'very dear Headmaster', visited him at the time he was writing the manuscript of what was to become *Stalky & Co.*, and told him that his tracts 'would be some time before they came to their own', Kipling's rueful acceptance of the truth of Uncle Crom's remark was not too dissimilar from Waugh's belief that the world was not yet ready for an exposé of the limitations of public-school education. Kipling took pride – and said so, in 1935, shortly before his death – that *Stalky & Co.* was still read, and remained 'a truly valuable collection of tracts'.[8] Waugh, writing in 1954, remained convinced of the truth of his presentation: more than four decades after its first printing he denied that it was a 'period piece', since it sold steadily from one year to the next, had become a title in Cassell's Pocket Library and turned into a Penguin and was reprinted by Methuen. 'Though England today is a different country, socially and economically, from what it was in 1911 when I went to Sherborne, I do not think that in essentials the life of the Public School boy has greatly changed.'[9] He had written his novel to 'expose' the inability or refusal of those in authority 'to recognise the true nature of school life', i.e. written it as a tract, even though his aim was to destroy the myth of the Brushwood Boy originated by Kipling.

The fundamental difference between Kipling and Waugh, however, was fully as important as any of their points of contact. Kipling, partly because of the near-sightedness that prevented him from becoming an athlete or even enjoying games, and partly because his closest friends, Lionel Charles Dunsterville (Stalky) and George C. Beresford (M'Turk), held defiantly secessionist views about cultural functions (e.g., Shakespearian readings of an actress in 'The flag of their country'), school spirit and organised games, believed firmly in the 'true' ideals of the public-school system. Those ideals remained vital despite the lies promulgated by professional patriots, the cant of some housemasters, the hypocrisy of some officials. The shaping of lives in the public schools that went on in indefinable ways was for the best. Little animals were being reborn as civilised human beings, and it did not matter that most of the educational process struck them as brutal; limits were necessary; as adults (and perhaps sooner rather than later) they would discover that what Kipling called the day's work had to be done. Kipling did not romanticise the formal elements of education at the college, which stressed translations, mechanical writing exercises, memorisation of mathematical 'solutions' and rote learning to a mind-numbing extreme. What went on in the classroom was seldom inspiring, rarely useful in any clearly explained way. Kipling never believed that his years at USC had been spent in the service of a progressive educational philosophy. But he saw a point to it all, even if much of his own learning had been picked up in bits and pieces, on his own and usually in defiance of the conventional wisdom. Discipline even in the form of arid and repetitive schoolwork forced a boy to recognise the power of higher authority, to limit his own selfish and hedonistic impulses, to prepare himself for later responsibility. The teachings of Carlyle proved particularly helpful because in *Sartor Resartus* Carlyle preached the work ethic, the value of working hard because the night was coming. (All of which helps to explain Kipling's strong revulsion, in 1890 and 1891, against the Decadent artists he met at the Savile Club, London, after he had completed his 'seven years' hard' as a journalist in India.) In brief, to Kipling the system of values at the college might well be picked apart as inadequate or wrong-headed or reactionary, but taken as a whole the system worked.[10]

The connection between school travails and the world of adult responsibility was much more difficult for Alec Waugh to establish. He conceded, late in life, that public schools retained their traditions and ideals. Despite his admission that he had been happy at Sherborne and had admired many of his masters, to whom he 'owed so much', the tone of the whole of *The Loom of Youth* was considerably darker than that of any of even the more severely judgemental 'tracts' contained in *Stalky & Co.* Gordon, its hero, identified himself passionately and completely with the Byron who protested, 'I have simplified my politics into an utter detestation of all existing governments.' Gordon's love of poetry derived from a sense that it expressed his own convictions. Byron's life and art were rebellious and became 'almost a religion with him'. Swinburne's finest line was to be discovered in the 'Hymn to Proserpine': 'I neither kneel nor adore them, but standing look to the end.'

And this 'Poetry of Revolt' matched perfectly his own mood:

> He would fight against these masters with their old-fashioned and puritanic notions; he would be the preacher of the new ideas.... He saw, or thought he saw, the mistakes of the system under which he lived; and – without pausing to consider its merits – wished to sweep away the whole foundation into the sea, and to build upon some illusory basis a new heaven and new earth.

Gordon was young, conceited, ignorant, at the time he declared his independence from the tyrants who poisoned his life in the sixth:

> But is there anyone who, having lived longer, having seen many bright dreams go down, having been disillusioned, and having realised that he is but a particle in an immense machine, would not change places with Gordon, and see life once more roseflushed with impossible loyalties?

Fully half the novel concerned itself with Gordon Caruthers in his final year at Fernhurst. His feelings were hotly intemperate and confused. Perhaps an unavoidable explanation of all these inchoate emotions was the fact that Gordon came before readers in 1917 as a young man innocent of family, home background and prior life. So determined was Waugh to give us the pathetic inadequacy of publicschool values, which failed to train us for 'Life' in all its appalling rigour, that it never seemed to have crossed his imagination how completely a fictional hero cut clean from all external ties was bound to be dependent on his immediate surroundings for whatever truths – higher or lower – he might discover. Gordon was destined to become a creature of circumstances, and to experience disillusionment. No public school advertised itself as a substitute for parents, God and all the eternal verities; only an adolescent would place his trust in such fancies. An aged man of the village wondered, after war had been declared, if the Germans were 'for us'. But during the senior final Gordon – almost equally ignorant – treated scholarship with cool contempt. He had already acquired the habit of writing a three-hour examination in ninety minutes or less, and a two-hour examination in less than forty-five minutes. The masters were on to him; he scored bottom in every paper. But here were the results of his paper on European history since 1914 (which he had been preparing for well over a year), the answers which took him fifteen minutes to record. He credited the unification of Italy to Cavour; no more than the name was set down. Since he had never heard of the Berlin decrees, he passed them by. His estimate of Napoleon III's character was borrowed from Holland Rose: 'A dreamer who unfortunately allowed his dreams to encroach on his waking moments.' Since the next two questions dealt with the 1848 revolution, 'a question that he had always said life was too short to worry about', he dismissed them as 'impossible'. To the last question, however, 'Illustrate by historical examples the truth of the statement "the people are the rulers of the rich"', he snorted, 'What an ass the man must be who set such a question!', and wrote, 'There are no illustrations of this theory in history.' Then, 'with the smile of one who has worked well, he blotted his papers, wrote his name at the top, and to the consternation of the master in charge showed them up and walked out'. Inevitably, he scored fifteen marks out of two hundred. (He may have been graded overgenerously.)

In time of war, with a sadly diminished student enrolment and the masters increasingly aged as those among their ranks fit to serve headed off to the Front, this bravura performance of a young hero impatient to be in uniform himself was understandable. But Gordon wrote sketchy responses to serious questions because he drew up an empty bucket from a very shallow well.

Waugh recorded far less about what went on in the classroom than Kipling did in *Stalky & Co*. Gordon entertained contempt for those who were supposed to be moulding the coming generation, and he offered no rebuttal when Tester, his friend, told him that

> The really brilliant men don't take up schoolmastering; it is the worst paid profession there is. Look at it, a man with a double-first at Oxford comes down to a place like Fernhurst and sweats his guts out day and night for two hundred pounds a year.

Students tormented their masters with insolent condescension, evaded their assignments, translated with illegal learning aids and treated would-be scholars as pariahs. The most mature among them were fifteen and sixteen years of age. Gordon, told to buy a textbook on modern Europe for 7s. 6d., put his bet on a history notebook left behind, years ago, by a brilliant student. The master assigned questions that had been used over and over again, and the answers, recorded in the notebook, were copied out by his students: 'Mary de Medici: was she an unmixed evil?' 'Compare Richelieu and Mazarin.'

> Then Gordon would have recourse to the unfailing authority, Van Hepworth. Sometimes he felt too slack to copy out the questions at all. On such occasions he would simply read Van Hepworth's essay straight out of the old, battered book.
> 'I hope you won't mind my reading this to you, but I was in rather a hurry and I doubt if you could quite read my handwriting.'
> Finnemore would listen with the greatest interest.
> 'Very nice indeed, Caruthers, very sound attitude to adopt. An essay well worth preserving. You will copy it out neatly, won't you?'
> 'Oh yes, sir.'

This tacit conspiracy between a doddering master and an unscrupulous student was clearly drawn, and the smell of it was right. Another student, Foster, 'absolutely' bamboozled his Latin master. He could not construe, he failed to score in Latin prose and yet he never received an imposition. He pointed out how hard he worked, and he often stayed behind to ask polite questions. 'But manners always win in the end. Foster showed so much zeal, such an honest willingness to learn, that Claremont finally classed him as a hard-working, keen, friendly, but amazingly stupid boy.' Claremont was unaware, even as Foster enquired 'why the subject of an active verb could not be in the ablative', that he had been taken as 'one more pawn in the gigantic game of bluff'.

Masters fought on severely pitted ground, and often lost. Waugh presented these matters as grim and even appalling evidence of the criminal negligence of a public-school administration, as testamentary proof of the twentieth-century's Condition of England. But he could not have it both ways: the bloods were what they were because public-school traditions made them irresponsibly obsessed with sports, in which case the traditions had to be changed, or because the bloods irresponsibly strengthened unworthy public-school traditions, in which case the major need was to re-educate them by emphasising traditional academic subjects.

The Stoics society was a case in point. Everyone above IVa, with a life subscription of sixpence, was entitled to attend meetings every other week. Of the more than one hundred members fewer than half regularly attended, and fewer than half of those paid any attention to the proceedings. The debates dealt with significant topics, for example 'Classical and modern education', but the speakers were intent on 'rolling off absurdly dogmatic statements that were based solely on ignorance and arrogance', and believed that 'a sufficient amount of conceit and self-possession would carry anyone through'. Ferrers, the mathematics teacher who delighted in smashing idols, spoke against classical education, and held the audience spellbound: 'Here was something new, something worth listening to.' But what did he say, specifically? 'There is no free thought. Classic men do very well in the Foreign Offices, but they can't think. . . . What do classics do in the literary world? Nothing. Chesterton, Lloyd George, Symons, Wells – all the best men never went to a Public School.' If organised sports and the frenzy that surrounded any particular game were repressive forces at Fernhurst, what, we may ask of Gordon, might be the alternative to the blind worship of games? Ferrers blamed the nation's fascination with Chelsea and West Ham United for England's failure to meet the challenge of Germany, which had been plotting and piling up armaments. Games were all right in their place, but, Gordon cried in a speech that 'really made an impression',

> We can like a thing without bowing down to it, and that's how we have got to treat games. Some fool said 'the battle of Waterloo was won on the playing fields of Eton'; and a fool he was, too. Games don't win battles, but brains do, and brains aren't trained on the footer field. It is time we realised that.

When Gordon's side won by an enormous majority, he left no cliché on its dusty shelf: 'Yes, "we have lit this day a candle that, by the grace of God, shall never be put out!"'

It was a little hard on the doctrine of physical fitness to blame it (as Ferrers did, and as Gordon did with no less passion) for creating England's unreadiness for German militarism. Gordon was entitled to change his mind about the value of sports and a school career spent in earning a footer cap. He had the right to reject 'mature philosophy', 'school successes', 'calf-bound prizes and tasselled caps', because poetry, so filled with 'colour and youth', had opened his eyes. His pantheon of new gods included Marlowe:

> Is it not brave to be a king?
> It is not passing brave to be a king
> And ride in triumph through Persepolis?

'Marlowe had been right, Marlowe with the pagan soul that loved material things, glitter and splendour, crowns and roses, red lips and gleaming arms.' Gordon moved away from 'the battle-cry of Byron' and 'the rebel flag of Swinburne' to the poetry of Ernest Dowson, in which he read 'something of his own failure to realise the things he had hoped for', of John Keats, who distracted him from 'the hoarse babble of voices' on all sides, and of John Milton, whose *Comus* lulled him 'into a temporary security with its abundance of perfect imagery'.

What a whirling chaos of ideas and sensations! None of it was sorted out; the anger against athleticism approached hysteria; and there was no guarantee that Gordon's love of poetry, new-formed, would last.

In Book IV, 'The weaving', we read of those fateful days in August 1914, when 'a great nation [England] forgot its greatness, and Europe trembled on the brink of war'. Would England enter into the contest, or would it shirk its duty? When the West End cinema flashed on the screen the news that England had declared war on Germany ('God Save the King!'), Ferrers declared his faith in war as the thing that was both wanted and needed.

> It will wake us up from sleeping; stir us into life; inflame our literature. There's a real chance now of sweeping away the old outworn traditions. In a great fire they will all be burnt. Then we can build afresh. . . . This war is going to save England and everything! Glorious!

Gordon shared the wild enthusiasm of Ferrers:

> Throughout the long summer holidays this feeling of rejoicing sustained Gordon's heart. He saw an age rising out of these purging fires that would rival the Elizabethan. He saw a second Marlowe and a second Webster. His soul was aflame with hope. He had no doubt as to the result.

Even after the retreat from Mons, which did not shake his confidence, he believed that the war

> had awakened England from her slumber of a hundred years; the old tattered clothes had fallen off her; she was now a queen in a rainbow garment. And Gordon, from the depth of his heart, poured forth his

thanksgiving to whatever gods might be, that the great hour had come while he was in the flush of youth, when he could himself drink the cup of glory to its dregs.

As the months passed, Ferrers wrote a long article for *The Country* on 'The public schools and the war', which 'bubbled over with enthusiasm'. Even though Tester returned in uniform to Fernhust, telling Gordon that their generation had been sacrificed (inevitable, but 'rather hard'), and that the days of roses were over, Gordon could scarcely credit the possibility that there would be nothing better for England after the war. 'No one can go through this without having his senses dulled', Tester said, 'his individuality knocked out of him. It will take at least twenty years to recover what we have lost, and there won't be much fire left in you and me by then.' Gordon, not ready yet to surrender belief in the possibility of redemption, though he was not to don a uniform until after Easter term, still searched for certitude. There came, in one remarkable moment, even the desire 'to surrender himself completely, to fling away his own aims and inclinations, and abandon himself to a life of quiet devotion from the world'. This amounted to a flirtation with Roman Catholicism. He visited Uphill, a school with its 'noble Cavalry' rising from the flowers, an Abbey watching over the place, and 'monks in long black robes' moving about 'slowly, magisterially'. He impulsively spoke to a monk about the confusing 'toleration of various doctrines' within Protestantism, as opposed to the certainties of Rome. Despite the calmness of the conversation, and the expected paternalism of the monk ('The Church loves her children far too much to wish them to leave her even for a minute. She wants them entirely, hers and hers alone'), he decided to wait. Material thoughts invaded his most sacred moments.

> A chance phrase, a word even, and there would suddenly rise before him the spectre of his own failure. And he was forced to realise that as yet he was unfit to lay down the imperious burden of his own personality. The hold of life was too strong. He still wanted the praise of the populace, 'the triumph and the roses and the wine'.

Gordon, at the novel's end, had the grace to appreciate how few worthwhile standards of his own he could claim, even while he recognised the inadequacy of the false gods of the playing-field and the limitations of life within the public-school system. 'Youth with its rainbow colours, its laughter, and its tears, was as fugitive as the sunlight.' Human existence outside the walls of Fernhurst was not so bad, and eventually there would come the pleasures of female companionship. Even service in the army would provide its compensations in terms of male bonding. If everything that had gone before needed sifting and re-evaluation, Gordon's adolescent years formed way-stations along the road to self-discovery. No one was more conscious than Gordon of how temporary any answer – English poetry, the honours of triumphant games, religion, military service – must be reckoned. Indeed, Gordon's odyssey possessed a rich value as a record of what a generation of bloods accomplished. If the bloods failed to do what the young hero of *The Loom of Youth* believed was necessary, they paid overgenerously for their sins of omission during the war years.

Chapter 12

Wyndham Lewis's *Tarr* (1918)

The Great War did not intrude seriously on the art-centred, ego-mad deliberations of the dramatis personae of Wyndham Lewis's *Tarr*. Nevertheless, there exists some obscurity in the dating of the draft, and in determining how much of it had been written before the war began. In *Rude Assignment*, an unconventional and not always trustworthy account of his own life, Lewis wrote of his poverty-stricken years just prior to the Great War, and mentioned having been confined to bed with a 'troublesome infection'.[1] That would have been in autumn 1913, when he was collecting material for a second number of *Blast*. His aim in writing a novel was to accomplish something major before joining the army (1915) and heading off to the trenches in France. Lewis claimed that he 'wanted to leave this token book, lest the worst should happen (although as then written in its first uncouth form, it would not have been a very satisfactory testament)'.

A large part of the novel appeared as a serial in *The Egoist*, running from 1 April 1916, to November 1917, and it followed the serialised version of James Joyce's *A Portrait of the Artist as a Young Man*. A prologue in *The Egoist* said that Lewis began writing the novel in 1910. Ezra Pound, who admired the novel greatly, said that it was finished before the war began. However, the preface that Lewis contributed to the Chatto and Windus edition of 1928 (the completely revised version on which Lewis expended considerable time and energy) stated flatly that 'it was written with extreme haste, during the first year of the War, during a period of illness and restless convalescence'. At any rate, the hard-bound edition of the novel appeared in July 1918, in London (The Egoist Ltd.) and in New York (Alfred A. Knopf).

Lewis, if he had wished to do so, could have written about a Paris conscious of a war about to begin, or actually at war. There was not a single allusion to soldiers mobilising for a war, or to any major war-related topic of conversation in France during 1914–15. Nor did Lewis, in his final months of writing the draft, concede that the French frontier leading to Germany had been closed to civilians. An important episode dealt with precisely this last point: in the novel, a German artist, fleeing from Paris because he had murdered a Pole accidentally in a serio-comic duel, could have easily crossed the frontier if he chose to do so.

Lewis said a good many things about this artist, unpleasantly related to his Germanness. Otto Kreisler, an impoverished German sculptor drifting towards his inevitable self-destruction, was intended by Lewis to be a German 'and nothing else', as he wrote in *The Egoist* prologue. In his autobiography Lewis entitled his twenty-eighth chapter 'The *Schicksal*. – the German in my fiction', and his choice of a German as his liveliest and most consistently disagreeable character had been carefully premeditated. He expressed some regret about his 'patriotic' argument of 1918 that Kreisler was 'a *German* – he was *a bad man* – the Germans are our *enemies* – all our enemies are bad men naturally – the Germans are all bad men'.[2] But the heroine, Bertha Lunken, was also a German, of the kind encountered in the creative works of Hauptmann and Sudermann, and her Germanness had also made her an alien living on the bounty of French culture, an *Ausländer* no less than Kreisler. 'Otto Kreisler represents the melodramatic nihilism of the generations succeeding to the great era of philosophical pessimism', Lewis conceded, noting that Nietzsche was in part responsible for the 'infection', and confessing himself unable to decide whether national socialism was the ultimate form of that malady. Lewis had been an intermittent student at the Heymann Academy in Munich during the first decade of this century, and he believed that he knew the Kreisler type: a ponderous German who lived on his father's meagre allowance, an untalented artist who despised his betters, an animal who used women as his 'Theatre', a middle-aging non-entity who accepted violence as 'the natural end to a violent Beserk nature'.[3] Moreover, in Paris Lewis had moved freely among a number of German friends, most of them 'bourgeois-bohemians'.

How accurately did Kreisler's unlovableness prefigure the brutality, hysteria and moral bankruptcy of Hitler? Lewis believed that Hitler (about whom he wrote a singularly obtuse series of articles in 1931) operated under the same influences as Kreisler; that Hitler, like Kreisler, sought to avenge himself on society for the fate that had overtaken him; that he was a machine, his life 'an empty mechanical tragedy', his death 'a foregone conclusion'.

Lewis's emphasis on the word 'machine' and on its corollary word 'Puppet' strongly suggested that Lewis believed in a *Schicksal* that predetermined the character of the Kreislers of Germany because they were German. Even the few facts he selected for his brief description of Kreisler's character provided something similar to 'a demonstration in predestination'. D. G. Bridson has noted that the anti-hero Kreisler 'embodied all the German traits which had made Nazism possible: he was not only the explanation of Nazism, he was its embodiment'.[4] To sketch such a personality adequately, the style had to be adjusted; the images, as a consequence, had to become hard and external and visible.[5] Lewis austerely stripped from his narrative 'all fleshly verbiage'. He clipped the text, 'rhetoric was under an interdict', he abstained from 'the use of any clichés (even the inoffensive mates of more gregarious words), eschewed sentimental archaisms, and all *pretty language*'.[6] He even employed – to the verge of distraction, and on an inconsistent basis – an equal sign between sentences. It never was clear why such a sign should follow one sentence, and not another; the 'idiosyncratic punctuation', as Hugh Kenner pointed out, was 'yet another device for preventing the prose from *flowing*',[7] and although most readers welcomed the 1928 version, which dropped the equal-sign device, smoothed transitions, and clarified meanings,[8] the original text of 1918, with its emphasis on a jagged, energy-nervous appearance on the printed page, translated faithfully the workings of Lewis's mind. This kind of writing attempted to verbalise Vorticist effects. The language, self-conscious and hard-edged,[9] repaid close reading precisely because it said so much within encapsulated spaces.

There was (in addition to his ferocious emphasis on style) a theory-driven concept of character. Kreisler not only believed that he was a puppet of fate, he acted like one; he invited his own undoing by misbehaving at a dance with a boorishness so heavy and near-incredible in its completeness that he seemed to be moving under some cataleptic spell.

Lewis was determined to impress upon the reader Kreisler's inability to do anything else but what he did. He was 'Doomed, Evidently' (the partial title of the section in which he first appeared).

He was now thirty-six years old; a failed human being; a recluse who lived in a room that resembled a funeral chamber, a 'rock-hewn death-house'. A German artist 'of a mock-realistic and degenerate school', he was predestined, in his encounters with women, to experience failure, for love in his case always meant *'unhappy* love'. Lewis was unrelenting: 'The massive wrinkled brow of this "thinking" Mensch exhibited the big-dog pathos of his heavily-thinking german kind.'

Kreisler exhibited the stigmata of Lewis's overall view of men as automata. 'The ossature is my favourite part of a living animal organism, not its intestines', he wrote in *Satire and Fiction* (1930), an opinion that he repeated in *Men Without Art* (1934) and any number of other contexts. 'Hardness in the shell' was another way of saying that he saw his characters from the outside.[10] He wrote vigorously on the subject of puppets in his essay 'Inferior religions', intended to explain some of his intentions in the writing of the stories in *The Wild Body: A soldier of humour and other stories* (1927). He evidently liked to think of many of his fictional creations as 'only shadows of energy, not living beings'. He was partial to mechanisms with a logical structure, and cited 'Boswell's Johnson, Mr. Veneering, Malvolio, Bouvard and Pécuchet, and the "commissaire" in *Crime and Punishment*', as analogous types.

We have not exhausted the catalogue of Kreisler's limitations as a human being when we acknowledge the pejorative power of the word 'German' (always lower-case in *Tarr*), or the depressing connotations of the word 'machine' when used as a descriptive tag for Kreisler. Because Kreisler could not accommodate himself to the needs or the fantasies of women, he took out his aggression in violent rape; the ugliness of the rape episode was not palliated by Lewis's virtuoso technique in dramatising its after-effects. In a classic study, SueEllen Campbell identified both of the major characters, Kreisler and Tarr, as versions of the 'Enemy-like figure' that haunted Lewis's imagination for fully half a century[11] – Kreisler challenged a Pole to a duel, and then by mischance murdered him. Finally, in despair, he hung himself in a French prison cell.

Lewis, delighted at the reviews that greeted *Tarr* (which were more favourable than he had expected), wrote to John Quinn in 1919 about how those who liked the novel described Kreisler as 'a dark and living figure, plunging, jolting, bursting his way through a gathering of Flaubertesque phantoms'.[12] Frederick Tarr (the English artist–

intellectual after whom the novel was named) was a less important character than Kreisler. On this point we have the testimony of Lewis himself. In *Rude Assignment* Lewis wrote that Tarr (named after a well-known cricketer) was a secondary character; for him, Kreisler was more important. He confessed that he had toyed with several names for his novel, ranging from 'Otto Kreisler's death' to 'The bourgeois bohemians' before deciding, in May 1917, that he should fix on the title *Tarr*. Even so, as early as 1909 Lewis had mentioned to T. Sturge Moore that he was working on a story named 'Otto Kreisler'; its length finally expanded into a novel; and Kreisler was, at least for long periods of time, uppermost in Lewis's imagination.

Lewis was correct in arguing that his novel was primarily about Kreisler, and derived much of its narrative power from Kreisler's behaviour; he was mistaken in his decision to name the novel after the relatively pallid and passive Tarr.

Hugh Kenner came closest to the mark in his judgement that 'The characters are all a little dead. They seem coherently conceived, inviolable to protests of reason or of sentiment. Yet they never *interact*.'[13] The stylistic excesses, severely reduced in the 1928 version, proved not to be necessary elements, and Lewis was glad to get rid of them. But there remains for the average reader Lewis's delight in language, his vigour of expression, that fairly won the cultist audience it has attracted over the years.

Part IV

Novels about the war

Chapter 13

The last year of the war

An English private, paid one shilling a day, soon lost any enthusiasm with which he and his fellow-soldiers may have begun the war.

Well before the end of 1914 the British Expeditionary Force – six infantry divisions, plus one cavalry division, plus practically all the Regulars who could be rushed back from the outposts of the Empire – was assigned to ferocious fighting. The Territorial Force, consisting of part-time soldiers, was also committed within a matter of weeks. Field-Marshal Lord Kitchener's appeal to patriotism, made in his capacity as minister of war, met with an astonishing response from Parliament: the authorisation of eighteen new divisions, a 'New Army' of 500,000 men. 'Pals Battalions' were raised by city councils; the 'Commercials' were recruited from shops and offices by Chambers of Commerce; the Public Schools Battalion, the Scottish brigades and the Ulster Volunteer Force (the 36th Division) swelled the ranks in 1915. By the end of the first full year of fighting, the front line, the support and the reserve – known as the trench system – were well established, and the concept of a No Man's Land between opposing trenches was widely approved as a means of minimising casualties. By the spring of 1916 four British armies had taken up positions on the Western Front; their size was unprecedented. The British were responsible for eighty-five miles of front, all of them within fifty miles of the North Sea or the English Channel. Inevitably, however, disillusionment with war leaders and with the generals who squandered lives swept through the divisions. Back in England, in 1915 and 1916, more than 5 million working days were lost to 'stoppages'. These evidences of labour unrest struck the soldiers as unpatriotic, and contributed to a demoralisation of their fighting temper (consistently misjudged by officers as being higher than it was).

General Sir Douglas Haig, who had been appointed commander-in-chief in December 1915, was at first reluctant to authorise a 'Big Push' because of intelligence reports documenting the fact that the enemy was superbly prepared for any offensive. However, bolstered by the urgings of Marshal Joffre, he began to believe that he could cut the German Army in two in one day. On 24 June, more than 1½ million artillery rounds were fired, preparatory to the command 'Over the top!' – but they did not destroy the German works, nor did they demolish barbed-wire defences. By the end of the first day some 20,000 dead British soldiers and an additional 40,000 British casualties had become official statistics. Haig refused to cut his losses; the battle continued; and not until 18 November did it finally grind to a halt. The gain in territory was, all things considered, insignificant. By the end of the year another 607,784 members of the British military had been put out of action, adding to the appalling casualties of 1914 and 1915. Two consequences, noted with sourness by the infantry, were the squandering of the surprise element when armoured tanks were introduced (too few were used, and these clumsily), and the elevation of both Haig and Joffre to the rank of field marshal. As late as the end of this pivotal year, both Haig and Joffre were contradicting, with vehemence, Lloyd George's opinion that cavalry had outlived its usefulness.

The idealism animating British soldiers on the Western Front could not, and did not, survive the carnage of the Battle of the Somme. This battle divided the history of the war. Nothing that followed could do more than deepen the disgust, the nausea and the feeling of hopelessness of the average infantryman. It did not matter that the Germans suffered almost equal casualties. The almost universal judgement was that everything had been staked, and nothing worthwhile had been gained, while much had been lost, forever. The poets Edmund Blunden, Siegfried Sassoon, Robert Graves and John Masefield were there, and bore witness; they were appalled. The Battle of the Somme, in short, proved to be England's Verdun, and its memory would scar more than one generation.[1]

My concern, in this survey of novels representing the best and the most readable fiction of a four-year period, has been with a predominant romantic strain. It was never seriously challenged by the doctrines of Realism. The lengthening of the Great War did not radically alter the themes or the tone of best-selling fiction, and an awareness of what had gone wrong in the Battle of the Somme did not affect in a major way the kinds of fiction written between 1916 and 1918.

A market grew for biographies of war heroes and memoirs of war experiences, written mostly by officers and to that extent unrepresentative of the feelings of enlisted men (who, it must be remembered, had declared a spontaneous, unofficial truce at the Front between Christmas and New Year's Day of 1914): Coulson Kernahan's *The Experiences of a Recruiting Officer* (1915), Sir Mortimer Durand's *A Life of Field-Marshal Sir George White, V.C.* (1915), Arnold Bennett's edition of Flight-Lieutenant Harold Rosher's correspondence, *In the Royal Naval Air Service: War letters of the late Harold Rosher to his family* (1916), Major A. Corbett-Smith's *Retreat from Mons* (1916), Major William Redmond's *Trench Pictures from France* (1917), Major H. M. Alexander's *On Two Fronts* (1917), Captain H. G. Gilliland's *My German Prisons: Being the experience of an officer during two-and-a-half years as a prisoner of war* (1918) and Captain R. Hugh Knyvett's *Over There!*, an account of Australian troops under fire in both Gallipoli and France (1918). These books exhibited two strong elements: a cheerfulness about the ultimate outcome of the conflict, and firm convictions about both the importance and the righteousness of 'the cause'. These non-fiction books were not untruthful about what was seen or experienced, but in general they failed to acknowledge growing rips in the social, cultural, political and economic fabric of the homeland their authors had left behind.

Fully one hundred of one hundred and fifty best-selling titles in W. H. Smith shops (October 1915) dealt with the war, and carried titles like *The German Spy System in France*, *Germany's Swelled Head*, *J'Accuse* (an attack on German pretensions), *My Adventures as a Spy*, *How Belgium Saved Europe*, *The Hero of Liège*, *Secrets of the German War Office*, *On the Side of the Angels* and *Remember Louvain*. These eye-witness accounts were fully as much polemic as journalism or first drafts of historical studies. H. G. Wells's *The War that Will End War* (1914) enjoyed a very wide sale, and the phrase became a slogan of some importance in the negotiation of the Treaty of Versailles as well as in the thinking of post-war prime ministers.

The case of Rudyard Kipling was paradigmatic. Though the winner of the Nobel Prize for Literature (1907) had long since renounced a belief in war as a glorious adventure, he had been preaching for many years the need to accelerate an armaments programme to match the German threat. His instant response to the outbreak of war was the writing of 'For all we have and are':

> For all we have and are,
> For all our children's fate,
> Stand up and take the war.
> The Hun is at the gate!

Kipling invoked 'the old Commandments', denounced Germany as 'a crazed and driven foe', and warned sternly that only 'iron sacrifice/ Of body, will, and soul' would bring the nation through.

> There is but one task for all –
> One life for each to give.
> What stands if Freedom fall?
> Who dies if England live?

Printed in *The Times*, instantly reprinted by American periodicals, and widely quoted, the poem expressed a national mood; 'The Hun is at the gate!' became an inescapable slogan. Kipling's short stories and poems remained very popular with the book-buying public throughout the war, and Kipling wrote about the navy and army after living aboard naval vessels and touring the Western Front (including Italy) with patriotic ardour. The death of his only son, John, in the Battle of Loos (27 September 1915), darkened his life. He and his wife Carrie hoped desperately against hope that John, marked down as 'missing in action', might by some good chance turn up in a prison or a military hospital. This illusory conviction lingered until finally Oliver Baldwin talked to Sergeant Farrell of the Irish Guards, who had been with John when he was shot through the head at Chalk-pit Wood; in the confused fighting that continued for days, the body disappeared, and became one of 10,000 unidentified bodies.

Kipling received a number of letters (a few coming from Germany) that exulted in God's revenge on him for having, in some mysterious way, provoked the war. These counted with him for much more than they should have, particularly since a much larger number of letters of sympathy from friends and well-wishers poured in from all quarters. Kipling's hatred of Germany intensified; indeed, he became convinced by the end of 1916 that another world war was inevitable, and that Germany would be responsible for starting it. Even so, Kipling's

'Epitaphs of the war' was astonishingly bleak; the enemy here was not Germany or its allies, but war itself. Most of the epitaphs were written during the second half of the Great War, when the full consequences of uninspired leadership both at home and on all sectors of the Western Front became more clear. Kipling wrote about 'A son':

> My son was killed while laughing at some jest. I would I knew
> What it was, and it might serve me in a time when jests are few.

He understood what 'The coward' might feel:

> I could not look on Death, which being known,
> Men led me to him, blindfold and alone.

The mood of Kipling's hard-earned knowledge about the price of war was recorded in 'Common form':

> If any question why we died,
> Tell them because our fathers lied.

Kipling's admiration of soldiers and sailors – the servants of the Empire – yielded to a different set of feelings as the war progressed; by 1917 he was an embittered observer; by 1918 only a sense of duty to see it through kept him (and then barely) from despair.

The poets, of course, traced an arc of disillusionment more swiftly and perhaps even more convincingly than novelists were able to do; the lyric mode functioned in the same manner as a light-switch. 'The modern soldier is portrayed as a passive and often degraded victim of circumstances', John H. Johnston has written in his history.

> Siegfried Sassoon's infantrymen, for example, succumb to hysteria ('Lamentations'), take their own lives ('Suicide in the Trenches'), or perish in an ill-conceived attack ('The General'). In 'Third Ypres' Edmund Blunden's soldiers die ignominiously or, stunned and helpless, crouch amid the ruins of a shell-blasted pillbox. The weapons of modern warfare add new terrors to death: mutilation, dismemberment, the agony of poison gas (Wilfred Owen's 'Dulce et Decorum Est'). In terms that reverse all idealistic conceptions of death in warfare, Isaac Rosenberg's 'Dead Man's Dump' depicts the pitiable degradation of the slain.[2]

By far the bleakest reading of the human condition published in a wartime novel had nothing to do directly with the war, even though

Somerset Maugham corrected its proofs while under gunfire in Ypres. *Of Human Bondage* contained (among many other characters based on real people) the character of Cronshaw, a reincarnation of the notorious Aleisteir Crowley, poet, dabbler in black arts and 'illuminist'. The meaning of life (Cronshaw told Philip Carey, hero of the novel) was to be found in a Persian rug. After puzzling over what Cronshaw might possibly have meant, Philip finally decided he understood the message. The meaning of life was that there was no meaning. Man by living served no end. 'It was immaterial whether he was born or not born, whether he lived or ceased to live. Life was insignificant and death without consequence.' A pattern in a rug might serve the pleasure of the weaver's aesthetic sense, but it served no larger end.

Millions of soldiers gave up their personal responsibility for discovering a pattern in the Persian rug of life, and did so no later than the spring of 1917. Bitterness and rage at the sheer waste of human life formed their dominant mood. Among them grew an awareness of the impossibility of reconstructing the world of pre-1914 values.

Even so, four years after August 1914, one might find notices of Corporal Ward Muir's *Observations of an Orderly* winning an ever-widening audience because the RAMC experiences were told in 'humorous, sympathetic stories'; *Short Flights with the Cloud Cavalry*, by 'Spin', which gave a reader 'breezy and entertaining tales of the amusing or exciting things that happen in the daily life of the aviator on service in France and elsewhere'; Dorota Flatau's *Yellow English*, a novel warning English readers of the danger of allowing the naturalised German 'to live freely amongst us and wield subtle influence in high places'; Henry Erskine South's *The Destroyers, and Other Stories of the Royal Navy*, which provided 'plenty of adventure and ... thrilling incident', and a 'pleasant love idyll' leavening the espionage yarn at the end; and a host of novels which resolutely looked backwards to an era when

> there were no bombs dropped from the skies, no aeroplanes to drop them, no inventions to breathe out gas, to squirt out fire. Happy times: the golden age of warfare when man went out to kill brother man in a fair give-and-take way, and each combatant had a sporting chance.

A novel that looked ahead to the end of the war ('through its pages', wrote a reviewer of F. E. Mills Young's *The Laws of Chance*, 'we are able to glimpse the happier future that may some day come to us') was greeted with relief by many readers. The battles of Belgium and

France – one may all too easily conclude after reading the book news, the advertisements, the reviews and the literary essays of countless periodicals – had become *tiresome*.

A few voices protested against this make-believe fiction. W. L. George, in his collection of essays, *A Novelist on Novels* (1918), fiercely attacked 'unreality, extravagance, stage tears, offensive piety, ridiculous abductions and machinery'. A reviewer of John Ayscough's *The Tideway* (Long) cleared his throat: 'The themes of most of the stories ... have been well worn in the popular magazines.' The *Morning Post*, thinking back on the autumn novels of 1917, lamented that fewer than one in three deserved a review, and added that 'Distinguished contributions by quite new hands are few.' (Grant Richards, quoting this opinion in his widely read weekly column, did not demur.) Back-scratching and puffery were occasionally called to order. Sir James Barrie, in his introduction to Leonard Merrick's *Conrad in Quest of his Youth* (1918), conjured up the memory of Laurence Sterne's *Sentimental Journey through France and Italy*, and said, 'I know scarcely a novel by any living Englishman except a score or more of Mr. Hardy's, that I would rather have written.' (Hardy wrote fifteen novels, one of which was never published. Barrie's 'score or more' is overgenerous.) This was too much for several reviewers, who entertained harsher views of Merrick's interesting but unequal works; they objected to the names of Sterne and Hardy being employed frivolously to inflate a less than first-rate talent.

The professional bookmen – Sir Arthur Quiller-Couch, for example, who published his lectures at Cambridge University (he was King Edward VII Professor of English Literature), and who gave to them the title *Studies in Literature* (1918) – did not pay much attention to modern literature, and even less to the modern novel. Sir Edmund Gosse told his readers that he wrote to please rather than to instruct, and that his primary aim was to spread abroad his own enjoyment of reading. George Edward Bateman Saintsbury, as a matter of policy, avoided writing about his living contemporaries in a seemingly unending stream of reviews, essays and magisterial surveys.

When Hugh Walpole's *The Green Mirror* appeared early in 1918, the anonymous *TLS* reviewer stamped his approval on the modesty of Walpole's story-telling ambitions:

> He has a true insight into the nature of domesticity. He can render perfectly the 'friendly confused smell of hams and medicine, which is the Stores note of welcome'. The psychology of a lady charged with the

exciting duty of buying three hot-water bottles is no secret to him. We have seldom met a better account of a long Sunday in the country and the cold supper with which it ends. On this occasion the servants were out, and there was no soup. These are the small things in which Mr. Walpole is invariably happy, and in our view it is no disparagement to a writer to say that his gift is for the small things rather than for the large.[3]

These illustrations are drawn, for the most part, from the final year of a war that had gone on so long that field marshals and generals, as well as infantrymen, were prophesying uncountable years ahead of trench combat, with inconclusive attacks and counter-attacks, despite the moving into place of the American Expeditionary Forces. In 1918 the hunger for gossip about authors was insatiable; Sax Rohmer, who believed in the doctrine of reincarnation and habitually worked in the midst of a collection of Oriental vessels and implements 'formerly used for purposes of sorcery', guaranteed by the publication of such exotic information the enlargement of interest in the sequels he intended to write to *The Mystery of Dr. Fu-Manchu*. Romance, comedy and vicarious thrills remained the staples of lending-library fiction.

But no matter how vague the outlines of the post-war era as described in futurist predictions, and no matter how similar the novels of 1918 might seem to those of 1915, publishing firms were suffering from the stresses of depleted ranks and spiralling costs of production. More than one critic noted how threadbare the subject-matter of certain kinds of plots had become (e.g., stories about German espionage). And it was becoming very difficult for Englishmen to light up a lucifer 'and smile, smile, smile' – after the disasters of the Somme, the failure of General Nivelle's Aisne offensive of 1917, the collapse of the Eastern Front and the Second Battle of the Marne.

Michael Joseph, in his candid *The Adventure of Publishing* (1949), defined the act of judgement involved in publishing novels (as well as other books) in the modern era:

> Publishing is not therefore a matter of choosing the right books to publish from the manuscripts submitted. A publisher must be able not only to visualise what will be to the public's taste; he must also be able to create and reshape books himself. It does not follow, however, that the most successful publishers are those who are best able to gauge public taste and satisfy it. Their success can at best be commercial and ephemeral: ephemeral because public taste is always changing and no enduring 'back list' can be built up from books which are merely popular in their day.[4]

Nevertheless, public taste in novel-reading did not change very much between 1914 and 1918. The most remarkable single aspect of English novels during the Great War was that they accommodated that taste for so long.

The English book market after the Armistice enjoyed a transient surge of prosperity as 'normalcy' returned, but publishers needed to rethink the structure of their trade. Vacant places had to be filled on their staffs. Overhead and salary costs kept climbing in step with inflationary pressures on the national economy. The growing importance of literary agents, the increasing willingness of authors to change publishing firms and to enter into new contracts, and the proliferation of 'business types' in both old and new firms meant that old ways of transacting arrangements were inevitably altered: in the minds of many, for the worse. 'In the thick of such a struggle anything like the cherished courtesy of the Publishers' Circle was unthinkable', Arthur Waugh wrote in his chapter 'Years of change',

> and one of the first problems of the Board-room was how to get hold of a new author, and inspire him with the idea for a new book; while the most urgent and anxious of all problems was how to retain your hold upon your author, when once you had secured him on your list.[5]

From this perspective 'modern commercialism' was the enemy. Mass-production, 'the gospel of to-day',[6] destroyed the small concern, run by a book-lover who liked to think of a cordial relationship with an author as the primary reason for being in publishing.

> Just as the unit of the state is the home, so the unit of commerce is the small business, whose proprietor is proud of his connection, and keen to satisfy his client, individually as well as collectively. Possession is the secret of prosperity. . . . The break-up of the small business all over the country leads to a decline in personal pride, in individual initiative, in ambition, and in contentment. It swells the record of the unemployed, and packs the football stands with vast and purposeless crowds, whose only pleasure seems to lie in making the greatest possible noise.[7]

Advertising of each new book as a 'masterpiece', bigger typography, more flamboyant epithets and incautious reviews compounded the problem.[8]

We may discount some of Arthur Waugh's nostalgia for a golden age of publisher–author relationships as a generalisation about conditions that never universally prevailed. Nevertheless, his summing-up was corroborated to a surprisingly large degree by a large number of reliable witnesses. After 1918 there took place a drastic sea-change in the publishing industry. The interest of the public in the lives and personalities of writers of fiction, the prices of both hard-bound and paperback editions of novels and the consensus on the high value of entertainment in a time of great crisis underwent a startling metamorphosis within a decade. Though the house of fiction during the Great War was well built and handsome, redesigning some rooms and changing the dimensions of others proved inevitable.

No English novel published between 1914 and 1918 came close to the honesty about trench warfare exhibited by Henri Barbusse's *Le Feu: journal d'une escouade*, published in 1916. The English translation (1917) was greeted with lukewarm and even patronising reviews. In 1929, more than ten years after the Armistice, the popularity of Erich Maria Remarque's *Im Westen nicht Neues* (translated into English immediately) signified that nothing close to its sober anti-war message had yet been written or published by an English novelist, and no English novel about the war during the first post-war decade achieved anything like its success.

The price of a 6s. novel, which had remained remarkably constant for four years, began to rise very slowly in 1917. The problem of containing costs was compounded by overproduction of novels, and by a popular opinion that a novel was a throw-away product, an opinion guaranteeing a shelf-life in bookstores of only three months, and a circulating-library life of only six months. (Books by unknown authors rarely lasted more than three.[9]) One striking aspect of this craze for publishing more novels than the market could accommodate was the rise in popularity of short-story anthologies, which had enjoyed only very small sales before 1914. Frank Swinnerton, who had been astonished to discover that supposed best-sellers during the war years had difficulty in reaching the thousand-mark, was really testifying to the diffuseness of the book-buying public and the exaggerations contained in advertising copy; but the demand for reading matter meant that the publishing of novels proved commercially successful even if press runs were relatively small. What overproduction in the post-war years demonstrated, however, was that probably nearly as many book publishers lost money as made it.[10]

Chapter 14

What the reviewers of the *Times Literary Supplement* wrote in 1918

By 1918, when the fourth year of the war was beginning to melt drearily into the fifth, and at a time when prophecies of an armistice within the foreseeable future had subsided to a despairing mutter, the market for fiction was expanding significantly. Despite a rise in price of what was increasingly seen as the basic commodity of the trade (not merely of lending libraries), those who could afford 6s. for a hardback in 1914 did not object too strenuously to the new prices of 7s. or 8s.; the miracle was that the 6s. price had remained stable for so long.

One sign of the changing interest in fiction was related to the multiplying number of columns in periodicals that concentrated on the latest works of ficton. A fair sampling of the reviews of Arnold Bennett's *The Pretty Lady* (released early in 1918) would include selections from the *Manchester Guardian*, the *Star*, the *Daily Telegraph* and the *Staffordshire Sentinel*; equally lengthy – and often equally discerning – notices were printed in the *Daily News*, the *Globe*, the *Evening News*, the *Times Literary Supplement*, *Punch*, the *Sunday Chronicle*, the *Pall Mall Gazette*, the *Nation*, *Country Life*, *Outlook*, *New Statesman*, the *Athenaeum* (twice), the *Daily Express* and the *Westminster Gazette*.[1] *The Pretty Lady* seriously divided Bennett's critics; it was, to be sure, an unusually controversial novel; but all the reviewers shared an interest in ascertaining whether Bennett's novel was adequately entertaining, moral or artistically satisfying.

They wrote as self-appointed guides to the common reader, though they were remarkably restricted to many of the concerns that had been stressed by Edwardian reviewers, even by reviewers of the 1890s. Inventing or devising new terms to grapple with original literary

165

techniques was not (in Henry James's phrase) a *felt need*, primarily because the overwhelming majority of novels published between 1914 and 1918 did not attempt to tell a story in a new way.

Of all the reviewing media the *Times Literary Supplement* may be accounted the most comprehensive and lively: Arnold Bennett, in addressing a letter to the editor (January 1919), was only expressing a widely held view when he called it 'the chief literary organ'. Its notices of 'New Novels' and 'Fiction' served as guides to thousands of readers during the troubled war years, and the following survey of what its reviewers had to say about novels in 1918 should be read as a fair summary of what representative critics thought about the latest and best specimens of the novel genre. Not a single new English novel received a front-page notice, even though a few novels regarded as classics might win the envied space. A very few novels won separate reviews on other pages, but not because they dealt with current war issues. Indeed, if generalisations are in order, novels about life in the services, and novels totally unrelated to war concerns – escapist entertainments, historical romances, family chronicles – outnumbered all the novels that sought to be up to date. Nor were these trends considered a matter for melancholy reflection by the reviewers, who never once called for a full-scale examination of life in the trenches; or by the readers who wrote letters to *TLS*; or by the editors who frequently spoke directly to the public, who selected for the correspondence columns the particular letters that would interest the widest audience, and in any case assigned the best of the new novels to their reviewing staff.

A few novels were reviewed because they were, in fact, war novels. Francesco Sapori's *La Trincea*, for example, was called the best *Italian* novel yet. 'We realize to the full horrors of the fighting in this barren, rocky desert', wrote the reviewer (Sapori was writing about the Carso front). Its hero, Rosselli, had no love for war; he was, after all, a sensitive musician, but the novel within which he moved and had his being, though it bore the stamp of truth, was not realistic. 'The ideal aspect of the war' (whatever that might be) was never far from Sapori's thought.[2]

The Crescent Moon, by Francis Brett Young, dealt with German East Africa on the eve of the outbreak of the war and during its first weeks; but, as the critic made haste to point out, the novel was really about the 'mystery' of mysterious Africa. 'As is Egdon Heath to *The Return of the Native*, so is the African scene to this much slighter, easier tale.'[3]

Surely, one might think, a novel in which the villain was none other than the Kaiser might be accounted a war novel. *The Island Mystery*, by G. A. Birmingham, dealt with an island in the Aegean Sea, whereon one might discover a cave with petrol in it for submarines: indeed, 'cisterns and cisterns' of petrol. 'We use the censorious term, villain', wrote the reviewer,

> for Mr. Birmingham is not one of those namby-pamby people whose pose is detachment. He has his code of morals, his conception of villainy. What fills him with noble indignation is not, of course, the intentional commission of evil, but forethought and efficiency in carrying it out. His hell is paved with good intentions.

It turned out, therefore, that this 'extravaganza of a novel' was not a serious effort to describe the war as most Englishmen under arms knew it; it was, rather, a romance for stay-at-homes.[4]

There were the usual operatic stories. J. S. Fletcher's *The Amaranth Club* concentrated on the contents of naval despatches sold to the Germans as well as the unmasking of a murderer; altogether, the reviewer wrote with satisfaction, 'a rush of exciting developments for the reader, who will thoroughly enjoy the tale'.[5]

'John Ayscough', a pseudonym, wrote *Jacqueline*, also about German espionage; but it made no pretence of being true. The scene was Boon Court, the country seat of Lady Berengaria de Bohun, the elder daughter of the thirteenth Earl of Lambeth; synopsising what went on in Ayscough's pages proved almost too much for the reviewer.[6]

Ethel Sidgwick's *Jamesie* tried, with some determination, to consider the 'real world'. Hers was a story of the small boy of Lord and Lady Iveagh Suit, and their kinfolk, just before and during the war. Told through letters, the novel did cope with the grimness of unmerited death. But the war, which was responsible for Jamesie's death (not to mention those of several other characters) was, nevertheless, 'a thing seen at a distance, something horrible', which was 'too big for the canvas'.[7]

Espionage attracted many novelists, who found it more attractive subject-matter than trench warfare. E. Phillips Oppenheim, for example, chose as his hero in *The Double Traitor* a member of the British Diplomatic Service who accepted money from a German masterspy in England, but consistently handed him false and misleading reports. This improbable yarn was 'nicely embroidered with fact', the reviewer wrote, perhaps with some complacency.[8]

William Le Queux also wrote about nefarious German machinations in *The Yellow Ribbon*. These provided 'an inexhaustible mine of sensations', and, the reviewer added, 'there are plenty of them in this tale'.[9]

Richard Deban's *That Which Hath Wings* provided a reader with 'a bewildering medley of society slang, German spies, heroic Boy Scouts, young women, either enormously tall or extremely short, but alike endowed with hearts of ample size': the novel turned into an 'unblushing juggling with the emotions of a tragic time' (the reviewer could not, in good conscience, recommend it).[10]

Less crass but more overtly didactic, and hardly fiction of a higher order, was Dorota Flatau's *Yellow English*. Its hero, Sir Frederick Schultz, was a naturalised alien who was demonstratively British, though he worked for the German interest. The reviewer drew the line at the crudeness of the message.[11]

Equally unlikely, but more entertaining, was W. Douglas Newton's *The War Cache*: 'a breathless tale of German spies and hidden war treasure on the East Coast, and in the fourth year of the war too, when petrol is scarce except to the munitions chemist, and to the Hun'.[12]

Indeed, one might speculate as to whether German spy stories were ever intended to represent the fruits of serious research on the practices of real agents. F. Thickness-Woodington's *Swayneford*, dealing with a pre-war situation, was considered 'quite good enough to please the average lover of sensation novels'.[13] Mrs Belloc Lowndes's *Out of the War* concentrated on the exploits of a British naval officer who turned out to be a German and a spy; but he had partially redeeming qualities, since he was driven by 'a holy passion', and he was consistently characterised as 'brave'. His wife, Betty, however, was a 'fool' for being taken in, 'for all her pluck and her warm heart'.[14]

Without a useful theory of what might constitute verisimilitude in fiction, reviewers often fell back on their sense of what might reasonably happen to characters who existed only within the pages of a book. *Wastralls*, by C. A. Dawson Scott, was 'neither a big nor a smooth story', but the reviewer noted with some satisfaction that the people in it moved and the events in it happened; 'and if the movements are crude and the events are harsh, the author has had the sure instinct which presents them in their true proportions'.[15]

In *Up and Down* E. F. Benson described the activities of an Englishman who lived on an island at the mouth of the Bay of Naples, and who returned to England when the war broke out. His services in France and Italy led directly to the winning of the Victoria Cross, and finally to his death of cancer in his Italian home. Most of the book, however, showed us a middle-aged man who stayed at home, and its interest lay in what it told the reader about the impact of the war on the middle class. Benson, the reviewer admitted, did not take the reader very high or very deep. 'He startles us with no very acute analysis or blinding revelation. His thoughts are not so remote or subtle that anyone will find a difficulty in following him.' But therein resided the value of the book, 'the cause why it will be welcomed by thousands. . . . It offers hope, consolation, and grounds for faith.'[16]

Similar reasons were used to justify a reviewer's liking of W. B. Maxwell's *The Mirror and the Lamp*. 'The Rev. Mr. Waladen simply "is"; if Tolstoy had been an Englishman, this is the Mr. Waladen whom he might have given us', and the reviewer added: 'the sergeant is perfectly a sergeant, through Mr. Maxwell's almost unerring instinct for dialogue'.[17]

E. M. Delafield's *The Pelicans* provided the reader with fascinating information about a Mrs Tregaskis. As the novel progressed, so did the author's sympathy for her. The reader's knowledge derived directly from the writer 'in her omniscient capacity of creator'. This, in turn, the reviewer found 'better than impartiality'.[18]

In the very last week of the war Frederick Sleath's *Sniper Jackson* was noticed as a first novel with a minor love interest. Perhaps, the reviewer mused, this was neither a conventional novel nor fiction at all. The story, such as it was, told of a Scotsman at Ypres who commanded a sniping section and led dangerous expeditions into No Man's Land. 'He is dealing with real live men who are really doing things': the words 'real' and 'really' served as talismanic epithets.[19]

It is clear, at any rate, that reviewers appreciated the chance to like fictional characters, though they might disguise their sympathies in the amiable language of a reviewer. Elinor Mordaunt, in her novel *The Pendulum*, wrote 'an engrossing tale chiefly because the people and the setting all seem so "real" . . . so real, indeed, that we can hardly think of them as characters in a novel'.[20]

Reviewers were, in short, baffled by the length and intensity of the war no less than were the leaders of the nation, and knew that their judgements of novels meant for the passing moment could not bear the weight of the highest literary standards. 'Fiction is probably the most living form of literature in England at the present moment', wrote one bemused critic early in the year, and for that reason it is the most difficult to judge. Far from having reached its full height, it is in a state of growth and development; we scarcely know on opening a new novel what to expect; the most sagacious has difficulty in deciding where to draw the line, and nowhere perhaps do our personal prejudices so confuse what should be our aesthetic judgments.[21]

It was a difficult time for the formulation of imperious literary dicta. In a summary of a novel that dealt with Poland in 1914–15 (*Love and Sacrifice*, by Beatrice Baskerville), one reviewer paused to reflect that one could hardly speculate on what the poets and novelists of the future might make of the Great War. The war, he continued, was 'so huge, so terrible, so inconceivable, that an author who "lets it tell itself" may very well be choosing the best way to get the effect of bringing it home.'[22]

The best novel need not deal with war events at all. Gilbert Cannan, for example, chose to write about a nineteenth-century Lancashire journalist who worried about the world's indifference; he was 'strong enough to suffer, but not strong enough to achieve; and so he breaks himself'. *The Stucco House* might be condemned, as a consequence, as a novel that turned back into the past, 'away from the complexities of to-day and from the great difficulties that war puts in the way of reasonable living'. Was one justified in saying that this seemed to be 'sheer evasion'? The reviewer thought that it was best to ignore Cannan's dates, and to take his story as a modern one. 'Then it will be found a moving, breathless, headlong, and sometimes incoherent protest against the civilization of industrialism.'[23]

It was necessary, above all, to move on, to win the war, since the British Empire, sorely tried, had become 'the champion of mankind, as Athens was the champion of mankind at Marathon'. It was not desirable to debate – in fiction any more than in any other kind of writing – what mistakes may have been made, or whether the world could recover from a struggle so long and desperate, or whether indeed the English had been in the past 'worthy' of the present cause.[24]

The fuzzy religiosity of *Mr. Britling Sees It Through* had appealed to a very large audience, and one need not disparage the impulse to suggest a greater good at work than one might see easily through the clouds of wartime, or read into novels with an uplifting message a crass commercial impulse; but such messages certainly proliferated in the months that led up to the Armistice. A few examples might be cited, beginning with a popular romance, containing time-tested ingredients, by Bernard Capes. *Where England Sets Her Feet* was an historical recreation of the times of Queen Elizabeth.

> The story is as familiar as can be; yet it is ever new; and newer than ever, perhaps, now, when it is told by an author who can set running through its pages a light of love for England, of passionate admiration for England menaced by a mighty enemy.

Walter Raleigh, Richard Grenville, Leicester: these men had helped to save a nation, despite personal differences, despite egos and selfishness, despite their own natures. *And England would do it again.*[25]

H. Rider Haggard, in *Love Eternal*, wrote about a soldier who went to war in France, and performed dangerous work in Africa, while his heroine turned her great house in Essex into a hospital. Zeppelins appeared; but they could not destroy an eternal love. The reviewer noted that in this somewhat unorthodox treatment of the Christian faith, love, goodness and life were easily interchangeable as verbal counters. Haggard might not be a literary artist, but he had 'enthusiasm, directness, and simplicity', and his virtues were twofold: his novel would bring 'comfort and consolation to many who in these days need it, besides pleasantly whiling away an hour or two for the others'.[26]

Another novel like it: *The Rough Road*, by W. J. Locke, neither better nor worse. It stressed the redemptive powers of the national crisis. In the hero, Doggie, who drank tumblers of whisky and indulged in bad language before he married a wonderful French wife and reformed as a soldier, Locke dramatised his conviction that something better was yet to come once the war ended. 'The great charm of Mr. Locke's work', wrote the reviewer,

> lies in the assurance that is wafted us by innumerable touches of irrepressible good nature that the worse the disease the more certain the cure; the darker the cloud the brighter the lining; the steeper the hill – but Mr. Locke puts it at greater length and more persuasively than we can.

English men and women who travelled down 'the rough road' were on their way to a vindication of the reasons why the journey was undertaken in the first place.[27]

Notions of how they were to become 'more clear-sighted, more unselfish, and necessarily more hard-working' were common enough in the relatively few novels that spoke of what might come after an armistice. *The New Moon*, by Oliver Onions, was set in the world of tomorrow, i.e., ten years from whenever an armistice might be signed; it stressed the importance of electricity in fashioning a better world; but the vision dissolved into a dream in the last chapter, a fact that suggested a failure of nerve accompanying Onions's inability to conceive an improvement in the moral and ethical behaviour of human beings in this post-war world.[28]

In general, reviewers had small patience with bad writing, and considered it their duty to warn readers to shun novels that misused grammar or split infinitives (*The Sheep Path*, by Harry Tighe); employed 'curiously indolent anachronisms', as in a novel about eighteenth-century Scotland (*Over the Hills and Far Away*, by Guy Fleming); indulged in improbabilities (*The Bag of Saffron*, by Baroness von Hutten); repeated stale devices that diminished a reader's respect for the tale (*Sir Isumbras at the Ford*, by D. K. Broster); argued a theory and a conviction not based upon insight and experience (*Nevertheless*, by Olive Wadsley); depended on stereotypes without realising that they had been outworn by previous generations of story-tellers (*The Foolishness of Lilian*, by Jessie Champion); insisted on the reader's suffering through the antics of charmless characters (*A Marrying Man*, by J. B. Stern, and many others); presented the public with a sequel that coarsened the sensationalism already rampant in the original (*The Return of Tarzan*, by Edgar Rice Burroughs, which followed by one year the publication of the first Tarzan novel in 1917); failed to communicate belief in the writer's own extravaganza (*Pieces of Eight*, by Richard Le Gallienne); dared the reader to greet as original the intertwinings of 'Love and War' (*The Last Bout*, by Rosamond Southey); talked too relentlessly about things the war-weary reader would rather forget (butter beans, war diets, the war-time potato patch, as in *The Silent Legion*, by J. E. Buckrose); repeated the foolish things said at the outbreak and during the early months of the war, despite the fact that so much had intervened (*The Test*, by Sybil Spottiswoode); spun fantasies that were neither real nor possible, though the writer might delude herself that she had drawn a portrait of an authentic soldier (*The Return of the Soldier*, by Rebecca West); insisted on treating mental illness 'of a kind no less unpleasant than those which are commonly recognized as vicious and commonly held to be unfit material for fiction' (*God's Counterpoint*, by J. D. Beresford); raised members of the lower class to a higher class merely because they were beautiful and virtuous (*The Telephone Girl*, by Alice and

Claude Askew); contradicted the received wisdom about German nastiness (*Towards Morning*, by I. A. R. Wylie); became shrill in an unseemly way about the sins and weaknesses of the national foe (*The Fire of Green Boughs*, by Mrs Victor Rickard); talked about the hopelessness of capital–labour conflicts (as in *Heronshawe Main: The story of a Yorkshire colliery*, by J. S. Fletcher, a rather unusual treatment of a theme repellent to most reviewers in that, with the arrival of 4 August 1914, 'patriotism and magnanimity win the day at last'); or employed the techniques of realism to no truly heart-warming end (as in *The Burning Glass*, by Marjorie Bowen, with its endless chatter about furniture, clothes and the heroine's toilets).

Whenever a good read came along, however, it was generously praised. Max Pemberton's *The Man of Silver Mount* offered 'a fine operatic display' as it recounted the story of a Mexican bravo fleeing from Mexico in 1913 'into the unknown in a fast destroyer'. Not a word of reproof could be found in a brief notice of *The Riddle of the Purple Emperor*, by Thomas W. and Mary E. Hanshew. Cleek, the 'Vanishing Cracksman' with his 'Forty Faces', had become involved with the theft of 'a big diamond' from an Indian temple, and the chapter headings provided ample warning that a pleasant night lay ahead in Cleek's company: 'The cry in the night', 'The woman in the case', 'The plot thickens', 'What they found in the bedroom', 'A twisted clue' and 'Unravelling threads'. *Miss Pim's Camouflage*, a mild imagining of what might happen if Miss Pim, commissioned by the commander-in-chief, crossed over to the German lines as an invisible person, visited the Kaiser's bedroom, nearly shot the Kaiser and strayed into a conference of generals, 'where to her horror she [became] visible, when Hindenburg's hand [was] at her throat', so intrigued the staff of the *Times Literary Supplement* ('a wonderful deal of entertainment', 'admirably done', 'full of scenes and moments which are both exciting and enjoyable') that it received *two* reviews, in the issues of 2 May and 9 May. *Piccadilly Jim*, by P. G. Wodehouse, was described as 'very diverting and exciting'. The reviewers forgave themselves even as they commended an inferior product: *A Sin of Silence*, by Ottwell Binns, was 'a good enough tale of a not high class'. Leonard Merrick's *While Paris Laughed* displayed 'quickness, lightness, and dexterity', even though the reviewer admitted that Merrick remained an unpopular author ('we confess ourselves unable to guess the reason'). *An English Rose*, by David Lyall, told 'a pretty, not very likely, tale of an "English Rose"' who went out from France as a VAD nurse and met two orderlies who had fought for France in the Foreign Legion; not more than a 'harmless romance', it was still worth recommending as a way to pass time pleasantly. *Karen*, by Mrs Sedgwick, was the story of a spirited English girl who married a German, and lived in Germany before and during the war. The reviewer conceded that 'of real feeling, the emotional response of consciousness to consciousness, there is little', but insisted (for the benefit of a readership that genuinely wished to know), 'As a novel, though, it is excellent company from beginning to end.' It was the reviewer's hope – and his joy when the hope was realised – that a professional entertainer would run true to form. When Dorothy Percival published *Footsteps*, the review expressed gratitude that nothing more nor less than what a common reader had a right to expect had, in fact, been delivered:

> Miss Percival tells her story clearly and simply, with a very fair instinct for what is and what is not important to it; and succeeds in expressing the idea that lies behind it without preaching and without talking at us independently of her characters.[29]

Frank Swinnerton's *Shops and Houses* also lived up to expectations. Swinnerton was more than a disembodied and cruel spectator. The reviewer wrote approvingly that he had 'enough sympathy to show us, at any rate through the eyes of Louis Vechantor, that there were possibilities and varieties among the people of Beckwith which make them momentarily attractive and intermittently pathetic'.[30]

And Anthony Hope's *Captain Dieppe* fulfilled every wish for the kind of story that would hold an intrigued reader by the fireside. Mr Hope, the reviewer wrote, 'breathes easily in the light atmosphere on his own creation. He knows exactly what he is about, and he never forgets the key he is writing in.'[31] Here, as elsewhere, the exact nature of what happened in the plot was slighted in favour of the reviewer's approval of what had been done so adroitly.

It would be pleasant to report that 1918 was the year in which the *Times Literary Supplement* recognised the inevitability of change in form and content of the novel genre, or that occasionally its reviewers might express impatience with hackneyed themes on the basis of a clearer sense of what was wanted. That cannot be done without contradicting the record. The year 1918 was recognisably like 1914 in its fictional interests, in the kinds of novels that authors thought worth writing and common readers thought worth purchasing; more of the past than of the present moved through the pages of even the best-written novels; and in a world of revolution and cacophony, blood and mire, and the obliteration of an entire generation of youth, the typical English novel remained much as it had been during the Edwardian era.

The editor of the *Times Literary Supplement* recognised his inability to cope with the extraordinary events of the war. The leader of the first issue printed after the Armistice confessed to a numbness of feeling:

> In all things, we well know, we are unequal to the events of this hour. Not only cannot we express what we feel; we cannot even feel what we would express. We are dazed spectators of that which but lately we thought we ourselves were doing. We watch the will working in the world, and know now that it is not our will.[32]

The statement amounted to a valedictory; a phase in the history of the English novel was ending.

At this point, finally, we come to a consideration of several novels that spoke directly of the German enemy, and of the experiences of war: John Buchan's *The Thirty-Nine Steps* and *Greenmantle*, H. G. Wells's *Mr. Britling Sees It Through*, Arnold Bennett's *The Pretty Lady*, and the anonymously written *The Love of an Unknown Soldier: Found in a dug-out*. The reader will judge the difficulties confronted by an author who had to balance the factors of entertainment and reader satisfaction against a sense of the seriousness of the issues for which the war was being fought.

Chapter 15

John Buchan's *The Thirty-Nine Steps* (1915) and *Greenmantle* (1916)

From 1912 on John Buchan's attacks of illness – at first incorrectly diagnosed as indigestion, then more accurately interpreted as a duodenal ulcer – intensified. Indeed, they were never wholly to leave him for the rest of his life. His doctor sent him to bed as soon as the symptoms became severe, and ordered him to stay there. 'There' was at Broadstairs, a watering-place close to Margate, famed for its associations with Dickens. Several homes nearby used stairways to descend to the sea; hence, the code-word in Buchan's title for a new novel, *The Thirty-Nine Steps*; but the tone of his new novel reflected Buchan's sense that Broadstairs was a dismal hide-away even while he continued to write as a convalescent patient.

Published in October 1915, the novel sold 25,000 copies before the end of the year, many of which parents sent to soldiers at the Front as suitable reading-matter. Buchan called it 'that elementary type of tale which Americans call the "dime novel"', and added that, in this type of romance, 'the incidents defy the probabilities, and march just inside the borders of the possible'. His judgement was at once diffident and just.

Richard Hannay, the major character, was an Englishman who had lived in foreign parts since the age of six. He had made his money as a mining engineer, enough to make an early retirement possible. Now, back in London at the age of thirty-seven, he found himself overwhelmed by ennui, and regarded himself as 'the best-bored man in the United Kingdom'. A ceaseless round of restaurants, theatres, race meetings and dinners with strangers uninterested in his personality or thoughts had palled. He was sick of the talk of an ordinary

177

Englishman. Schoolmasters from New Zealand and editors from Vancouver – 'the dismalest business of all' – seemed similarly at their wits' end, adrift in London; and he intended to return to the South African veld. After his overnight guest, Scudder, became a murder victim in his flat – 'There was a long knife through his heart, which skewered him to the floor' – he realised that he could not call on the police for assistance. He feared for his own safety, and he was to learn, though in a tantalisingly incomplete form, the dead man's secret: the Greek premier who planned to visit England would be the target of assassins. Hannay worked out the complexities of a code in the dead man's notes even as he fled from London to Scotland and as he made his weary, increasingly exhausted way across the countryside. Every man's hand seemed to be raised against him. A relentlessly searching aeroplane hovered above, then approached with 'an ominous beat', dropped several hundred feet and began to circle 'round the knot of hill in narrowing circles, just as a hawk wheels before it pounces'.

Hannay at one point lay imprisoned in a store-room, and discovered lentonite, a blasting explosive. The criticism of some early reviewers, that it seemed highly unlikely he would have known what to do with it, was unfair. Hannay, a mining engineer by trade, was fully capable of rigging a detonator to a length of fuse, and knew how to protect himself before the blast went off.

Yet this was not a romance to be judged, overall, by its plausibility. Why would the police believe instantly that Hannay, in seeking to escape from them, should take one of the *northern* lines out of London? Why would he not bury himself in the heart of the world's biggest city? The malevolent certainty of the pilot of the aeroplane scouring the countryside looking for Hannay was not made more credible simply because, at long last, the pilot discovered him. The two appearances of Marmaduke Jopley – described as 'an offence to creation', one who did his business by 'toadying eldest sons and rich young peers and foolish old ladies' – were presented, implausibly, as coincidences. At a critical moment, someone made up to look like the First Sea Lord, Lord Alloa, sat down at a table with old acquaintances from both the Army and Navy, but they did not see through the imposture. The judgement of Sir Walter Bullivant, after he heard Hannay's explanation of the meaning of the Black Stone (*Der Schwarzestein*), seemed about right: 'It reads like some wild melodrama.' He added sombrely, 'It's like a penny novelette.'

The Thirty-Nine Steps had its literary antecedents in the fiction of

Rider Haggard and Conan Doyle, both of whom Buchan mentioned, with reverence, in an early chapter, as well as Robert Louis Stevenson, whom he did not mention. A literary innkeeper quoted Kipling's line, 'Romance bringing up the nine-fifteen', to reassure us that adventure was not only to be found 'in the tropics or among gentry in red shirts'. For Buchan's readers, Hannay's fear of the enemy was not seen as paranoid, and novels about an impending German invasion had been written by (among others) Erskine Childers and H. H. Munro. Moreover, the geography of the scenes in the 'high heathery mountains' of Scotland was carefully drawn, and imparted a degree of reasonableness to the factitious events. As an entertainment, the story, a superior example of the genre, gave good value for money.

But from another point of view *The Thirty-Nine Steps* was fairly close to a classic statement of a widespread English attitude early in the war. What Hannay did, not what he thought, was pretty much all there was to him. He harboured few large thoughts about the causes leading to the then-impending war, and he remained remarkably consistent. He always found it hard to put up with others, with himself, too, for that matter, if adventure were not available, or if he could not identify an appropriate way to bash the opposition. He had little Latin (though he did recognise a brief quotation when someone flung it at him), and less Greek. He lied with ease to his servant Paddock, knowing that Paddock, utterly loyal, would forgive him. He did not object when anti-Semitic slurs were uttered in his presence (here and in other novels starring Hannay); but on this score the defence has often been made that Buchan should not be identified carelessly with the characters who make the remarks.[1]

Above all, he was an ordinary Englishman called to greatness by extraordinary circumstances that tested his ingenuity, courage and patriotism. He surprised the reader no more often than he astonished himself. In one memorable scene, after being mistaken for a Free Trader at a meeting convened in a Masonic Hall, he was called upon to make a speech. 'I woke them up a bit when I started in to tell them the kind of glorious business I thought could be made out of the Empire if we really put our backs into it', he said, to rousing acclaim. When he impersonated a roadman in order to escape a search party in Galloway, and succeeded in his impersonation, he demonstrated English ingenuity, English pluck. Surely he more than compensated, by mid-narrative, for his credulity in trusting Scudder's wild story, told originally in order to secure a night's lodging. The story turned out to be false in almost every essential detail; but Hannay penetrated to the truth soon enough to frustrate the German agent Franz.

The leader of the enemy, Franz's employer, was somehow not human in Buchan's rendering. Though at first he resembled Mr Pickwick, with big glasses stuck on the end of his nose and the top of his head 'as bright and bare as a glass bottle', his look transfixed Hannay:

> There was something weird and devilish in those eyes, cold, malignant, unearthly, and most hellishly clever. They fascinated me like the bright eyes of a snake. I had a strong impulse to throw myself on his mercy and offer to join his side, and if you consider the way I felt about the whole thing, you will see that that impulse must have been purely physical, the weakness of a brain mesmerised and mastered by a stronger spirit.

Later still, disguised as a Mr Appleton of Trafalgar Lodge at the Ruff – 'the big chalk headland in Kent, close to Bradgate' – he may have seemed normal, or English, but Hannay was under no illusions: 'Mystery and darkness had hung about the men who hunted me over the Scotch moors in aeroplane and motor-car, and notably about the infernal antiquarian.' Eventually, Mr Appleton's secrets revealed themselves:

> Now I saw cruelty and truthlessness where before I had only seen good-humour. . . . He was sheer brain, icy, cool, calculating, as ruthless as a steam hammer. Now that my eyes were opened I wondered where I had seen the benevolence. His jaw was like chilled steel, and his eyes had the inhuman luminosity of a bird's.

Mr Appleton's scheme failed, however. The agent Franz was captured by English sailors who took over the *Ariadne*, the German yacht to which he fled; but before he learned that Hannay was triumphant, he believed, for the briefest of moments, that '*Der Schwarzestein ist in der Siegeskrone.*'

'There was more in those eyes than any common triumph', Hannay wrote (some time after the event).

> They had been hooded like a bird of prey, and now they flamed with a hawk's pride. A white fanatic heat burned in them, and I realised for the first time the terrible thing I had been up against. This man was more than a spy; in his foul way he had been a patriot.

Buchan unfairly characterised his novel as a 'shocker'. It was, for all its limitations as a character study, a patriotic statement of some significance to readers – both civilian and military – in the second year of the war. In his 'foul way' Mr Appleton may have been a patriot; but he turned out, finally, to be no match for Hannay's dash and verve – for Hannay as a resourceful Englishman.

Buchan dedicated *The Thirty-Nine Steps* to Thomas Arthur Nelson, whom he admired all his life as the one-time captain of the Oxford rugby team and as a player for Scotland. He served as the literary adviser to Nelson's publishing firm after Nelson became its head, and he responded with enthusiasm to Nelson's invitation to write about the campaign in France and Flanders. His reports, in turn, developed into the *Nelson History of the War*, which appeared in fortnightly parts. The twenty-four 'volumes' of the *History* averaged 50,000 words apiece, and ran to 1,200,000 words. It rivalled in literary grace, lucidity and topical appeal *The British Campaign in France and Flanders*, the multi-volume work on which Sir Arthur Conan Doyle was engaged during the same years.

At the same time that he was writing the *History*, Buchan accepted invitations to lecture, in Scottish and English lecture-halls, on the progress of the fighting. *The Times*, impressed by his lucidity in explaining complicated strategy, asked him, in 1915, to report on the second battle of Ypres. These signed articles (the fact that they were not anonymous constituted a signal distinction) personalised the war for a large home-front audience, and earned the respect of the Tommies themselves. They were strikingly candid about the problems of inadequate stores of ammunition and shells that official bulletins had minimised. As part of his reporting duties, Buchan interviewed leading officers of the British staff, from General Haig down; he escorted a delegation of Russians to Scapa Flow; he witnessed the bombardments of the Battle of Loos; in Walt Whitman's celebrated phrase, he suffered, he was there.

With the assistance of only one individual (who served as a checker of facts, and who helped prepare maps and synopsise bulky reports) Buchan wrote the whole of his extraordinary *History*, which ran from February 1915 to July 1919. After that, he undertook a large-scale revision and rewriting for the edition of 1922. 'My aim has been to write a clear narrative of one of the greatest epochs in history', Buchan wrote in his preface,

> showing not only the changing tides of battle, but the intricate political, economic, and social transformations which were involved in a strife

not of armies but of peoples. I have tried – with what success is for others to judge – to give my story something of the movement and colour which it deserves, and to avoid the formlessness of a mere compilation.[2]

In these aims he was remarkably successful. The coolness of tone with which he analysed the motivations and degrees of success of major statesmen and generals remains impressive to this day. He admitted (without regret) that he had placed more emphasis on the role played by Great Britain than on that of any other participant. He confessed that he had not attempted to 'lay open sealed archives' (though without the disappointment expressed by Doyle, who knew that his *British Campaign* had suffered as a consequence); and he knew that 'there must inevitably be mistakes'.

Miscalculation, as in previous wars, had played a significant role in determining whether war would come to the Continent. Buchan placed moderate blame on the disastrous policy followed by Britain in Ireland, on an overgenerous mandate given by the voters to the Liberal Government in 1906 and on the misreading of German intentions (only partly during Lord Haldane's mission to Berlin, in 1912, and more critically in the crucial year following his discussions with the Emperor, Bethmann-Hollweg, and Admiral von Tirpitz). France, recovering from the disaster of 1870 ('one of the marvels of history'), had been oscillating violently between nationalism and extreme internationalism. The cynicism with which the average Frenchman regarded politics undermined the prestige of the central government, and allowed other nations to believe that France had become 'effete, steeped in anti-nationalism, distracted by narrow class interests, sunk deep in matter'.[3] The dual monarchy of Austria–Hungary was wildly unrepresentative of recent population shifts and current interests in its parliamentary assemblies; 'too weak to desire more than to hold what they had', they were easily swayed from Berlin.[4] And Buchan's summation of his own lengthy analysis of Germany's share of culpability must take some sort of prize for anticlimax:

> With a flamboyant emperor ambitious of ranking with the great makers of history, an army burning to prove its perfection to the world, an aristocracy intolerant of all ideals of democratic progress, the rulers of industry at once exultant and nervous, the popular teachers preaching a gospel of race arrogance, and throughout the nation a vague half-mystical striving towards a new destiny, Germany was an unquiet member of the European family.[5]

Buchan's characterisation of Bismarck was surprisingly generous. This 'very great statesman' avoided dogma, thought that war was not the best way to achieve a nation's goals (though his 'blood and iron' speech to the Prussian Diet on 29 September 1862 was often quoted by his critics as proof to the contrary), and would have led Germany in a direction other than the one it followed in August 1914. But 'The Imperial Government was neither representative nor responsible', and power passed to the autocrat William.

Buchan gave full marks to the Kaiser's charm of manner, the dignity of his appearances in various fine uniforms, his receptivity to new ideals, even his sense of humour. But the emperor 'had an acute, if perverted, sense of history' ('mystic medievalism');[6] was over-impressed by the doctrine of divine right; enjoyed too strenuously the life of a 'bagman' who worshipped the power of money; and loved the pageantry of war without understanding its practical meaning. He was a disaster for his country, because once the pilot had been dropped, there was no strong chancellor to direct his energies to worthy ends. Buchan saw comparable problems in the ascendancy of the squirearchy of Prussia, the army chiefs and the new kings of trade, the industrial magnates. To them had fallen 'the kingdoms of the earth . . . and, like Jeshurun, they waxed fat and kicked'.[7]

Buchan's *History* was crowded with sharply observed details, a strong sense of the incompatible impulses within men that had led to an international tragedy, and a powerful faith in the usefulness of maps, statistics, battle orders and printed records. But he never entertained a doubt in its pages that the war had been right and necessary. He bore personal losses bravely, reserving his eulogies for Tommy Nelson, Jack Wortley, Raymond Asquith, Bron Lucas, Basil Blackwood and others in two separate volumes, *These for Remembrance* (Medici Society, Chiswick Press, 1919), and *Francis and Riversdale Grenfell* (Thomas Nelson, 1920). Buchan assessed correctly the importance of America's entry into the war; he repudiated the notion that the German civilians had lost the war which the soldiers could have won ('the High Command were themselves the principal architects of their country's defeat'[8]); looking back on it, Buchan saw clearly that it had been a war of nations rather than governments, demanding 'the sustained endurance of every class in the community'; and his summing-up of what had been gained and lost as a consequence of the waging of the war was poignant, and rang true.

'The sacrifice was chiefly of innocence and youth', said Buchan, 'and in computing it there can be no distinction between friend and enemy.'[9] He believed, with great magnanimity of spirit, that most men who fell died 'for honourable things', and these included love of country and home, comradeship, loyalty to manly virtues, the indomitable questing of youth. But the final message – despite his awareness of the horrors of No Man's Land and elsewhere – was romantically determined to see a greater hope for the coming day than he could possibly have believed in more than three years after the Armistice:

> Innocence does not perish in vain, against such a spirit the gates of death cannot prevail, and the endurance of their work is more certain than the coming of spring. The world is poor indeed without them, for they were the flower of their race, the straightest of limb, the keenest of brain, the most eager of spirit. . . . Yet to look back upon the gallant procession of those who offered their all and had the gift accepted, is to know exultation as well as sorrow. The youth which died almost before it had gazed on the world, the poets with their songs unsung, the makers and the doers who left their tasks unfinished, found immortal achievement in their death. Their memory will abide so long as men are found to set honour before ease, and a nation lives not for its ledgers alone but for some purpose of virtue. They have become, in the fancy of Henry Vaughan, the shining spires of that city to which we travel.[10]

It is impossible to argue that Buchan's perspective was objective, or even realistic, since the peroration of his lucid, heroically proportioned *History* grew from a conviction that all the follies, mistakes and millions of deaths were somehow justified by a better world that had not yet come into being. However, one should point out that his optimistic rhetoric is consistent with the tone of the novel *Greenmantle*, published by Hodder and Stoughton in 1916. Its background, Germany and the Middle East, was as carefully drawn as the scenes of the 'high heathery mountains' of Scotland in *The Thirty-Nine Steps*. Buchan's forays through the bazaars of Constantinople in the spring of 1910, which he thought of as 'pure Arabian Nights', mixed with impressions of young Turks, conversations with the Sultan's brother as well as British Embassy officials, rug-bartering and his enjoyment of Turkish delight (Buchan's wife, Susan, remembered with pleasure how 'beautifully clean Turks slapped and manipulated a glutinous substance' into its final, miraculous transformation[11]). These memories had been stored away for future reference during a yachting cruise aboard the *Rannoch*, owned by a friend Gerard Craig-Sellar. Though the novel had a 'gipsy begetting', in Buchan's own phrase, and though it was written 'in every kind of odd place and moment', its topography continues to impress generations of readers as authentic.

The novel – twice as long as *The Thirty-Nine Steps* – began with Hannay at a country house in Hampshire, where he was convalescing after hard-fought battles at Loos. The Western Front, though it played no role in the ensuing narrative, was described unsentimentally. Hannay as a soldier had performed heroically, but he hated his job: preventing his subalterns from 'going to glory'. The battlefront, he admitted, was both 'glorious and bloody', and he saw some purpose in the relentless grinding-down of troops on both sides of No Man's Land.

London, to which Hannay travelled in response to a telegram from Bullivant (director of intelligence operations in *The Thirty-Nine Steps*), was dreadfully remote from the real action:

> It seems to have lost its bearings and broken out into all manner of badges and uniforms . . . . One felt the war more in its streets than in the field, or rather one felt the confusion of war without feeling the purpose. I dare say it was all right; but since August 1914 I never spent a day in town without coming home depressed to my boots.

Much of this information was put to good use in *Greenmantle*, and what he had seen of large stretches of European landscape before the war underpinned his guess as to what a wartime journey on a Berlin-bound train might be like:

> I could see from the window the lights of little villages, and now and then the blaze of ironworks and forges . . . . As we went eastward the lighting seemed to grow more generous. After the murk of London it was queer to slip through garish stations with a hundred arc lights glowing, and to see long lines of lamps running to the horizon.

The descriptions of a hunting lodge, a German river steamer followed by six barges and the Golden Horn ('a lot of moth-eaten barges and some queer little boats like gondolas', and Turks who looked like 'London old-clothes men'), were all authentic-sounding.

The Cossack charge that captured Erzurum, in one of the great set battles of the Near East campaign, must have seemed to Buchan to be, in its own way, a celebration of courage that allowed room for individual initiative. Nevertheless, *Greenmantle* did not deal with trench warfare. Buchan's narrative allowed room for movement. The novel took full advantage of an opportunity to explore more than half of Europe, as well as a respectable fraction of Asia.

Moreover, *Greenmantle* benefited from Buchan's developing skills in fictionalising the traits of real people. General von Einem was the name of a real German, printed in a dispatch to *The Times*; hence the name of Hilda von Einem, that diabolical deviser of the whole scheme of a Moslem uprising inspired by the German-directed fanaticism of a leader named Greenmantle. Hannay himself had been drawn from life, from a man named Edmund Ironside (later a field-marshal); Hannay's South African background proved more important to *Greenmantle* than to *The Thirty-Nine Steps*, for on several occasions Hannay talked the language of the Boers in order to deceive his German hosts, and the memory of the veld and of veld-craft turned out to be important in several plot developments. Aubrey Herbert was the original of Sandy Arbuthnot, one of Hannay's confederates. Herbert, a contemporary of his at Balliol (Buchan attended Brasenose), had travelled much more widely than he; Herbert's real-life exploits made romantic fiction seem drab. Sandy, in the words of one biographer, was 'one of the best documented, as well as one of the least probable, of Buchan's creations'.[12] Blenkiron was a composite picture of various American businessmen and journalists who encountered Buchan both before and during the war. The fact that Blenkiron was warm-hearted and wholly admirable testified to Buchan's lifelong love of Americans. As Blenkiron said when explaining to Hannay his reasons for being in Europe at a time when his country was supposedly neutral:

> 'I have counted myself out of the bloodshed business, but, as your poet sings, peace has its victories not less renowned than war, and I reckon that means that a nootral can have a share in a scrap as well as a belligerent.'
> 'That's the best kind of neutrality I've ever heard of,' I said.
> 'It's the right kind,' he replied solemnly.

Peter Pienaar was the kind of man with whom Hannay could do business; indeed, trust with his life. Buchan had met many likeable Boers when he had visited South Africa shortly before the end of the Boer War (1901–3), when he was acting on a commission from L. S. Amery. Buchan was sketching his small army of characters on the basis of closer personal observation than he had felt free to do in Hannay's first adventure. His 'missionaries' rang true as a consequence.

The restless surging from one locale to the next prevented detailed individualisation of more than a few characters, however. The most provocative of all the characterisations was that of the Kaiser, who interviewed the disguised Hannay, presumably on his way to the Near East to serve the German Empire. Sir Walter Scott had introduced genuine historical figures in minor roles to authenticate the settings and bestow the necessary grace for solving otherwise impossible human problems. Close to Buchan's time was Émile Zola, who had presented a burned-out, pathetic Napoleon III in *La Débâcle*, which dealt with the humiliating defeat suffered by France in 1871. The French emperor could not wrest a victory from the dilemma created by his misguided policies; Zola's startling achievement lay in the authenticity of his suggestion that, at some late stage of war, events passed beyond human control. Those presumably in command – and, more specifically, Napoleon III, who had eagerly anticipated the opportunity to lead French troops towards an easy victory and glory – found themselves haunted by the same problems that confronted ordinary foot-soldiers. Similarly, Buchan drew the Kaiser as a dynast who had finally realised the probability of failure. Like the French emperor, Kaiser Wilhelm had been a jingo, and had encouraged his all-too-willing general staff to plan a war that would lay waste large areas of Europe. By 1916 the fruits of easy victory, still hanging on the bough, had turned to ashes. 'Below the helmet was a face the colour of grey paper', Hannay noted, 'from which shone curious sombre restless eyes with dark pouches beneath them.' The Kaiser was swift to denounce the English as a traitorous race: 'Some Englishman once said that he would call in the New World to redress the balance of the Old. We Germans will summon the whole earth to suppress the infamies of England.' Yet Buchan also saw him as a man tormented. 'I did not seek the war', he told a startled Hannay.

> It was forced on me.... I laboured for peace.... The blood of millions is on the heads of England and Russia, but England most of all. God will yet avenge it. He that takes the sword will perish by the sword. Mine was forced from the scabbard in self-defence, and I am guiltless.

The Kaiser resembled Thomas Hardy's Napoleon, in the wood of Bossu after the defeat at Waterloo, when he became most aware of the working of the Immanent Will (*The Dynasts*, III, VII, IX). Indeed, Hannay observed at one point that the Kaiser's features were better known to the world than those of any man since Napoleon. But his most striking comment was an afterword, when the Kaiser departed for his own destination:

> The last I saw of him was a figure moving like a sleep-walker, with no spring in his step, amid his tall suite. I felt I was looking on at a far bigger tragedy than any I had seen in action. Here was one that had loosed Hell, and the furies of Hell had got hold of him.

Hannay escaped from the archetypal German officer Stumm in one of the more harrowing passages of the novel. This heroic exertion was followed by great pain and a debilitating illness that required an extended stay in the garret bed of a poor German woman. Her husband was fighting on the Eastern Front; she might never hear from him again. 'The struggle meant little to her', Hannay discovered. 'It was an act of God, a thunderbolt out of the sky, which had taken a husband from her, and might soon make her a widow and her children fatherless. She knew nothing of its causes and purposes.' Buchan went beyond any casual assumption, harboured by those who believed in the righteousness of the reasons for their fighting, that an entire population would have to be punished once the fighting had ended. When Hannay reflected on the probability that the peasant-woman did not want to entertain bitterness against the Russians, and only wanted them to spare her man, he realised 'the crazy folly of war'. Hannay had been to Ypres; he had heard 'hideous tales of German doings', and he 'used to want to see the whole land of the Boche given up to fire and sword'. Now, however, he understood that the civilian population deserved better than that:

> that woodcutter's cottage cured me of such nightmares. I was punishing the guilty but letting the innocent go free. It was our business to thank God and keep our hands clean from the ugly blunders to which Germany's madness had driven her. What good would it do Christian folk to burn poor little huts like this and leave children's bodies by the wayside? To be able to laugh and to be merciful are the only things that make man better than the beasts.

This deepening note of compassion redeemed the melodrama of any number of scenes (such as the fist-fight in which the heavily disadvantaged Hannay defeated the murderous Stumm). An engineer could transcend national boundaries. Hannay's 'good hours' work' for Captain Schenk, carried on in the engine-room of an Essen barge, was the kind of professionalism which Kipling and Conrad, in such fictions as 'The ship that found herself' and *Lord Jim*, respected as earning a man the right to travel anywhere, and to be recognised as a brother. *Greenmantle* was filled with a love for life, an enlightened view of morality (Buchan had been brought up to respect the humane side of Presbyterian doctrine) and an eagerness to identify just reasons for sympathising with the poor.

Buchan failed to create a single convincing woman character in either of his wartime novels. Hilda von Einem, with her 'strange potent eyes' that resembled 'a burning searchlight which showed up every cranny and crack of the soul', conjured up for Hannay a vision of 'one of the old gods looking down on human nature from a great height, a figure disdainful and passionless, but with its own magnificence'. The sight of Hilda kindled Hannay's imagination; but the readers of *Greenmantle* had met this creature before, in the fiction of Rider Haggard and W. H. Hudson. The passions of a woman with bright hair and an exquisite oval face led to an extraordinary series of scenes in the *castrol* ('a rough circle about ten yards in diameter, its interior filled with boulders and loose stones, and its parapet about four feet high') near Erzurum. Buchan clearly recognised the impossibility of rendering justice to Hilda's personality. As Hannay mused:

> I had never before thought of her as beautiful. Strange, uncanny, wonderful, if you like, but the word beauty had too kindly and human a sound for such a face. But as she stood with heightened colour, her eyes like stars, her poise like a wild bird's, I had to confess that she had her own loveliness. She might be a devil, but she was also a queen.

Of all the novels dealing with wartime conditions prior to the publication of *All Quiet on the Western Front*, *Greenmantle*, despite its exotic flavouring and its remoteness from the main theatres of action on the Continent, may have lasted best. Hannay's sense of duty was more complicated, and troubled, than that of countless fictional soldiers sent out on impossible missions. While the emphasis on Hannay's exploits in *The Thirty-Nine Steps* created a closed and even solipsistic universe, in which Hannay had little time to think of any save himself, or of how to engineer his new escape, *Greenmantle* offered readers a large and varied case of fellow sufferers (or fellow adventurers) along with Hannay. Rather surprisingly, but refreshingly new as a matter of technique, Peter Pienaar told, in the third person, his adventures in going 'to the wars'. The flashback sequence filled in several details crucial to the plot, otherwise unknown to Hannay at the time the events occurred. *Greenmantle* also paid its respects to the urgency of religious impulses – the Islamic notion of Holy War, for instance, with which Hannay had little sympathy or even understanding, and which he found far removed from the quiet services of the Church of Scotland or the Church of England. The novel was a superior example of war fiction that entertained even while it informed a stay-at-home audience about the courage of determined Englishmen far from home.

Chapter 16

H. G. Wells's *Mr. Britling Sees It Through* (1916)

To be reminded of the fate of a best-seller closely tied in subject-matter and perspective to contemporary events is useful at this point. Those who urge novelists to concern themselves with the headlines of the day need only look at the decline in critical approval of one of the most popular novels in the early part of this century, *Mr. Britling Sees It Through*.

It helped to re-establish the flagging reputation of its author, H. G. Wells. When the Great War began, Wells, with £20,000 to his name, was a reasonably wealthy man (the pound sterling had a purchasing power in 1914 at least eight times that of the pound in the 1990s); but he was a prodigal spender, too, investing recklessly in pleasure, real estate and his determination to keep up with current fashions and much richer party-givers in the near vicinity of Easton Glebe, Essex, his newly acquired home. By the end of 1915 his 'fortune' had dwindled to £5,000.

Cassells, a publisher that treated *Mr. Britling Sees It Through* gingerly at first, brought it out in September 1916. Its success was immediate, and startlingly so. Within three months it had been reprinted eight times; by the year's end, thirteen times. Translations (French, Russian and German) were rapidly prepared, and several cheap editions came out with Wells's blessing. The fact that 38,000 copies had been sold by Cassells persuaded Ernest Benn to pay Wells £3,000 down for a new manuscript, and an astonishing 27½ per cent royalty for another six books (Benn wound up some £5,000 in the red after all the profits and losses had been reckoned).[1] Anthony West is the authority for the statistic that within eighteen months Wells earned from *Mr. Britling* some £50,000, and Wells has told us that some £20,000 of that came from the United States.[2] The royalties amounted to a small fortune, and, of course, the success of this wartime novel ended the dry Fabian-dominated phase of his career. The lasting success of his relaunch of a flagging career – Wells as populariser of the new sciences, of *all* the sciences, as a master narrator – was ensured by the publication of *The Outline of History* in 1920.

Mr. Britling Sees It Through was clearly autobiographical, though only a few of the elements taken from Wells's own life need to be identified here. Two sisters were described as attractive, witty and young; they are named Cecily and Letty; these are the names of 'Rebecca West' – a pseudonym for Cecily Isabel Fairfield – and her sister Letitia. (Wells sometimes was very lazy about changing the names of minor characters from the names of their originals.) There were the countless references to well-known historical figures, perhaps most strikingly the Kaiser, Lloyd George, Bernard Shaw and Winston Churchill. Lady Homartyn was patterned after the former mistress of Edward vii, the Countess of Warwick, on the edge of whose estate Easton Glebe had been built. Kurt Bütow, tutor to the Wells children, was used as the partial inspiration for the Herr Heinrich who went off to war and died on the Eastern Front. Mrs Harrowdean was best seen as a fictional treatment of Elizabeth von Arnim, an author, a writer of passionate letters of love and abuse and (by 1916) a former sweetheart. Edgar Wilkins (Book ii, 'Matching's Easy at war: Taking part'), who proposed a 'tremendous scheme for universal volunteering', may be found in *Ann Veronica* and *The New Machiavelli* as a comic counterpart of Wells, who on occasion could back off and see himself as a slightly ludicrous writer given to hyperbole and unseemly enthusiasms.[3]

Easton Glebe did not change significantly when it turned into Matching's Easy. It had the same general dimensions. On its lawn the guests played an exhaustingly strenuous version of hockey. Wells, like Britling, enjoyed bullying his company into organising dances. The plain Jane who found herself unable to satisfy Wells's sexual needs was recreated here as the pathetic, and finally tragic, figure of Mrs Edith Britling – the second wife who could only fall short of Mr Britling's first wife, the splendidly loving and self-sacrificing Mary, who had died prematurely.

Nevertheless, some facts were changed and some characters invented. Mr Direck, the American visitor to Matching's Easy, was a cartoonish picture of Yankee tourists with intellectual pretensions, not clearly based on any of Wells's American acquaintances; the religious conversion which overtook Britling was much more extreme than any transformation of religious belief experienced by Wells; and Wells's two sons, too young to fight in the war, were patently not the basis of the characterisation of Hugh Britling, the son who died in the trenches.

Yet, overall, this book will be best remembered as a charting of Wells's own shifts of attitude towards 'the war that will end war' (the title of a small book written by Wells, and published at a cheap price in 1914). If at its beginning the novel seemed to deal with ordinary events in that long Edwardian summer, moving slowly for more than 100 pages, a novelist's defence must be that the world seemed to be much the same for most of 1914, and any revolutionary change in its status must have seemed unthinkable to ordinary English men and women. One had the opportunity to act on the assumption that tomorrow would be much like today. Wells certainly believed in the growing democratisation of world societies, in a steady improvement in liberal and humane sentiments. He knew that huge problems existed, but in the novel these seem to be largely restricted to the incapacities of public statesmen, whose identities would inevitably change, thus affording room for hope that the new holders of public office would improve the moral and ethical atmosphere of England. The most pressing issue of a political nature seems to have been the centuries-old Irish question, which had already brought down more than one prime minister. Germany, because of family ties with the British queen, was talked about more as a naughty neighbour than as an Empire-threatening rival.

So far as its literary structure is concerned, *Mr. Britling Sees It Through* was not very much of a novel, despite its marvellous timeliness and its self-assured treatment of important themes. The title, for one thing, suggested that it covered more of the war than simply a single year (it ended in October 1915), and its proposed solution to the problems of Britling's family tragedy – an increase in religiosity, a reaching-out to the enemy, a faith in a League of Nations, a United States of the World – was never very convincing, despite a reader's deepest wish to acquiesce.[4] Moreover, the opening chapters made much of Mr Direck, who served as secretary to the Massachusetts

Society for the Study of Contemporary Thought (he was 'rather underworked and rather over-salaried'). He came to Essex on the branch line of 'the little old Great Eastern Railway' in order to invite Mr Britling to give a lecture in the United States. Mr Direck never seemed to follow through on his assigned responsibility; we never learn whether Mr Britling was disposed to act favourably on the invitation: and attention was soon distracted by the chaotically cheerful life at Matching's Easy, with weekend parties, casual visitations and intense conversations about an astonishingly wide variety of topics. Mr Direck fell in love with Cecily and that, too, received considerable attention and space.

Eventually his romance was submerged by a rushing flood of other events. Mr Britling, who began as a caricature of Wells, unstoppable as a talker, a reckless and incompetent driver of a newfangled automobile and an essayist whose plush life-style seemed to be due more to a wealthy patron's largesse than to his own ability, turned into the dominant character, a serious man indeed, energetically concentrated on using his writing skills, concerned about his need to convert fellow countrymen to an awareness of their danger and their need for acting collectively. As the anonymous reviewer in the *Times Literary Supplement* remarked,

> it is easy to see that Mr. Wells himself has never written a novel more shapeless and wasteful than this. He starts a score of people and lavishes all his art on them, only to drop them, forget them, pick a few of them up spasmodically again, and drop them once more, as the tide of his dissertation gathers and spreads.[5]

Hugh, the adolescent who lied about his age in order to enter the army as a private, became the major link between his father and the horrid realities of trench warfare. But Hugh was not important for well over half the novel, and his father referred to him somewhat brutally as being, at the age of seventeen, 'juvenile, doing a juvenile share, no sort of man yet'.

Hugh Britling Senior was so egocentric that he would not willingly yield place to anyone else's perspective – he would not credit the possibility of war with Germany, or (once the war began) of a protracted war, or of any one of a vast number of possibilities that, in the inevitable fashion of the history that shaped us all, came true. He could not foresee that his son would become a man under the pressures of war. He was not ready for almost anything that would happen to himself or to others. He was more fatuous about himself, his family, his affair with Mrs Harrowdean and his nation than he understood. Because he spoke so directly for Wells, for a whole generation of well-intentioned Englishmen, he was more blandly inane about a host of topics than Wells appreciated.

Hugh's perspective should have been treated earlier, and with more respect: what did *Hugh* think about Sarajevo, about the flurry of war declarations, about his generation of public-school students? If the reader of 1916 was intended to appreciate fully his maturation into the prototypical hero who died for England, he needed more information about how Hugh became transformed; and for that matter, what he was like before the metamorphosis took place.

Such an emphasis would have made Hugh a major character at the expense of the considerable fun that was poked (rather unfairly) at an American do-gooder; it would have reduced Mr Britling's maunderings about the reasons why he was repeatedly unfaithful to his wife; and it might have created space for a more detailed and circumstantial treatment of the family relationships that Wells evidently intended to present as a microcosm of English society. It would also have lessened the reliance, in the last third of the novel, on letters: both those of the young soldier who was hardening under the hammer-blows of his military service and the lengthy message that Mr Britling composed for the benefit of the family of Herr Heinrich, more specifically Heinrich's father, who was assumed to be a German of good will, and who (presumably) would turn into the chief hope of a resurrected, more democratic Germany after the end of the war. (Herr Heinrich was tutor to Mr Britling's children.) A fuller treatment of Hugh would thus minimise the problems created by the changes associated with the development of an epistolary novel, namely, those created by a change in pacing; the sense that Hugh's voice was heard as if from the end of a tunnel; and the failure in imagination that gave us letters rather than dramatic scenes.

Richard Hauer Costa is not the only writer who makes an important point of the use of central intelligences in both Henry James and H. G. Wells, and who concedes the lessening interest of Wells in the private intelligence, 'central or otherwise', at the time of his break with James. Wells declared a truce 'between strategies of *action* and – increasingly vital to him – *reaction*. . . . Plausibility for Wells, in midcareer dialogue novels like *Mr. Britling*, is whatever enabled Britling to react – an orchestration *outward*.[6] This balanced tension between what Britling saw and heard, and what he thought, arises from the opposition of public and private selves. Much can be said on behalf of Costa's notion that the Wells hero 'must, as befits *his* creator, combine private and cosmic angst'.[7]

But that, in turn, presupposes that Wells thought of Britling as a public man who harboured a separate and secret private personality. After the ingratiating, even disarming opening chapters that depicted an Edwardian idyll at Matching's Easy, that distinction (if it ever was made by Wells) seemed to have been lost. Mr Britling (i.e., a 'little Briton') gave himself uncomplainingly to the cause of victory for England; he renounced Mrs Harrowdean (with some relief, because she had been hard on him, reminding him of romantic obligations that she insisted he must meet despite the existence of a wife). He wrote pamphlets and leaders for the press as well as letters that exhorted and proselytised, and he spoke on platforms to audiences that respected his wisdom and looked to him for guidance. He had no private or inner self. And when Hugh enlisted, it was as much for his father, who symbolised decency and middle-class concepts of honour in England, as for the nation which welcomed him into the service.

Britling's mind may have been chaotic with rushing and self-contradictory ideas (his 'cognitive dissonance'), and he may not have sorted out all the alternatives, or anticipated the full consequences of any of the courses of action he recommended so enthusiastically to his countrymen. But he was vividly alive, if not always credible, and one watched, as at a good show, the development of Wells's characterisation of a man who 'sniffed at the heels of reality', and who entertained ideas 'in the utmost profusion about races and empires and social order and political institutions and gardens and automobiles and the future of Indiana and China and aesthetics and America and the education of mankind in general'. Who could dislike a first-rate temperament that was 'always lively, sometimes spacious, and never vile'? The topics of his talk cascaded on the ears of each listener. 'He talked about everything, he had ideas about everything'. But there was no depth to him; he was what he seemed to be, neither more nor less. Moreover, those who lived by the newspapers – Britling read them, quoted them, wrote for them, and perhaps most disconcerting of all, believed them despite the lies he knew or suspected they were printing – would inevitably become their victim. '*Punch* was delicately funny about him; he was represented as wearing a preposterous cocked hat of his own design, designing cocked hats for every one.' And there were other indications that the nation's press found something risible about his strident campaigning for 'new ideas' and reformed standards of international behaviour.

Hugh was not the only individual who suffered from Wells's narcissistic love affair with Mr Britling. Surely no one respected the potentialities of the female intelligence more than Wells, or understood better that the phenomenon of the new woman would not go away in a few years. A reader's complaint against the sketchiness of the portrait of Edith Britling, for example, need not be based on any uneasiness about Wells's scorn of the homemaker type. Wells did not scorn Edith. The generosity with which Wells conceded Edith's virtues – her calmness, her steadiness, her pride in her husband's achievements, 'her consistent honourableness' – was genuine enough. All of this, however, did not convincingly explain the reasons why her husband tired of her so quickly, beginning with chess games that first revealed 'extensive difficulties of sympathy', because they invariably ended in defeat (games of chess 'led to such dreadful fits of anger that he had to renounce the game altogether'). Even less did it justify her husband's dreadful philandering. The problem, again, was novelistic: Wells simply did not see the world from Edith's point of view even for the length of a single conversation.

Edith was just as much Hugh's mother as Mr Britling was his father. We would like to know how she responded to Hugh's succumbing to war hysteria (so persistently pushed along by her husband's propaganda); what she thought of Hugh's joining up, beyond the hackneyed response of a mother simultaneously glad for her country's sake and fearful for her son's personal safety; and whether her thoughts on reading his letters from the front coincided with the emotional impressions and mercurial responses of her husband. Wells paid serious attention to every emotion and thought of Mr Britling. The second half of the novel showed Mr Britling changing in accordance with developments in wartime strategy. He reordered his priorities, rethought his prejudices, etc. Each dawn new headlines were printed; these allowed – nay, encouraged – him to remake his opinions. An individual opinion might not have mattered (though, taken as a whole, Mr Britling's opinions were roughly consistent). But Wells lacked any real interest in conceding Edith the right to change, too.

When Hugh died, or – more precisely speaking – when the telegram announcing his death came to the Britlings, the story reached a point where Hugh's parents might well become reconciled because of their sorrow, or reach a moment of realisation that their paths through life had permanently diverged. Hugh's death should have changed both his parents, who, we have been told many times, loved him dearly. The emphasis, however, fell on Mr Britling's reaction to the telegram. 'He read the final, unqualified statement, the terse regrets. He stood quite still for a moment or so, staring at the words'. When he saw his wife coming down the alley between the roses, he was

> wrenched by emotions as odd and unaccountable as the emotions of adolescence. He had exactly the same feeling now that he had had when in his boyhood some unpleasant admission had to be made to his parents. He felt he could not go through a scene with her yet, that he could not endure the task of telling her, of being observed. He turned abruptly to his left. He walked away as if he had not seen her, across his lawn towards the little summer-house upon a knoll that commanded the high road. She called to him, but he did not answer.

He worried whether she was following him. 'Safe in the summer-house he could glance back', and then, amazingly, he thought, 'It was all right. She was going into the house.'

Inevitably, she learned of Hugh's death, and her instinct was to wonder what she could say to her husband. (Nothing Mr Britling did since he received the telegram indicated that he had worried about what he should say to Edith.) Edith's desire to comfort her husband battered down her 'timidity, her self-criticism, her deeply ingrained habit of never letting herself go'. Her compassion for the stricken animal that her husband had become pushed to the back of her mind any thought of Hugh. She came forward to him, late at night, while he brooded by the fire: 'It is so dreadful for you', she said, 'it is so dreadful for you. I know how you loved him'. But she could not reach him. She knew she was failing in her effort. If her husband momentarily reassured her to 'make her feel that she was of value to him', that was not his major thought at the moment; rather, if it were not for Edith, he thought that he could kill himself. (What did he think Edith might do? Or did he think that it did not matter what Edith thought?) At any rate, when she did leave him, he closed the door softly behind her, and, at that instant, he forgot her: 'Instantly he was alone again, utterly alone. He was alone in an empty world.'

This scene was widely praised in 1916. Reviewers were much taken with Wells's description of Mr Britling's nocturnal walk, alone in the world despite the 'troublesome noise of night-jars and a distant roaring of stags, black trees, blacknesses, the sky clear and remote with a great company of stars.' Mr Britling suddenly felt that 'his boy was all about him, playing, climbing the cedars, twisting miraculously about the lawn on a bicycle, discoursing gravely upon his future, lying on the grass, breathing very hard and drawing preposterous caricatures'. Mr Britling addressed his son directly: 'I will work to-morrow again, but to-night – to-night . . . . To-night is yours . . . . Can you hear me, can you hear? Your father . . . who had counted on you'. Then he made his way to the seat in the arbour and became 'very still with his arm upon the back of the seat and his head upon his arm.' One can wonder whether the sentimentality of the scene went over the edge, even as the impact of its raw emotionalism, comforting thousands of Wells's readers at the midpoint of the Great War, may be felt.[8] But the solipsism of Mr Britling's repsonse is not in question, for it is complete and, in its completeness, oblivious to the missed opportunity to imagine Edith's point of view as having value, or even of being *there*.

After that evening of shocked and self-imposed solitude Mr Britling grew into a new, more optimistic state of mind. He told Letty (who was overwhelmed by the supposed confirmation of the death of her husband Teddy, Mr Britling's secretary) that he was neither angry nor depressed. He choked and put his face between his hands, shuddered and became still. The average reader must be as astonished as Letty by what Mr Britling says next:

> The only possible government in Albania is a group of republican cantons after the Swiss pattern. I can see no other solution that is not offensive to God. It does not matter in the least what we owe to Serbia or what we owe to Italy. We have got to set this world on a different footing. We have got to set up the world at last – on justice and reason.

Wells, who did not believe that the war could possibly last beyond 1916, was expressing his faith in a Supreme Being. God, as Mr Britling conceived him, was fallible, finite and struggling to succeed 'in his great and comprehensive way as we struggle in our weak and silly way – who is *with* us – that is the essence of all real religion.'

Mr Britling's religion was not Christian, or recognisably anything else; it was hyperbolically framed, just as his prescription for a post-war Albania was 'the only possible' solution, just as what he recommended for the nations of the world was something 'we have got' to do. Those who believed otherwise had 'silly absolute ideas', and if they worshipped God as 'the maker of Heaven and Earth' (Letty's phrase), Mr Britling saw through them and their 'Quack God', their 'Panacea'. 'I see it so plain', he said, 'that I am amazed that I have not always seen it. . . . But it's so plain to me.'

Religiosity did not shake Mr Britling's conviction that Germany's arrogance had been responsible for the war. Later, he would write to Heinrich's father to that effect. Germany, in the decade that ended with its defeat of France in 1871, 'turned her face towards evil', refused to treat France generously and shook off friendship with other great powers. But Mr Britling was dissatisfied with the dryness and generalness of what he wrote (both in his essay 'of preposterous ambitions', which was entitled 'The better government of the world', and in his letter to Heinrich's family in Pomerania). A new, strange, overpowering conviction interrupted his thoughts.

> Never had it been so plain to Mr. Britling that he was a weak, silly, ill-informed and hasty-minded writer, and never had he felt so invincible a conviction that the Spirit of God was in him. . . . And for the first time clearly he felt a Presence of which he had thought very many times in the last few weeks, a Presence so close to him that it was behind his eyes and in his brain and hands. It was no trick of his vision; it was a feeling of immediate reality. . . . It was as if he had been groping all this time in the darkness, thinking himself alone amidst rocks and pitfalls and pitiless things, and suddenly a hand, a firm strong hand, had touched his own. And a voice within him bade him be of good courage. There was no magic trickery in that moment; he was still weak and weary, a discouraged rhetorician, a good intention ill-equipped; but he was no longer lonely and wretched, no longer in the same world with despair. God was beside him and within him and about him.

The revelation was the 'crucial moment' of his life. Mr Britling now understood that 'the King was coming to his own'.

Hugh had shown God to Mr Britling; his son had been a means whereby Mr Britling found God within himself; and from here on he would seek to establish the World Republic because he was in God's service. As a vision, perhaps this was neither better nor worse than comparable moments of revelation in the novels of Lloyd C. Douglas or A. J. Cronin; it was certainly more agreeable than Letty's desire to murder Germans six months after the war as revenge for her husband's death ('by a campaign of pursuit and assassination that will go on for years and years after the war itself is over'), and it hardly would be reasonable to expect a Wellsian hero to settle down in numb apathy for very long after the loss of a much-loved son. Still, the vagueness of this particular solution, the nebulousness of Mr Britling's God, and the rock-hard certainty that this was the best, and in fact the one feasible, solution to the emotional turmoil caused by mass slaughters on the Western Front, implied a great deal about Mr Britling's conversion. Mr Britling was bound to change his mind again, and still again, as the newspaper headlines changed; his hallmark was a disconcerting volatility; his receptivity to new ideas meant, most of all, that no old ideas were sacrosanct, including his own. As Sidney Dark wrote,

> Wells's God is his own God. . . . It would be untrue to suggest that the war convinced the mass of the people of England, or of any other country, of the need of God. In this respect Wells cannot be taken as typical of his nation. His fellows shared his bewilderment but a very few of them shared his discovery. That is what always happens.[9]

(Dark wrote these lines in 1922.)

Hence, *Mr. Britling Sees It Through* was a war novel because it dealt with the experiences of a middle-aged writer on the home front during a stupendous conflict between European powers. It came off the press right in the midst of raging battles that had no certain or predestined outcome. Its enthusiastic reception by the book-buying public certified the truth of the statement that it struck deep chords during an emotion-laden moment of English history. And yet it was an odd performance, and in some ways not a novel at all. It was less a book about England's entering into Gethsemane than about H. G. Wells moving around frenetically at the centre of the universe. Anatole France once began a book by saying that he intended to write about himself concerning Shakespeare. Wells doubtless planned at first to define his relationship to the Great War by describing a large house in Essex, populating it with characters based on people he knew and retracing the evolution of the war month by month. But as the novel developed, Wells became more important than the war in *Mr. Britling Sees It Through*, and all the characters served to illustrate his reasons for believing thus and so, or changing his reasons for believing. He sketched the sombre spectacle of his movement from grief for young friends killed in combat (like Ben Keeling, the Fabian at Cambridge University whom he greatly admired) to his experiencing the presence of God. It must have been difficult for most readers to object at the time. In mid-war it was much more difficult to discern the true subject-matter of *Mr. Britling Sees It*

Through, and doubtless it would have been futile for reviewers to nag about the egocentricity of the fiction. An air of good-humoured innocence pervaded every page. 'If it happened this way', Wells seemed to be saying, 'and more important, if it happened this way to *me*, it is bound to interest *you*, my readers.' And so, in 1916, it did.

On the occasion of its reissue by the Hogarth Press in 1985, Christopher Priest, in an Introduction, noted that the novel had been unavailable for years, outside libraries and second-hand shops. Any reception study of the sales of Wells's books would have to correlate his declining royalties after the Second World War with the steady fall in reputation of any number of other Edwardian gurus, like Arnold Bennett, George Bernard Shaw, John Galsworthy and Beatrice and Sidney Webb.

It may be that 'Wells shares are rising on the stock exchange: slowly, perhaps, but rising', as a recent biographer says ('He still speaks to us all – and a Wellsian world awaits, as it has always done, for those who are willing to use their brains and their will').[10] But it is easier now to appreciate the comic elements of *Mr. Britling Sees It Through* – the ludicrous efforts of Mr Britling to drive a recalcitrant automobile, Mr Direck's unavailing efforts to break in on Mr Britling's non-stop lecture–monologue, the endearing stiffness of the German tutor Herr Heinrich, the dressing-up in bright costumes for a vividly described dance, the extraordinary hockey game at the Dower House at Matching's Easy, Mr Direck's clumsy courtship of Cecily Corner – all of which are recorded in the first third of the novel. It is also possible to build, in the mind's eye, the personality of Hugh as it unfolds in letter after letter written from training camp and from the Front, and to admire Hugh as an individual rather than as an Englishman of the upper middle class (no mean achievement in a frankly didactic novel). And we must not underestimate the portrayal of Mr Britling himself, a thinly disguised portrayal of an aging author who now used the novel for ulterior motives only fitfully connected with the reasons that had lain behind his writing of scientific romances, short stories and serious novels between 1895 and 1910. In this novel, however, Wells's diagnosis of what went wrong in our time will not convince many. His suggested solution, a religious awakening to the reality of the God within, will convince even fewer readers at the end of the twentieth century. But his earnestness, his idealism and his ferocious energy in trying to do what was right, and to convince others that it was right, remain impressive.

Chapter 17

On the home front: Arnold Bennett's *The Pretty Lady* (1918)

Arnold Bennett's patriotic support of the English cause found expression in a *War Journal 1914–1918*; a weekly series of articles for the *London Daily News* (earning at first £21 per essay, and later £37); a series of 'Observations' for the *New Statesman*; still another series for *Lloyd's Weekly Newspaper*; a pamphlet entitled *Liberty! A statement of the British case* (1914); and a series of five articles for the *Illustrated London News* and the *Saturday Evening Post* that Bennett subsequently reprinted in book form (he added a sixth essay), entitled *Over There: War scenes on the Western Front* (1915). It was possible, he admitted, that Russia rather than Germany may have been the real enemy, and that England's initial belligerency may have been a mistake. But, despite his conviction that war was hell (he was quoting the American aphorism), and idiotic to boot, he never wavered in his public championing of the declaration of war by his government. 'We don't want to argue about it', he wrote in *Liberty!*

> And we are fighting about it.... We are convinced that our new ideal is a finer one than the ideal of the German military caste, that the two ideals cannot flourish together, and therefore that one of them must go down. If Germany triumphs, her ideal (the word is seldom off her lips) will envelop the earth, and every race will have to kneel and whimper to her, 'Please, may I exist?' And slavery will be re-born.... We have a silly, sentimental, illogical objection to being enslaved. We reckon liberty – the right of every individual to call his soul his own – as the most glorious end. It is for liberty we are fighting. We have lived in alarm, and liberty has been jeopardized too long.[1]

He served as a military representative on the Thorpe Division

Emergency Committee and helped to plan a suitable defence against any German invasion of the east coast. He was deeply moved, shortly after the outbreak of war, by a meeting that had been called by C. F. G. Masterman, Chancellor of the Duchy of Lancaster; eminent authors were asked by Masterman to consider what they might do to further war aims, and clarify for the public what the government's principles amounted to. Like Thomas Hardy, G. K. Chesterton, H. G. Wells, Sir James Barrie, Sir Henry Newbolt, J. W. Mackail, G. M. Trevelyan, Anthony Hope Hawkins, John Masefield, Robert Bridges, Gilbert Murray, A. C. Benson and R. H. Benson and Sir Owen Seaman (all of whom were present), Bennett wanted to do the honourable thing, and to use his considerable talents as creative artist, journalist, literary critic and propagandist. In mid-1915 he went on a semi-official 25-day tour of the Western Front. Lord Beaverbrook was probably never more inspired in fitting a writer to a given task than when he asked Bennett to serve as Director of British Propaganda in France; less than six months later (September 1918) Bennett was appointed Director of Propaganda in the Ministry of Information.

These activities alone were more intense than the sum total of what he had been doing in the years immediately preceding Germany's invasion of Belgium. His work was complicated by increasing strains in his marriage to Marguerite Soulie (they would separate formally in October 1921). He was ill and suffered from fits of nervous exhaustion. He collected some of his published essays in two volumes. *Books and Persons: Being comments on a past epoch, 1808–1911* (1917) was a selection of the 'Books and persons' columns that he had written for Orage's *New Age* under the pen-name of Jacob Tonson. *Self and Self-Management: Essays about existing* (1918) devoted only one essay to his war work, or to a war issue. His yachting experiences aboard his 50-ton Dutch-built barge (Frank Swinnerton made it an important character in *Nocturne*) were recorded in a travel book, *From the Log of the 'Velsa'* (scrialised in the *Century Magazine*, 1914; published as a book in 1920). *The Lion's Share*, written for the *Strand Magazine*, was rejected by its editor for dealing with women's suffrage, a taboo subject; it proved an artistic and commercial disappointment. His agent, J. B. Pinker, had difficulty in placing it; the *Metropolitan Magazine* of New York finally published it (1915), and Cassell brought it out as a book late in 1916. Much more successful, though perhaps no more distinguished as literature, was Bennett's play *The Title* (1918). Its subject-matter – a man refuses a title, braving his wife's opposition, until he learns that an impostor will accept the title in his place (whereupon he accepts his nomination for the Honours List) – proved an embarrassment when, a few years later, Bennett was offered a knighthood for his war work; he felt obliged to refuse it.

What emerges clearly from a review of Bennett's war years is the substantial financial sacrifice that Bennett made in order to support the war effort. His topical writings paid only modest returns; his income fell sharply from the level he had enjoyed in the five years just before the war. He worked through several serious bouts of neuralgia, even barely controlled hysteria, before he found himself focusing his energies on the tasks that Lord Beaverbrook turned over to him – energies that were very inadequately recompensed by the government during the half-year that he served.[2]

His largest financial success came from the publication of *The Pretty Lady*, in April 1918. It was a novel about the home front, but it could not usefully be compared to *Mr. Britling Sees It Through*, a novel with idealism and hopes for a better tomorrow. Perhaps only Bennett would have dared to interpret the significance of the war from the perspectives of Christine, a French prostitute who had escaped to England early in the war; G. J. Hoape, a middle-aged bachelor who kept her as a mistress, but whose calculations for his own future happiness never included the thought of marrying her; Queenie, a high-living society woman who recklessly exposed herself to danger during an air-raid, and died as a consequence; and Concepcion, her friend, who narrowly escaped a nervous breakdown when she learned her husband had died at the Front, who then collapsed after working in a munitions factory, and who seriously contemplated suicide as a solution to all her problems. Even the barest summary of the episodic plot will identify these four lost souls as deeply unhappy people. Though they interacted throughout the novel, they were locked fast within their separate selves.

The Pretty Lady proved an immediate hit with the public, and went into a second edition within two weeks; it sold 17,500 copies within a month, and 30,000 by mid-September. Bennett had hoped not to shock the 'B.P.' (British public), but he could not have been completely surprised by the outcry from some quarters. The reviewer for the *Times Literary Supplement* wrote, with distaste, that portions of the novel were 'unpleasantly frank'. H. M. Richardson, in the *Sunday Chronicle* (14 April), attacked it as 'decadent, ignoble and corrupting . . . an abomination'. Though Hugh Walpole, George Moore and

Rebecca West admired it (and Lord Beaverbrook thought so well of it that he tendered Bennett the offer of the British Directorship of Propaganda in France), Bennett wrote that most of the reviews were 'specially footling', and added, with asperity, 'Astonishing the number of critics who daren't *mention* that the chief character is a whore!'[3] Booksellers in Cambridge and Bath boycotted it. Less than a month after publication W. H. Smith banned it from the stalls and libraries under its control. The honorary lay secretary of the Catholic Federation threatened to take action against Cassell because the novel contained passages that offended Catholics. This move was followed by another, from the Honorary Secretary for the Catholic Truth Society, who wrote (also in May) that *The Pretty Lady* dealt 'in the crudest way with subjects which it was not usual to present in a story intended for general circulation', and that Catholics took offence at the manner in which Bennett had treated matters connected with Catholicism. Bennett's nimble defence included the sending of a copy to the Attorney General, another copy to Lord Birkenhead and a ringing declaration to Cassell that he would not suppress or change any part of his novel; but he lived through some nervous moments before he realised that Cassell would support him fully.

Bennett wrote to George Doran, his American publisher (13 May), that he objected to the charges made against the novel.

> Some of the good reviews have said that it is decadent and cynical, and that it gives an entirely ruthless picture of heartless people in London. This is not so, and I particularly want you to note that the war has a good effect on the three principal characters, namely, Christine, Concepcion and G. J., all of whom do what they can. The book is emphatically not cynical. Nor does it portray heartless people, and I should like this to be insisted on.[4]

The Pretty Lady was an unusual performance for the Bennett who had written *Liberty!*; who exerted himself heroically on behalf of his nation, endangering his health, destabilising his standard of living and increasing the strains of his domestic arrangements. War, in this novel, was depicted with grim consistency as an ugly fact, both in itself and in its consequences. For one thing, the soldier befriended by Christine, the cocotte, was a young man who drank carelessly. His personality, so far as one could infer from his behaviour, was self-destructive; and he was destined to die in France. In one extraordinary scene, during a zeppelin raid, G. J. Hoape, looking for his walking stick, discovered the 'sole object of interest . . . a child's severed arm, with a fragment of brown frock on it and a tinsel ring on one of the fingers of the dirty little hand'.

In another, Nurse Smaith, reporting to the members of a committee who had the power to reimburse her for expenses incurred in helping the wounded and dying of a Serbian unit, spoke with 'the purity of a cockney accent undefiled by Continental experiences', and vividly described the horrors of the Front. She begged for her modest travel expenses with only limited prospects of success. Her plea led directly to Concepcion's violent outburst: 'Even if it is public funds, can't you give ninety-five francs in memory of those three saucepans?'

Concepcion, in still another scene, recounted the story of a factory girl, in the valley of the Clyde, who earned £2 a week ('nearly'); laughing, she threw back her head, got her hair entangled in the machine behind her, and had 'the whole of her scalp ripped clean off'.

Though Bennett had no occasion to describe the war experiences of soldiers at the front (his attention concentrated on the London scene), he also chose not to stress the exhilaration of even a single group of English men and women working together for a common set of goals. A sourness permeated the text, despite Bennett's disclaimer that his novel was 'emphatically not cynical'. In one extraordinary scene – Dickensian in detail, perhaps even in conception – G. J. Hoape passed through 'the cardiac region of St. James's' in order to arrive at his bootmaker, 'bearing a name famous from Peru to Hong Kong'. His left boot, of a new pair, was 'not quite comfortable on the toes'. The manager, appalled, swore to make things right for his patron: 'God in any case should not suffer.' To polish them, he conjured up, from a trap-door in the floor of the shop, a 'horrible, pallid, weak, cringing man', who knelt before G. J. even more submissively than the manager had knelt.

> He never looked up, never spoke. When he had made the boots like mirrors he gathered together his implements and vanished, silent and dutifully bent, through the trap-door back into the earth of St. James's. And because the trap-door had not shut properly the manager stamped on it and stamped down the pale man definitely into the darkness underneath. And then G. J. was wafted out of the shop with smiles and bows.

Bennett's sardonic style was well matched to his selection of useable materials, despite the comments of some critics who have seen in this particular anecdote a characteristic failure of the author to integrate his materials with an overarching vision. Bennett's indictment of the rottenness of the top strata of English society was not limited to a few such happenings.[5] A weightier censure might be based on a closer examination of G. J.'s final assessment of what the war was all about. The possibility was raised, on Bennett's penultimate page, that the war had sprung, 'not out of this crime or that, but out of the secret invisible roots of humanity', and that its spread 'defied conclusions and rendered equally impossible both hope and despair'. Pride and faith in England had not diminished as the months passed, despite the failure of the new Somme offensive in the north. 'Was victory possible? Was victory deserved?' G. J., like Bennett himself, had seen too many instances of 'official selfishness, folly, ignorance, stupidity, and sloth, French as well as British'. His conclusion proceeded to a logical destination:

> The supreme lesson of the war was its revelation of what human nature actually was. And the solace of that lesson, the hope for triumph, lay in the fact that human nature must be substantially the same throughout the world. If we were humanly imperfect, so at least was the enemy.

At this point in the narrative G. J. had a right to feel depressed. He misunderstood Christine's conversation with soldiers in Piccadilly, and he had cut her off permanently; Queenie had died, 'due to an extremely small piece of shrapnel which struck [her] head slightly above the left ear, entering her brain'; and Concepcion had told him of her plan to do away with herself. A reader might derive some small measure of satisfaction from G. J.'s desperate lunge at a more optimistic reading of the future (after all, his name was Hoape): 'Perhaps civilisation, by its nobility and its elements of reason, and by the favour of destiny, would be saved from disaster after frightful danger.' The stumbling-block to any innocent faith in what was yet to come lay in the word 'perhaps'. G. J.'s desire to see Concepcion as the symbol of what might be rescued could not be grounded on certainty; despite the promise of birth and renewal implicit in the very name of Concepcion, Bennett remained obstinately unwilling to reassure his reader that she would not, at some later time, commit suicide.

The Pretty Lady dealt not with the war itself, despite all the narrator's talk about Belgian atrocities, the confusion of refugees at Ostend, the dreariness of war factories and the terror of ordinary people in the streets of London as bombs fell, so much as with attitudes towards the war held by the supposed leaders of society. For example, Bennett did not think much of the members of the monumental Club to which G. J. belonged. They discussed manoeuvres at the Marne as if they constituted a game conducted solely for their reading pleasure; one elderly gentleman summed up his impressions:

> Obviously the centre of gravity is no longer in the West – it's in the East. In the West, roughly, equilibrium has been established. Hence Poland is the decisive field, and the measure of the Russian success or failure is the measure of the Allied success or failure.

Another said 'cheerfully' that the expense of the war – one million a day, with a doubling of the income tax – could not be borne indefinitely by the country, despite the fact that the only hope for England rested on the nation's being able to stand it indefinitely. Hence, there was no hope, 'at any rate for unbiased minds. Facts are facts, I fear.' These were the views of old men, but they were also the views of the nation's leaders. One had been offered the Press Bureau, and had turned it down because he would have had no real power, but 'unlimited quantities of responsibility'. Another, urged by the Lord Chancellor to return to the Bench, 'and so save a pension to the nation', responded that he would begin to think about that when the Lord Chancellor had persuaded the Board of Works to ventilate his old court.

In another scene which showed the executive committee of the Lechford hospitals in action, debating its responsibilities in administering a special hospital in Paris, two convalescent homes in England and an important medical unit somewhere in Italy, Bennett's emphasis fell heavily on finances: 'philanthropists were unquestionably showing signs of fatigue'. The agenda of the committee members, obsessed by considerations of cost, seemed singularly devoid of a sense that what they were doing might help real people; bloodless considerations of the respect due to power and position affected their votes on any issue that came before them.

Was Bennett, in denying that he had written about heartless people, defending the proposition that the four major characters in his novel had 'heart' in the customarily understood sense? That, too, was arguable. G. J. Hoape estimated to a nicety whatever rewards or liabilities might attend his slightest world-weary motion. He furnished his flat by combining 'the somewhat massive dignity suitable to a bachelor of middling age with the bright, unconquerable colours which the eternal twilight of London' demanded. He thought of himself as a specialist in friendships, yet throughout the years that the unfolding of the narrative required, a reader might judge that those he greeted at the Club, at board meetings or at social gatherings were mere acquaintances. Even the women with whom he had most to do sought from him transient advantages rather than love; he encouraged the formation of such reciprocities because they lessened his responsibilities towards them.

His mistress, Christine, moved in a world of practical concerns. She pleased G. J. because she was stylish and young, and because his séances with her at her flat provided him with the illusion that he was in the Orient. Though Bennett took pains to identify the qualities which made her 'a modest success' as a prostitute, he did not estimate the hardness which made Christine impatient with the thought of marriage ('an impossible prison for her'), terrified by thoughts of falling off her diet, and concerned about her health and complexion ('the source of money'). All Christine desired – before her looks would flee from her, as they inevitably would – was that G. J. should install her in a flat with her own belongings. As for the war, which had uprooted her from her beloved Paris, she understood little about its causes, but hated the Germans with a burning passion.

> She believed them to be capable of all villainies whatsoever. She believed every charge brought against them, never troubling about evidence. She would have imprisoned on bread and water all Germans and all persons with German names in England. She was really shocked by the transparent idiocy of Britons who opposed the retirement of Prince Louis of Battenberg from the Navy . . . . She had a vision of England as overrun with innumerable German spies who moved freely at inexpressible speed about the country in high-powered grey automobiles with dazzling headlights, while the marvelously stupid and blind British police touched their hats to them.

An equally important side to Christine existed: her mystical adoration of saints. By the Oratory of St Philip at Brompton she put herself under the protection of the Miraculous Infant Jesus of Prague – 'in her own esteem she was still an honest Catholic' – and she prayed to the Virgin of the vii Dolours. The drunken soldier who invaded her flat 'at the moment when she was kneeling at the altar' at the Oratory must have been 'part of a miracle' which had granted her pardon and peace. She therefore believed that she 'had a duty to him, and her duty was to brighten his destiny, to give him joy, not to let him go without a charming memory of her soft womanly acquiescences'. But he returned to the war, and to his guaranteed death; Christine, unable to help herself, went forth into the night searching for another soldier in need of her ministrations, hoping for a second miracle.

The second of the three women with whom G. J. dealt was Queenie Paulle, the heiress to a vast fortune who had an intense desire to enjoy life, though her values were those of what Bennett consistently characterised as an unworthy aristocracy. Her idea of war-work was to commission Roger Fry to design a first-aid station that would provide 'Help for Distressed Beauties'. She loved watching air-raids over London: 'They dropped two bombs close to the National Gallery', she told G. J. in a voice 'as ecstatic as a young maid at her first dance.'

> Pity they couldn't have destroyed a Landseer or two while they were so near! There were either seven or eight killed and eighteen wounded, so far as is known. But there were probably more. There was quite a fire, too, but that was soon got under. We saw it all except the explosion of the bombs. We weren't looking in the right place – no luck!

This harum-scarum hoyden may have been based on Diana Manners (Lady Diana Cooper), though Bennett had not met her prior to publication of his novel. He had had ample opportunity to become acquainted with her high-spirited behaviour through the gossip columns, and, as Margaret Drabble has shown, a number of coincidences between what she did in her 'Corrupt Coterie' and what Queenie did in the way of charity appearances, acting and partying suggests strongly that Lady Diana and Bennett were 'on the same wavelength'.[6] Queenie believed the war to be an 'extremely complex' happening. Reviewing her extensive store of information, gathered from her 'private sources', she gave G. J. ('in the vein of exclusive gossip') a fast summary of the war. Thus did she trivialise the imminent entry of Bulgaria into the war, the maturing Salonika expedition, the confidential terrible utterances of K. on recruiting, and, of course, the misfortune (due to causes which Queenie had at her finger ends) 'round about Loos'. G. J. introduced her to an officer just returned from Sulva. She, radiant with sex, expressed her delight at a new acquaintance even as she invited him to tea: 'you must be oozing with interest and actuality.' (The conversation took place at a gallery exhibition of the etchings of Felicien Rops, during the autumn of 1915.)

Bennett seems to have experienced more difficulty in integrating the experiences of Concepcion into an overall framework than he encountered with those of Christine and Queenie. Partly, his problem arose from the fact that Concepcion possessed 'very little physical charm' (a black mark), a masculine mind and egotism. But she was witty, wealthy, a leader of fashion and much talked-about; she had married for love; and her husband, who had enlisted, made her a widow unexpectedly. As she told G. J., in announcing her plan to shop at Debenham and Freebody's after receiving the War Office telegram announcing that her husband had been killed, 'I had to see if I could stand it. Because I've got to stand it, G. J. . . . And moreover, in our set it's a sacred duty to be original.'

Concepcion, nevertheless, had more of a sense of what was required from home-front civilians than anyone else. She suffered, and she understood the suffering of others. She sacrificed everything to work among 5,000 other girls in a Clyde Valley factory, taking their side in disputes with the works manager, even running a lathe on occasion, and radiating genuine compassion.

> Ours was the best factory on the Clyde, and the conditions were unspeakable, in spite of canteens, and rest-rooms, and libraries, and sanitation, and all this damned 'welfare'. Fancy a girl chained up for twelve hours every day to a thundering, whizzing, iron machine that never gets tired. The machine's just as fresh at six o'clock at night as it was at six o'clock in the morning.

Ultimately, her neurasthenia overcame her. She proved too fine-tuned an instrument for the coarse demands of wartime conditions. Though Bennett could not render convincingly G. J.'s final yearning to marry Concepcion, the very fact that G. J. learned to appreciate her attractive humanness came closer to redeeming him than any other impulse he felt at a late stage of the war.

The Pretty Lady suggested, overall, an exhaustion with the necessities of carrying on, of seeing the war effort through to completion. Most of Bennett's characters lacked lovableness (an aspect of characterisation that literary critics throughout the war had ranked very close to the top, right next to realistic, life-like portraiture). They entertained few large thoughts about the meaning of wartime sacrifice, and had ceased to wonder about what might come once the guns ceased their firing along the Western Front. Bennett's picture of England between 1915 and the end of 1917 suggested strongly that the insoluble problems created by war would be replaced by newer, equally insoluble problems whenever the Germans were defeated (of their defeat neither he nor G. J. entertained a doubt). Perhaps, as the reception of the novel demonstrated, such an interpretation of the dominant English mood was overstrained, too dark for comfort. But Bennett was correct in denying that he wrote cynically. There was no fatal disjunction between his journalism, his tracts, his propaganda efforts and his creative life. He was reporting on atmospherics, and in the last year of the war his reportage rang true. If the novel lacked finish, if the whole somehow did not successfully have the impact of individual chapters, if about the entire performance there hung the miasma of England's disappointed hopes and Bennett's sheer physical exhaustion, *The Pretty Lady*, even so, made a remarkable impression on novel-readers in 1918. On any number of counts, it must be remembered as one of the most powerful works of fiction published during the entire war.

Chapter 18

In the trenches: (Anonymous), *The Love of an Unknown Soldier: Found in a dug-out*

A young officer of the Royal Field Artillery, who discovered a bundle of papers in one of the dug-outs of an abandoned gun position, was intrigued by the fact that they had been wedged in between a post and the wall of one of the bunks. They did not deal with matters of military importance. Rather, they were the intimate notations of a brother officer, who may well have died in the endless bombardments that rendered untenable the position of those who had manned the dug-out. Who the soldier was could not be determined (he had never signed his name); who the girl was to whom he had addressed his letters was unknown, and would remain unknowable. She deserved to have the papers, because they had been written to her. However, it was not clear how to send them on to their rightful owner. 'The MS. in a red box' was taken to London by the young officer, who returned there, on leave from the front. He consulted the publisher John Lane, who in turn became fascinated by the literary value of the manuscript, and its record of a 'poignant' human experience. Publishing the papers, he finally decided, might be the best way of letting the unknown woman know that they existed; whenever she might appear in his office, he would hand them over to her. 'Meanwhile', Lane wrote, 'I ask her pardon for this necessary means of making known to the world the romance that she kindled in the heart of her lost soldier, which he himself did not tell her.'

Though the authenticity of battle descriptions may not be questioned, the diary (such as it is) can be, and should be, considered as a novel. Thus did the reviewers of 1918 interpret its literary form, in large part because the writer, a commissioned officer below the rank of captain, revealed himself on page after page as a well-read young man who had familiarised himself with literary models, and who continually tested them against his own sense of truth, based on his own experiences. He quoted Epictetus; he had pondered the problems of class status in H. G. Wells's *The Research Magnificent* (a novel dealing with the early phase of Wells's relationship to Rebecca West); he spoke of Matthew Arnold as a passionate soul hiding beneath the disguise of 'a perambulating refrigerator'; he scoffed at Thomas Hardy's novels as untrue to human nature; he scattered allusions to the New Testament throughout his text.

Anonymous though he remained, yet some evidence of his life before he entered the service could be gleaned. He had attended Oxford, where he rowed stroke, confessed being excited by Eights Week and had studied the Greek philosophers. He received his degree; because he was his father's son, he became a Member of Parliament, hoping that he might help to solve the problem of poverty within a decade; but disillusionment with the motives of his fellow MP's soon set in, and he went to live in the slums. 'There I learned that poverty is disturbingly contented, and that philanthropy is as untidy as it is unrewarding', he wrote. His next decision was to travel to Russia 'to sympathize with the revolution that was brewing'; again, he found himself forced to undeceive himself. Within him grew a sense that life was passing him by. When war broke out, he rejoiced. The crisis stripped English youths of their 'sham refinements', and clothed them in 'the armour of duty'. He continued:

> We hadn't known how to live wisely; God restored to us the chance to die for something worthy. He'd grown tired of seeing us charging windmills, so He set over against us the mustered hosts of hell. How real everything has become of late!

Since there are no precise dates to indicate when this fierce exaltation began, it is impossible to say whether the mood was sustained right up to the moment of his death. But it could not have deserted him entirely, if at all; his final notes were written during a period of maximum exposure to enemy shells and machine-gun bullets ('We are absolutely in the open and can now be seen every time we fire'), when he was still an idealist.

The writer of these letters – there are nineteen, though others may have been sent as well – was compassionate on behalf of his men. (Towards the end of this manuscript he mentioned, almost in passing,

The Love of an Unknown Soldier

that he commanded one hundred soldiers.) He identified a few: Jack Holt, who but recently married, and who slept with his head in a bag – which saved him during a trench cave-in; Bill Lane, who escaped death because he had been given a leave to visit Blighty; and Stephen, who gave up his leave so that Jack could visit his wife (she had become dangerously ill during her pregnancy). He admired their courage, and some of the things they said brought him close to tears. Just before the big offensive, one soldier admitted that he was 'pretty sure he's going to get it; he prefers it in his left arm, he says, because that will leave his right O.K. to place about the waist of his girl.' The author knew that danger made a difference, though he could not explain the psychology of his men.

> Out in the sunshine you can hear singing everywhere. The servants are polishing up their officer's leather and buttons, so that when the show starts they may look spick and span. My chap, without a word from me, has got out my swaggerest breeches and tunic. It's the same with the men. If we die, we shall die swells.

When the Huns commenced gassing, his men had to wear masks. 'It's no joke to wield a spade in a mask, but these chaps never stopped. . . . If gassed, we led him out of the barrage to recover; when he was better he invariably came back. Their pluck was superhuman.' The young officer, struggling to understand why they persevered despite the murderous crossfire, knew that they did so without regard to orders, pay or the hope of decorations.

> It is only the undiscussed nobility of their purpose that keeps them going. . . . It doesn't matter who or what our men were in civilian life, they all show the same capacity for sacrifice when in danger. Some of them were public-school men; some served behind counters; some were day-labourers. We have several who have been in gaol; they're every bit as good as the others.

He added: 'They usually carry out twice as much as they're ordered. They're rarely sullen. . . . They're almost always cheery and helpful.' In this universe of brave men, cowards do not exist, and only occasionally will a man suffering from shell-shock collapse under the strain.

The author's love of his fellow humans extended to the poor dumb horses who slithered like cats on the glass-like road, 'where ditches had overflowed and frozen'; who stood in the mud all winter ('It was pitiful to see them limping along, putting their last ounce of strength into dragging the guns'); and who, if they fell down, had difficulty in rising because the mud sucking them down was turning into glue. The hero understood, and forgave.

> Those men whom I saw piled high in trenches so loved their ideal that they could die for it. There is something god-like in such self-abnegation. 'God so loved the world that He gave His only begotten Son'; these men so loved the world that they gave themselves. Though the ideal for which they die may be mistaken, whether they be English, French, Germans, they seem somehow to strive up towards God's level. To do that is religion.

What we are dealing with here, in brief, is the portrait of a *verray, parfit, gentil knyght* whom Chaucer would have instantly recognised. The author, in sketching the similarities between his beloved and Joan of Arc, in speaking of Joan's visions in the woods about Domrémy, in reminding his reader of the divine madness of Marie Bashkirtseff (who loved Bastien-Lepage's painting of Joan in the Metropolitan Museum in New York City), in his quoting of Rossetti's poem about 'the emotion of a dedicated sympathy' in a bygone age and in his praise of the romance of the medieval spirit, shared the joy of life that Gaston de Foix, 'the gayest soldier of the Italian Renaissance', had celebrated in words and deeds. 'Every defeat was changed into victory by his presence', the unknown soldier wrote envyingly to his beloved.

> When the walls of a beleaguered city were so slippery with blood that nobody could climb them, he stripped off his hose and shoes, in a spirit of devilry bound his right arm behind him, fastened his lady's kerchief about his left and, grasping his sword, led the storming party to success. He took these long chances that he might add glory to the name of his lady.

Thus, the reader of 1918 knew something about the hero, though perhaps not enough to believe in him. He knew even less about the young woman with whom the subaltern was conducting the mildest of flirtations. The two had met after he, wounded at the front, had been sent as a convalescent to the United States to serve as a member of the British Mission (soon after America had declared war on Germany); he spoke to a public audience 'on the splendour of men's souls in the trenches'; and while the hall emptied, he was introduced to a nurse who was about to sail for France with a unit that was 'going to take care of little children in the devastated districts'. It was only right, only to be expected, that when he returned to Europe and called on the only girl he knew, he should find his new acquaintance staying with her. (Why should miracles be the exclusive property of medieval legends?) He spent his entire leave with her, walking with her on the Champs-Élysées, through the Luxembourg Gardens, down the Boule Miche to Notre-Dame; he extracted from her, at the very last moment, a promise to write to him: 'I shall be a better soldier because we have met. If I die, I shall die satisfied.' She was adept at the French language. She outranked him with her captain's bars, and (though not much was made of this), she came from a background of greater wealth (her family owned limousines and several houses): 'You spoke of this once, I remember, saying how difficult it was to have been born rich. Everything had been done; you weren't supposed to do anything.' Despite such touches, however, her personality remained clouded, perhaps even unreal; her love of children was talked about but not dramatised; her slight case of septic poisoning, and her subsequent convalescence at Monte Carlo, where 'dashing Serbian officers' surrounded her, was commented on, but not quoted directly from her letter.

Indeed, a reader might well have experienced difficulty in deciding whether the romance was a contrivance designed to allow the author an excuse to lament the hopelessness of normal emotions in the trenches, or whether the descriptions of activities at the front (some of them astonishingly vivid in communicating an immediacy of sensation) were recorded so that romantic interludes might lighten the burden of blood and sacrifice. Artifice, however, tainted the love story from the beginning, with the fortuitous discovery of the Red Cross nurse in the one Parisian apartment he had access to; the unrealistically expensive interludes at the Hotel Crillon, the Hotel Pavillon and the Café de Paris, as well as the flood of gifts he sent to her (on a subaltern's meagre salary); and his receiving a letter 'from a Sister in an American unit now in France', who heard him speak when he was in America, and who enclosed in the letter a photograph of two American nurses, one of whom was his beloved. 'Isn't that luck for me? . . . An accident! Yes, but so many accidents have happened to me and you. I begin to be superstitious – superstitiously hopeful.' Accident or fictional contrivance? (One might even begin to suspect John Lane's story of the lucky discovery of 'The MS. in a red box'.)

The Love of an Unknown Soldier was filled with sentimentality; some of it was very hard to take seriously. But it was not the excess of an essentially trashy sensibility. The failure of the nurse to respond with assurances of devotion to the soldier's love letters, and even the suggestion that till the end she remained ignorant of the depth of his attachment to her ('There are times when I think of you profanely, as if you were the mother of God Himself'), suggested a chasteness of attitude, a cloistered condition of the heart all the more impressive because of its very restraint.

The importance of this strange approximation of a novel, however, lay primarily in its depiction of a set of attitudes towards the war that identified the staying power of ideals even in the final year of the war, while providing, in horrifying fullness of incident, a record of the insanity of No Man's Land. The author genuinely believed in the modesty of the English:

> We English are quite conscious of our splendour, only we don't talk about it. We do magnificent things and voice them in the language of stable-boys. We're so terribly afraid of self-praise and sentiment. We feel intensely, but we keep up a pretence of carelessness.

Though at times he admitted to feeling a 'passionate contempt for the Hun', he put on a brave show, and even as shells rained down upon him and his men, even as a faint smell of gas permeated the dug-out, he spoke, through clenched teeth, of the 'festive Hun' who thus made his presence known. He feared giving himself away; self-pity, he said, was 'the worst enemy that a soldier can have'. How, then, could one endure when the temptation to show the white feather became almost irresistible? The answer: forget self, 'consider one's body, one's pain, everything personal as of no account. The game – the establishing of the ideal for which we fight – is the only thing that matters.'

What, then, did the subaltern think he was fighting for? That was harder to define, and anyhow he was too busy to worry about definitions of war goals. There were too many heroes for any individual to be noticed. 'We have become nations of heroes. To be brave is the work-a-day standard; not to be brave is the dastardly exception.' He concentrated on getting the next task done, cutting the wires to enable his soldiers to move across the next few yards of fortified trench, running the messages to the next command post; he had no time to worry about the reasons why any particular action might be commanded of him. 'Ever since war started', he told his beloved, 'I have hoped to die in France. So many others have died that it would not seem fair if I came back. This is the one chance I shall ever have of laying down my life for other people. I don't want to miss it.' In the

The Love of an Unknown Soldier

trenches, taking time out to think about ultimate objectives distracted one from immediate responsibilities. 'No words can convey the picture; it was horribly inhuman, pitiful and glorious. You won't understand the last adjective. No one could who had not been there. It was glorious because it was so immense.'

There are hopeless contradictions here: that one could still believe in the romance of war and in the existence of heroes when death was so impersonal; that this kind of warfare would guarantee the formation of a better world; that the Boche was one's brother because he shared in the miseries of Armageddon, though he was simultaneously the anti-Christ. The author was confounded by intolerable antilogies:

> The guns opened up; the night firing had commenced, shaking the walls of my narrow dwelling. I pictured the Hun carrying-party above which our shrapnel had begun to burst. They would throw away their burdens and scatter. We were sweeping and searching; we must surely kill some. Why should we kill them? We have never even seen these men. Life was ruthless. It withheld love till it was too late. It put weapons of slaughter into our hands, when all we desired was to live ourselves. It gave us glimpses, only glimpses, of the things we had desired, and then passed us on into another world.

The Love of an Unknown Soldier provided comfort for those who had not gone off to war, reassuring them that noble men were fighting for pure and virtuous women, for Blighty and for ideals that might be profaned if they were to be examined too specifically. Life was hellish in France. No one denied that. But men like the unknown soldier would win the war some day, somehow. To believe otherwise was unthinkable. And, in the midst of the Great War, to accuse the author of being sentimental was to apply irrelevant aesthetic criteria.

One rather wonders, now that the war is over, what is likely to be the immediate future of 'war-books', as regards popularity with the buying public. I do not know if it is possible to draw any analogy from the fate of the war-plays which were running at the time the armistice was signed; but I am credibly informed that the 'business' at all the theatres where such plays were in the bill fell off enormously as soon as peace was assured. Quite possibly it may be the same with the books, and in the first flush of peace the public may turn away from war literature, and for a while regard it with distaste. But, even if it is so, the turn of the war-books will assuredly come again later on, when we are sufficiently far removed from 'Armageddon' to be ready for a dispassionate study of its amazing and many-sided history.

'Jacob Omnium', *The Bookseller: A newspaper of British and foreign literature* (December 1918), p. 605.

Notes

1 At the turn of the century

1. Lafcadio Hearn, *Complete Lectures on Art, Literature and Philosophy*, edited by Ryuji Tanabé, Teisaburo Ochiai and Ichiro Nishizaki (Kanda, Tokyo: The Hokuseido Press, 1932), p. 368.
2. *ibid.*, p. 349.
3. *ibid.*, p. 357.
4. *ibid.*, p. 359.
5. *ibid.*, p. 360.
6. *ibid.*, p. 370.
7. *ibid.*, pp. 372–3.
8. *ibid.*, pp. 376–7.
9. *ibid.*, p. 380.
10. *ibid.*, p. 384.
11. *ibid.*, p. 385.
12. *ibid.*, p. v.
13. Mrs Oliphant and F. R. Oliphant, *The Victorian Age of English Literature* (London: Percival, 1892), vol. II, p. 172.
14. George Saintsbury, *A History of Nineteenth Century Literature* (New York and London: Macmillan, 1896), p. 323.
15. *ibid.*, p. 324.
16. Hugh Walker, *The Age of Tennyson* (London: George Bell, 1897), pp. 265–8; Walker repeats and elaborates his charges in *The Literature of the Victorian Era* (Cambridge: Cambridge University Press, 1910), pp. 729–47, *passim*.
17. Clement Shorter, *Victorian Literature: Sixty years of books and bookmen* (London: James Bowden, 1898), p. 53.
18. Saintsbury, *op. cit.*, p. 330.
19. Arthur Rickett, *The Vagabond in Literature* (London: J. M. Dent, 1906), p. 119.
20. *ibid.*, p. 121.

21. G. K. Chesterton, *Varied Types* (New York: Dodd and Mead, 1903), pp. 98–9.
22. *ibid.*, pp. 103–4.

2 The publishing world in 1914

1. Charles Morgan, *The House of Macmillan (1843–1943)* (New York: Macmillan, 1944), p. 210.
2. *ibid.*, p. 211.
3. Frank Swinnerton, *The Bookman's London* (London: John Baker, 1951), p. 73.
4. Arthur Waugh, *A Hundred Years of Publishing: Being the story of Chapman & Hall, Ltd.* (London: Chapman and Hall, 1930), pp. 277–83.
5. *ibid.*, p. 282.
6. Marjorie Plant, *The English Book Trade: An economic history of the making and sale of books* (London: George Allen and Unwin, 1939), pp. 445–50.
7. Derek Hudson, 'Reading', in Simon Nowell-Smith (ed.), *Edwardian England 1901–1914* (London: Oxford University Press, 1964), p. 309; see also Ian Norrie, in *Publishing and Bookselling*, Part One: *From the Earliest Times to 1870*, by Frank Arthur Mumby; Part Two: *1870–1970*, by Ian Norrie (London: Jonathan Cape, 1930; revised edition, 1974), *passim*.
8. Charles Morgan, *op. cit.*, p. 215.
9. *ibid.*, p. 216.
10. Fredric Warburg, 'What is publishing?' in Gerald Gross (ed.), *Publishers on Publishing*, (London: Secker and Warburg, 1961), p. 454.
11. Sir Stanley Unwin, 'Getting started', in Gross (ed.), *Publishers on Publishing*, p. 420.
12. John Gross, *The Rise and Fall of the Man of Letters: Aspects of English literary life since 1800* (London: Weidenfeld and Nicolson, 1969), pp. 199–200.
13. Amy Cruse, *After the Victorians* (London: George Allen and Unwin, 1938), p. 243.
14. *ibid.*, p. 247.

3 Authors and the reviewing media

1. Richard D. Altick, 'The sociology of authorship: The social origins, education, and occupations of 1,100 British writers, 1800–1935', in *Writers, Readers, and Occasions: Selected essays on Victorian literature and life* (Columbus: Ohio State University Press, 1989), pp. 95–109. Altick expanded a list of 350 authors whose social origins, education and non-literary occupations had been investigated by Raymond Williams in *The Long Revolution* (1961) to 1,100 British and Irish writers, born between 1750 and 1909, whose reputations were established between 1800 and 1935. Altick's survey, though it has serious limitations (generously conceded by Altick), and though it has not been updated since its original publication (1962), is a significant contribution to our improved understanding of where English

authors come from. See also John Sutherland's 'Victorian novelists: A survey', in *Critical Quarterly*, vol. 30 (spring 1988), pp. 50–61. However, no comparable study has focused on the writers of the Great War years.
2. Readers interested in fuller information about any of these periodicals should consult Alvin Sullivan (ed.), *British Literary Magazines*, vol. 3: *The Victorian and Edwardian Age, 1837–1913*, and vol. 4: *The Modern Age, 1914–1984* (New York: Greenwood Press, 1983).
3. Virginia Woolf, *The Second Common Reader* (New York: Harcourt Brace and Harvest Books, reprint of 1932 edition, pp. 244–5).
4. *The Times Literary Supplement* (1914), 19 March, pp. 133–4, and 2 April, pp. 157–8.
5. *ibid.*, 14 May, pp. 229–30.
6. *ibid.*, 15 January, p. 21.
7. *ibid.*, 22 January, p. 38.
8. *ibid.*, 5 March, p. 116.
9. *ibid.*, 5 February, p. 60.
10. *ibid.*, 12 March, p. 121.
11. *ibid.*, 9 April, p. 178.
12. *ibid.*, 21 May, p. 249.
13. *ibid.*, 15 January, p. 30.
14. *Ibid.*
15. *ibid.*, 16 April, p. 190.
16. *ibid.*, 30 April, p. 214.
17. *ibid.*, 5 February, p. 63.
18. *ibid.*, 12 February, p. 77.
19. *ibid.*, 12 March, p. 130.
20. *ibid.*, 16 July, p. 346.
21. *ibid.*, 30 July, p. 370.
22. *ibid.*, 29 January, p. 50.
23. *ibid.*, 12 March, p. 130.
24. *ibid.*, 26 March, p. 154.
25. *Ibid.*
26. *ibid.*, 2 April, p. 166.
27. *ibid.*, 23 April, p. 202.
28. *ibid.*, 30 April, p. 214.
29. *ibid.*, 7 May, p. 226.
30. *ibid.*
31. *ibid.*, 14 May, p. 238.
32. *Ibid.*
33. *ibid.*, 21 May, p. 249.
34. *Ibid.*
35. *ibid.*, 18 June, p. 298.
36. *ibid.*, 25 June, p. 311.
37. *ibid.*, 1 January, p. 6.
38. *ibid.*, 29 January, p. 49.
39. *ibid.*, 12 February, p. 66.
40. *ibid.*, 12 March, p. 129.
41. *ibid.*, 23 April, p. 199.

42. *ibid.*, 2 July, p. 322.
43. *Ibid.*
44. *ibid.*, 2 April, p. 167.
45. *ibid.*, 2 April, p. 162.
46. *ibid.*, 26 March, p. 153.
47. *ibid.*, 26 February, p. 116.
48. *ibid.*, 19 February, p. 90.
49. *ibid.*, 2 April, p. 167.
50. *ibid.*, 12 February, p. 74.
51. London: Hurst and Blackett, 1897, p. 2.

4 George Moore's *The Brook Kerith* (1916)

1. Quoted by Malcolm Brown in *George Moore: A reconsideration* (Seattle, Wash.: University of Washington Press, 1955), p. 207.
2. Janet Egleson Dunleavy (ed.), *George Moore in Perspective* (Naas, County Kildare: Malton Press; Gerrards Cross, Bucks.: Colin Smythe; Totowa, N.J.: Barnes and Noble, 1983), p. 18.
3. A. Norman Jeffares, *George Moore* (London: Longmans Green, 1965), p. 27.
4. Quoted by Joseph Hone, *The Life of George Moore* (New York: Macmillan, 1936), p. 333.
5. William Butler Yeats, 'Dramatis personae, 1896–1902', *Autobiographies* (London: Macmillan, 1955), p. 438.
6. George Moore, 'The nineness in the oneness,' *Century Magazine*, n.s., LXXXVII (Nov. 1919), p. 66.
7. Robert Porter Sechler, *George Moore: 'A disciple of Walter Pater* (Philadelphia: Folcraft Library Editions, 1976), p. 33. Sechler's study, originally a Ph.D. dissertation (1931), is the fullest treatment thus far of Moore's indebtedness to Pater's theories of style.
8. Graham Owens, 'The melodic line in narrative' in Graham Owens (ed.), *George Moore's Mind and Art* (Edinburgh: Oliver and Boyd, 1968), pp. 102–3.
9. Hone, *op. cit.*, p. 372.
10. Janet Egleson Dunleavy, *George Moore: The artist's vision, the storyteller's art* (Lewisburg, Pa.: Bucknell University Press, 1973), p. 140.
11. Anthony Farrow, *George Moore* (Boston, Mass.: Twayne, 1978), p. 139.
12. Jean C. Noël, '"The Brook Kerith": Heretical romance', in Douglas A. Hughes (ed.), *Critical Essays on George Moore* (New York: New York University Press, 1971), pp. 272–9.
13. Milton Chaikin, 'George Moore's early fiction,' in *George Moore's Mind and Art, op. cit.* p. 37.
14. Noël, *op. cit.*, p. 269.
15. Hone, *op. cit.*, pp. 313–17.
16. Frederick W. Seinfelt, *George Moore: Ireland's unconventional realist* (Philadelphia: Dorrance, 1975), *passim.*
17. Hone, *op. cit.*, p. 329.

5 Norman Douglas's *South Wind* (1917)

1. H. M. Tomlinson, *Norman Douglas* (London: Hutchinson, 1931; reprinted 1952), p. 66.
2. Norman Douglas, 'Introduction', *South Wind* (New York: Modern Library, Random House, 1925), pp. vi–vii.
3. Norman Douglas, *Alone* (London: Chapman and Hall, 1923), pp. 168–9.
4. *ibid.*, p. 169. Douglas's quotation, 'One dirty blackmailer', etc., is in Chapter XLIX of *South Wind*. Compare Norman Douglas, *Late Harvest* (London: Lindsay Drummond, 1946), p. 58:

    South Wind was the result of my craving to escape from the wearisome actualities of life. To picture yourself living in a society of such instability, of such 'jovial immoderation' and 'frolicsome perversity' that even a respectable bishop can be persuaded to approve of a murder – this was my aim.

5. Mark Holloway, *Norman Douglas: A biography* (London: Secker and Warburg, 1976), p. 241.
6. *ibid.*, pp. 229–32.
7. Douglas wrote this originally as an article for the *Anglo-Italian Review* (March 1920, pp. 53–61), and it later became part of the Introduction to *Alone*.
8. Tomlinson, *op. cit.*, p. 66.
9. Norman Douglas, *Looking Back: An autobiographical excursion* (New York: Harcourt Brace, 1933), p. 26.
10. Ralph D. Lindeman, *Norman Douglas* (New York: Twayne, 1965), pp. 137–9.
11. R. M. Dawkins, in *Norman Douglas* (London: Rupert Hart-Davis, 1952), is severe on this point:

    Of any feeling for the intellectual and imaginative attraction of mathematics there is not a trace [in *South Wind*] . . . . It is only by some study of mathematics that a man learns to distinguish between a cogent demonstration and the tentative conclusions which are often all that is in the reach of the humaner studies. (pp. 66–7)

12. Nancy Cunard, *Grand Man: Memories of Norman Douglas* (London: Secker and Warburg, 1954), pp. 278–9.
13. Constantine FitzGibbon, *Norman Douglas: A pictorial record* (London: The Richards Press, 1953), p. 34.
14. *ibid.*, p. 35.

6 Frank Swinnerton's *Nocturne* (1917)

1. Frank Swinnerton, *Background with Chorus: A footnote to changes in English literary fashion between 1901 and 1917* (London: Hutchinson, 1956), p. 215.

2. Frank Swinnerton, *Swinnerton: An autobiography* (New York: Doubleday and Doran, 1936), p. 182.
3. *ibid.*, p. 143.
4. P. M., 'A conversation about Frank Swinnerton', in *Personal Sketches by Arnold Bennett, H. G. Wells, Grant M. Overton* (New York: George H. Doran, 1920), p. 32.
5. *Swinnerton: An autobiography*, p. 138.
6. *ibid.*, p. 140.
7. Arnold Bennett, 'Frank Swinnerton: A personal sketch', in *Personal Sketches*, pp. 9–10.
8. *Swinnerton: An autobiography*, p. 181.
9. Swinnerton, *Background with Chorus*, p. 216.
10. *Swinnerton: An autobiography*, p. 184.
11. Swinnerton, *Background with Chorus*, p. 216.
12. See, for example, Frank Swinnerton's discussion of the reading public (Chapter IX) in Frank Swinnerton, *Authors and the Book Trade* (London: Gerald Howe, 1932), pp. 123–42.
13. Frank Swinnerton, *Figures in the Foreground: Literary reminiscences 1917–40* (London: Hutchinson, 1963), p. 237.
14. *ibid.*, p. 238.
15. *ibid.*, p. 251.
16. *ibid.*, p. 264.
17. *ibid.*, p. 266.
18. *ibid.*, p. 254.
19. H. G. Wells, 'Introduction', *Nocturne* (New York: George H. Doran, 1917), p. x.
20. *ibid.*, p. xi.
21. *ibid.*, p. xiv.
22. *ibid.*, pp. xii–xiii.
23. *Swinnerton: An autobiography*, p. 10.
24. Frank Swinnerton, *The Georgian Literary Scene 1910–1935: A panorama* (London: Dent, 1950), p. 37.
25. *Swinnerton: An autobiography*, p. 348.

7 Compton Mackenzie's *The Early Life and Adventures of Sylvia Scarlett* (1918)

1. Compton Mackenzie, 'Poetry and the modern novel', *Unconsidered Trifles* (London: Martin Secker, 1932), p. 255.
2. *ibid.*, p. 257.
3. *ibid.*, pp. 260–1.
4. David Thomas and Joyce Thomas, *Compton Mackenzie: A bibliography* (London and New York: Mansell, 1986), pp. 3–5.
5. *ibid.*, p. vi.
6. Compton Mackenzie, *My Life and Times; Octave Five: 1915–1923* (London: Chatto and Windus, 1966), p. 125.
7. *ibid.*, p. 122.

8. *ibid.*, p. 126.
9. Andro Linklater, *Compton Mackenzie: A life* (London: Chatto and Windus, 1987), p. 130.
10. Mackenzie, *My Life and Times, op cit.*, p. 178.
11. Compton Mackenzie, *Literature in My Time* (London: Rich and Cowan, 1933), p. 186.
12. Katherine Hepburn's ceaseless 'bright' chatter in the cinema version of *Sylvia Scarlett* (1935) perplexed audiences; film exhibitors voted Hepburn box-office poison, and came close to ending her career as a film star. Mackenzie dryly noted, 'Hollywood made as much a mess of Sylvia Scarlett as Crippen made of his wife' (David and Joyce Thomas, *op. cit.*, pp. 10–11).
13. Leo Robertson, *Compton Mackenzie: An appraisal of his literary work* (London: The Richards Press, 1954), p. 100.
14. Kenneth Young, in *Compton Mackenzie* (Longmans Green, 1968), asks whether Sylvia is 'consciously or otherwise a lesbian?' (p. 16).
15. D. J. Dooley, *Compton Mackenzie* (New York: Twayne, 1974), p. 61.
16. Quoted by Dooley, *ibid.*, p. [8].

8 Mary Webb's *The Golden Arrow* (1915)

1. Quoted in Michael Millgate's *Thomas Hardy: A biography* (Oxford: Oxford University Press, 1982), p. 502.
2. The Rt Hon. Stanley Baldwin, Introduction to Mary Webb's *Precious Bane* (London: Jonathan Cape, 1929), p. 7.
3. Quoted in Thomas Moult's *Mary Webb: Her life and work* (London: Jonathan Cape, 1932), p. 257. Additional biographical and critical materials of interest: Dorothy P. H. Wrenn's *Goodbye to Morning* (Shrewsbury: Wilding, 1964); Gladys Mary Coles's *The Flower of Light: A biography of Mary Webb* (Middletown, Conn.: Wesleyan University Press, 1986).

9 Joseph Conrad's *Victory* (1915)

1. Daniel R. Schwarz, *Conrad: The later fiction* (London: Macmillan, 1982), p. 61. See George Dangerfield's *The Strange Death of Liberal England, 1910–1914* (London: Nelson, 1936) and Samuel Hynes's *The Edwardian Turn of Mind* (Princeton, N.J.: Princeton University Press, 1968), *passim*, for comparable judgements on what Schwarz calls 'the ennui, anxiety, and moral and intellectual confusion of pre-war England' (*op. cit.*, p. 73).
2. Joseph Conrad, 'Some reflections on the loss of the *Titanic*', *Notes on Life and Letters* (London: J. M. Dent, 1924), p. 214.
3. *Ibid.*
4. *ibid.*, p. 217.
5. *ibid.*, p. 218.
6. *ibid.*, p. 227.
7. Joseph Conrad, 'Certain aspects of the admirable inquiry into the loss of the *Titanic*', *Notes on Life and Letters, op. cit.* p. 230.

230   *Notes*

8. *ibid.*, pp. 230–1.
9. *ibid.*, p. 242.
10. Later critics have been less certain of its status. F. R. Leavis ranked it lower than *Nostromo*, but listed it 'among those of Conrad's works which deserve to be current as representing his claim to classical standing' (*The Great Tradition* (London: Chatto and Windus, 1948, p. 253). This view is shared by M. C. Bradbrook and Morton D. Zabel. Frederick R. Karl speaks of the novel as 'the culmination of Conrad's achievement' ('*Victory*: Its origin and development', *Conradiana*, vol. xv, no. 1 (1983), p. 49). Yet Albert J. Guerard characterises *Victory* as 'very badly written and very roughly imagined', a prime example of 'imaginative collapse', containing 'extraordinary uncorrected lapses in syntax and diction' (*Conrad the Novelist* (Cambridge, Mass.: Harvard University Press, 1958, p. 255). He introduces his searing critique with the sentence, 'For this is one of the worst novels for which high claims have ever been made by critics of standing: an awkward popular romance built around certain imperfectly dramatized reflections on skepticism, withdrawal, isolation' (p. 272), adding, 'The time has come to drop *Victory* from the Conrad canon, at least to the degree that *The Trumpet-Major*, once so widely admired, has at last been dropped from Hardy's' (p. 273). Douglas Hewitt, Thomas Moser and Bernard Meyer have written comparably harsh judgements.
11. Arnold E. Davidson, *Conrad's Endings: A study of the five major novels* (Ann Arbor, Mich.: UMI Research Press, 1984), p. 5. Davidson is expanding an insight of Frank Kermode. For additional commentaries on the problems inherent in any close reading of *Victory*, see Leo Gurko's *Joseph Conrad: Giant in exile* (New York: Macmillan, 1979), pp. 212–21; Gary Geddes, *Conrad's Later Novels* (Montreal: McGill–Queen's University Press, 1980), pp. 41–80; Douglas Hewitt's *Conrad: A reassessment* (London: Bowes and Bowes, 1969), pp. 103–11; Frederick R. Karl's *A Reader's Guide to Joseph Conrad* (New York: H. Wolff, 1960), pp. 246–67; Paul L. Wiley's *Conrad's Measure of Man* (Madison, Wis.: University of Wisconsin Press, 1954), pp. 150–8; and Walter F. Wright's *Romance and Tragedy in Joseph Conrad* (Lincoln, Neb.: University of Nebraska Press, 1949), pp. 101–6.
12. *Ibid.*

10 Ford Madox Hueffer's *The Good Soldier* (1915)

1. Asa Briggs, 'The political scene', in Simon Nowell-Smith (ed.), *Edwardian England 1905–1914* (London: Oxford University Press, 1964), pp. 45–6.
2. Ford Madox Ford, 'Dedicatory letter to Stella Ford', in *The Good Soldier* (New York: Alfred A. Knopf, 1951), p. xix.
3. *ibid.*, p. xx.
4. Mark Schorer, 'An interpretation', in *The Good Soldier, op. cit.* This essay, printed originally in *The Princeton University Library Chronicle* (April 1948), was revised for *Horizon* (August 1949); and revised again for Knopf's edition of the novel in 1951. A few changes were made when *The Good*

Soldier was reprinted in 1957, but these were not significant, and I have used the text of the 1951 edition.
5. Carol Ohmann, *Ford Madox Ford: From apprentice to craftsman* (Middletown, Conn.: Wesleyan University Press, 1964), p. 111.

11 Alex Waugh's *The Loom of Youth* (1917)

1. Alex Waugh, *The Best Wine Last: An autobiography through the years 1932–1969* (London: W. H. Allen, 1978), p. 309.
2. Alex Waugh, Preface to new edition, *The Loom of Youth* (London: Methuen, 1984), p. 9.
3. Thomas Seccombe, Preface, *The Loom of Youth* (London: Grant Richards, 1921), p. 11.
4. *ibid.*, p. 14.
5. *ibid.*, p. 12.
6. *ibid.*, p. 16.
7. Alex Waugh, Preface to new edition, p. 12.
8. Rudyard Kipling, *Something of Myself: For my friends known and unknown* (New York: Doubleday and Doran, 1937), pp. 144–5.
9. Waugh, Preface to new edition, p. 13.
10. See Robert F. Moss, *Rudyard Kipling and the Fiction of Adolescence* (New York: St Martin's Press, 1982), pp. 75–82, and J. M. S. Tompkins, *The Art of Rudyard Kipling* (London: Methuen, 1959), pp. 241–2.

12 Wyndham Lewis's *Tarr* (1918)

1. Wyndham Lewis, *Rude Assignment: A narrative of my career up-to-date* (London: Hutchinson, 1951), p. 126.
2. *ibid.*, p. 149.
3. *ibid.*, p. 151.
4. D. G. Bridson, *The Filibuster: A study of the political ideas of Wyndham Lewis* (London: Cassell, 1972), p. 173.
5. Hugh Gordon Porteus, *Wyndham Lewis: A discursive exposition* (London: Desmond Harmsworth, 1932), pp. 124–5.
6. Lewis, *op. cit.*, p. 129.
7. Hugh Kenner, *Wyndham Lewis* (Norfolk, Conn.: New Directions Books, 1954), p. 30.
8. See, for example, William H. Pritchard's analysis of why he considers the revised text 'superior', in Chapter 2, 'The satirist's curse of humor', *Wyndham Lewis* (New York: Twayne, 1968), pp. 28–31. My quotations from *Tarr* are transcribed from the 1928 edition because they are easier to read, and represent Lewis's qualities as a writer more pleasingly than does the 1918 edition.
9. Jeffrey Meyers, *The Enemy: A biography of Wyndham Lewis* (London: Routledge and Kegan Paul, 1980), pp. 63–4.
10. E. W. Tomlin, in *Wyndham Lewis* (Writers and Their Work, no. 64),

(London: Longmans Green, 1955), p. 32, points out that 'while it is one thing to portray men as "machines governed by mere routine" (for a machine has no "inside"), it is another to maintain that they *are* machines.' Tomlin is quoting Hazlitt's comment on Ben Jonson.
11. SueEllen Campbell, *The Enemy Opposite: The outlaw criticism of Wyndham Lewis* (Athens: Ohio University Press, 1988), pp. 18–19.
12. A letter from Wyndham Lewis to John Quinn, dated 1 August 1919, in the John Quinn Memorial Collection, New York Public Library; quoted by Timothy Materer, *Wyndham Lewis the Novelist* (Detroit: Wayne State University Press, 1976), p. 58.
13. Kenner, *op. cit.*, p. 48.

13 The last year of the war

1. See Martin Middlebrook's *The First Day on the Somme, 1 July 1916* (London: Lane, 1971) for a well-written account of a crucial battle. A. J. P. Taylor, in *English History 1914–1945* (Oxford: Clarendon Press, 1965), supplies useful statistics and a strongly individualistic point of view in one of the better-written volumes of *The Oxford History of England.*
2. John H. Johnston, *English Poetry of the First World War: A study in the evolution of lyric and narrative form* (Princeton, N.J.: Princeton University Press, 1964), p. 10.
3. (Anon.), *Times Literary Supplement*, 24 January 1918, p. 43.
4. Michael Joseph, *The Adventure of Publishing* (London: Allan Wingate, 1949), p. 42.
5. Arthur Waugh, *A Hundred Years of Publishing: Being the story of Chapman & Hall, Ltd.* (London: Chapman and Hall, 1930), p. 289.
6. *ibid.*, p. 311.
7. *ibid.*, p. 312.
8. *ibid.*, p. 315.
9. F. R. Richardson, 'The circulating library', in John Hampden (ed.), *The Book World* (London: Thomas Nelson, 1935), pp. 200–1.
10. Sir Stanley Unwin, 'Introduction', in Hampden (ed.), *The Book World*, p. 9.

14 What the reviewers of *The Times Literary Supplement* wrote in 1918

1. *Arnold Bennett: The critical heritage*, edited by James Hepburn (London: Routledge and Kegan Paul, 1981), pp. 372–84.
2. *The Times Literary Supplement* (1919), 10 January, p. 17.
3. *ibid.*, 14 March, p. 128.
4. *ibid.*, 28 March, p. 152.
5. *ibid.*, 21 February, p. 24.
6. *ibid.*, 28 March, p. 152.

7. *ibid.*, 14 March, p. 128.
8. *ibid.*, 4 April, p. 160.
9. *ibid.*, 30 May, p. 255.
10. *ibid.*, 4 July, p. 312.
11. *ibid.*, p. 314.
12. *ibid.*, 29 August, p. 406.
13. *ibid.*, 26 September, p. 458.
14. *ibid.*, 3 October, p. 482.
15. *ibid.*, 4 July, p. 312.
16. *ibid.*, 1 August, p. 360.
17. *ibid.*, 19 September, p. 440.
18. *ibid.*, 3 October, p. 468.
19. *ibid.*, 7 November, p. 541.
20. *ibid.*, 16 May, p. 232.
21. *ibid.*, 25 April, p. 195.
22. *ibid.*, 17 October, p. 496.
23. *ibid.*, 17 January, p. 32.
24. *ibid.*, 4 April, p. 157.
25. *ibid.*, 21 March, p. 140.
26. *ibid.*, 4 April, p. 160.
27. *ibid.*, 24 October, p. 510.
28. *ibid.*, 15 August, p. 380.
29. *ibid.*, 29 August, p. 406.
30. *ibid.*, 10 October, p. 481.
31. *ibid.*, 8 August, p. 372.
32. *ibid.*, 14 November, p. 545.

15 John Buchan's *The Thirty-Nine Steps* (1915) and *Greenmantle* (1916)

1. David Daniell, *The Interpreter's House: A critical assessment of John Buchan* (London: Nelson, 1975), p. 206, offers the same kind of defence that Kipling's admirers put up for the Anglo-Indian tales: 'we have to allow for the obvious function of character. Scudder is a frightened American man hunted to death – why should he be supposed to speak for John Buchan?'
2. John Buchan, *A History of the Great War* (Boston: Houghton Mifflin; London: Thomas Nelson, 1922), vol. I, p. ix.
3. *ibid.*, p. 36.
4. *ibid.*, p. 32.
5. *ibid.*, pp. 28–9.
6. *ibid.*, p. 15.
7. *ibid.*, p. 21.
8. *ibid.*, vol. IV, p. 434.
9. *ibid.*, p. 443.
10. *ibid.*, pp. 443–4.

11. Susan (Grosvenor) Buchan, *John Buchan by his Wife and Friends* (London: Hodder and Stoughton, 1947), p. 53.
12. Janet Adam Smith, *John Buchan: A biography* (Boston: Little and Brown, 1965), p. 256. Compare Janet Smith's *John Buchan and his World* (London: Thames and Hudson, 1979), and William Buchan's *John Buchan: A memoir* (London: Buchan and Enright, 1982), *passim*.

16 H. G. Wells's *Mr. Britling Sees It Through* (1916)

1. Ernest Benn, in *Happier Days: Recollections and reflections* (London: Ernest Benn, 1949), pp. 160–2.
2. Anthony West, *H. G. Wells: Aspects of a life* (London: Hutchinson, 1984), p. 54.
3. Additional identifications are cited by Sidney Dark, editor of *John o' London's Weekly*, in *An Outline of Wells: The superman in the street* (New York and London: G. P. Putnam, 1922), pp. 122–3:

    Colonel Rendezvous is the highly competent soldier who for some time commanded the Canadian army in France and is now known as Lord Byng. The journalist is Ralph Blumenfeld, the American born editor of the 'Daily Express', Lawrence Carmine is Cranmer Byng, the oriental scholar and poet.

    The station-master was also drawn from life, as were several of the assembled company at Matching's Easy. As Lovat Dickson writes in *H. G. Wells: His turbulent life and times* (London: Macmillan, 1969), p. 261, *Mr. Britling* – the shortened name of the American edition – was 'demonstrably the most autobiographical of all his novels'.
4. The French translation was titled *Mr. Britling commence à voir clair*, which mis-states Wells's meaning; Mr Britling did not see through the pretensions of the war or of life (he was too immersed in the everyday crises of carrying on); but David C. Smith adds, perceptively, that 'that is a good title for the inner meaning of the book, of course'. See *H. G. Wells: Desperately mortal* (New Haven and London: Yale University Press, 1986), p. 224. The history of the translations of this novel illustrates the hunger of several nations for fiction that would make sense of the monstrous carnage on several war fronts. The Germans read almost as many copies as the English, and Maxim Gorky sponsored a Russian translation as soon as he read it.
5. Published on 21 September 1916, p. 451; reprinted in Patrick Parrinder (ed.), *H. G. Wells: The critical heritage* (London and Boston: Routledge and Kegan Paul, 1972), pp. 236–8.
6. Richard Hauer Costa, *H. G. Wells: Revised edition* (Boston: Twayne, 1985), p. 91.
7. *ibid.*, p. 94.
8. J. R. Hammond, *An H. G. Wells Companion* (London: Macmillan, 1979), p. 182.
9. Dark, *op. cit.*, p. 133.
10. Smith, *op. cit.*, p. 485.

17 On the home front: Arnold Bennett's *The Pretty Lady* (1918)

1. Arnold Bennett, *Liberty!: A statement of the British case* (New York: George H. Doran, 1914), pp. 46–8.
2. Kinley E. Roby, *A Writer at War: Arnold Bennett 1914–1918* (Baton Rouge: Louisiana State University, 1972), *passim*.
3. *Letters to Arnold Bennett*, edited by James Hepburn, vol. III: *1916–1931* (London: Oxford University Press, 1970), p. 55. The letter is addressed to Hugh Walpole.
4. *ibid.*, p. 58.
5. See, for example, James G. Hepburn, *The Art of Arnold Bennett* (Bloomington, Ind.: Indiana University Press, 1963), p. 134, and Roby, *op. cit.*, pp. 248–9.
6. Margaret Drabble, *Arnold Bennett* (New York: Alfred A. Knopf, 1974), pp. 235–6. In addition to the works cited above, additional critiques and useful primary materials are printed in Dudley Barker's *Writer by Trade: A portrait of Arnold Bennett* (New York: Atheneum, 1966), pp. 191–2; *Arnold Bennett: The centenary of his birth, an exhibition in the Berg Collection* (New York: New York Public Library, 1968), pp. 44–7; Olga R. R. Broomfield's *Arnold Bennett* (Boston: Twayne, 1984), pp. 99–102; John Lucas's *Arnold Bennett: A study of his fiction* (London: Methuen, 1974), pp. 180–6; Reginald Pound's *Arnold Bennett: A biography* (London: William Heinemann, 1952), pp. 269–72, 297–8; Walter F. Wright's *Arnold Bennett: Romantic realist* (Lincoln: University of Nebraska Press, 1971), pp. 182–3; and Kenneth Young's *Arnold Bennett* (London: Longman for the British Council, 1975), pp. 31–3.

Bibliography

This list of readings, largely separate from the works cited in the notes that accompany each chapter, includes (a) books published during the Great War, mostly by writers of fiction, aimed at persuading the English public of the righteousness of the Allied cause; (b) biographies of novelists that supply information about their wartime activities; (c) histories of the war itself; and (d) specialised treatments of English life between 1914 and 1918. These are not mutually exclusive categories, of course. It has become increasingly clear, with the passage of time, that the First World War was the true watershed of the century, much more so than the Second World War proved to be. This bibliography amply documents the truth of the generalisation.

Aldridge, John W., *After the Lost Generation: A critical study of the writers of two wars*, New York: McGraw-Hill, 1951.
Angell, Norman, *The Great Illusion*, London: William Heinemann, 1908.
Begbie, Harold, *On the Side of the Angels*, London: Hodder and Stoughton, 1915.
Bennett, Arnold, *Over There: War scenes on the Western Front*, London: Methuen, 1915.
Bennett, Arnold, *Letters*, edited by James Hepburn, London: Oxford University Press, 1968.
Bergonzi, Bernard, *Heroes' Twilight: A study of the literature of the Great War*, London: Constable, 1965.
Buchan, John, *Nelson's History of the War*, 24 vols, London: Nelson, 1915–19.
Buchan, John, *The Battle of the Somme: First phase*, London: Nelson, 1916.
Buchan, John, *The Future of the War*, London: Hodder and Stoughton, 1916.
Buchan, John, *Memory Hold-the-Door*, London: Hodder and Stoughton, 1940.
Buitenhuis, Peter, *The Great War of Words: British, American, and Canadian propaganda and fiction, 1914–1933*, Vancouver: University of British Columbia Press, 1987.
Campbell, Phyllis, *Back of the Front*, London: Newnes, 1915.
Ceadel, Martin, *Pacifism in Britain, 1914–45*, Oxford: Oxford University Press, 1980.

Chesterton, G. K., *The Crimes of England*, London: Palmer and Hayward, 1915.
Chesterton, G. K., *Autobiography*, London: Hutchinson, 1936.
Clarke, Ian Frederick, *Voices Prophesying War, 1763–1984*, London: Oxford University Press, 1966.
Cruttwell, Charles R. M. F., *A History of the Great War*, Oxford: Oxford University Press, 1970.
Dangerfield, George, *The Strange Death of Liberal England, 1910–1914*, London: Nelson, 1936.
Daniell, David, *The Interpreter's House: a critical assessment of John Buchan*, London: Nelson, 1975.
Davis, Richard Harding, *With the French in France and Salonika*, New York: Scribner's, 1916.
Delany, Paul, *D. H. Lawrence's Nightmare: The writer and his circle in the years of the Great War*, New York: Basic Books, 1978.
Dickson, Lovat, *H. G. Wells: His turbulent life and times*, London: Macmillan, 1969.
Doyle, Arthur Conan, *The German War*, London: Hodder and Stoughton, 1914.
Doyle, Arthur Conan, *A Visit to Three Fronts*, London: Hodder and Stoughton, 1916.
Doyle, Arthur Conan, *Memories and Adventures*, Boston: Little, Brown, 1924.
Falls, Cyril, *War Books: A critical guide*, London: Peter Davies, 1930.
Ferro, Marc, *The Great War, 1914–1918*, 1969; translated, London: Routledge and Kegan Paul, 1973.
Fussell, Paul, *The Great War and Modern Memory*, Oxford: Oxford University Press, 1979.
Fussell, Paul, *Abroad: British literary travelling between the wars*, Oxford: Oxford University Press, 1980.
Galsworthy, John, *A Sheaf*, London: Heinemann, 1916.
Gosse, Edmund, *Inter Arma, Being Essays Written in Time of War*, London: Heinemann, 1916.
Grattan, C. Hartley, *Why We Fought*, New York: Vanguard, 1929.
Graves, Robert, *Goodbye to All That*, London: J. Cape, 1929.
Green, Roger Lancelyn, *A. E. W. Mason*, London: Parrish, 1952.
Greicus, Michael S., *Prose Writers of World War I* (Writers and Their Work, no. 231), London: Longmans, 1973.
Hart, Basil Liddell, *A History of the World War 1914–1918*, London: Faber and Faber, 1934.
Haste, Cate, *Keep the Home Fires Burning: Propaganda in the First World War*, London: Lane, 1977.
Hay, Ian, *Carrying On: After the first hundred thousand*, Edinburgh and London: William Blackwood, 1917.
Hoffman, Frederick J., *The Mortal No: Death and the modern imagination*, Princeton, N.J.: Princeton University Press, 1964.
Hoffman, Frederick J., *The Twenties: American writing in the postwar decade*, New York: Free Press, 1966.
Hueffer, Ford Madox, *When Blood Is Their Argument: An analysis of Prussian culture*, London: Hodder and Stoughton, 1915.

Bibliography

Hynes, Samuel, *The Edwardian Turn of Mind*, Princeton, N.J.: Princeton University Press, 1968.
Hynes, Samuel, *A War Imagined: The First World War and English culture*, London: The Bodley Head, 1990.
James, Robert Rhodes, *Gallipoli*, New York: Macmillan, 1965.
Kipling, Rudyard, *France at War*, London: Macmillan, 1915.
Kipling, Rudyard, *The Fringes of the Fleet*, New York: Doubleday and Page, 1915.
Kipling, Rudyard, *The War in the Mountains*, New York: Scribner's, 1917.
Klein, Holger Michael (ed.), *The First World War in Fiction: A collection of critical essays*, London: Macmillan, 1978.
Knightley, Philip, *The First Casualty: From the Crimea to Vietnam: The war correspondent as hero, propagandist and myth maker*, New York: Harcourt Brace Jovanovich, 1975.
Lee, Dwight (ed.), *The Outbreak of the First World War*, Boston: D. C. Heath, 1966.
Leed, Eric J., *No Man's Land: Combat and identity in World War I*, Cambridge: Cambridge University Press, 1979.
Machen, Arthur, *The Bowmen and Other Legends of the War*, London: Simpkin, Marshall, 1915.
Mackail, Denis, *The Story of J. M. B.: a biography*, London: Hodder and Stoughton, 1918.
Marder, Arthur, *From Dreadnought to Scapa Flow*, London: Oxford University Press, 1966.
Masefield, John, *Gallipoli*, London: Heinemann, 1916.
Masefield, John, *The Old Front Line*, New York: Macmillan, 1917.
Masterman, Lucy, *C. F. G. Masterman*, London: Cassells, 1939.
Middlebrook, Martin, *The First Day on the Somme, 1 July 1916*, London: Lane, 1971.
Mock, James R., and Cedric Larson, *Words that Won the War*, Princeton, N.J.: Princeton University Press, 1939.
Montague, C. E., *Disenchantment*, London: McGibbon and Kee, 1922.
Morgan, Charles, *Reflections in a Mirror*, 2nd series, London: Macmillan, 1946.
Murray, Gilbert, *Faith, War, and Policy*, London: Oxford University Press, 1918.
Panichas, George A. (ed.), *Promise of Greatness: The war of 1914–1918*, London: Cassell, 1968.
Parfitt, George, *Fiction of the First World War: A study*, London: Faber and Faber, 1988.
Parker, Sir Gilbert, *Is England Apathetic?*, London: Darling, 1915.
Parker, Sir Gilbert, *What Is the Matter with England?*, London: Darling, 1915.
Parker, Sir Gilbert, *The World in the Crucible: An account of the origins and conduct of the Great War*, London: Murray, 1915.
Read, James Morgan, *Atrocity Propaganda*, New Haven, Conn.: Yale University Press, 1941.
Read, Herbert, *A Coat of Many Colours*, London: Routledge and Kegan Paul, 1957.

Roby, Kinley E., *A Writer at War: Arnold Bennett 1914–1918*, Baton Rouge, La.: Louisiana State University Press, 1972.
Russell, Bertrand, *Justice in War-Time*, London: Allen and Unwin, 1916.
Russell, Bertrand, *Autobiography: 1914–1944*, London: Allen and Unwin, 1967.
Sanders, Michael L. and Philip M. Taylor, *British Propaganda during the First World War, 1914–1918*, London: Macmillan, 1982.
Smith, Adam, *John Buchan: A biography*, London: Hart-Davis, 1968.
Smith, Constance Babington, *John Masefield, A Life*, Oxford: Oxford University Press, 1978.
Smith, David, *H. G. Wells: Desperately mortal: A biography*, New Haven and London: Yale University Press, 1986.
Squires, James Duane, *British Propaganda at Home and in the United States from 1914 to 1917*, Cambridge, Mass.: Harvard University Press, 1935.
Swinnerton, Frank, *The Georgian Literary Scene 1910–35: A panorama*, London: Dent, 1950.
Taylor, A. J. P., *The First World War: An illustrated history*, London: H. Hamilton, 1964.
Taylor, A. J. P., *Beaverbrook: A biography*, New York: Simon and Schuster, 1972.
Trevelyan, Janet Penross, *The Life of Mrs. Humphry Ward*, New York: Dodd, Mead, 1923.
Tuchman, Barbara, *The Proud Tower*, London: Macmillan, 1966.
Turner, Leonard C. F., *Origins of the First World War*, London: Arnold, 1970.
Vansittart, Peter (ed.), *Voices from the Great War*, London: Cape, 1981.
Ward, Alfred C., *The Nineteen-Twenties: Literature and ideas in the post-war decade*, London: Methuen, 1930.
Ward, Mrs Humphry, *Towards the Goal*, London: Murray, 1917.
Weintraub, Stanley, *Journey to Heartbreak: The crucible years of Bernard Shaw, 1914–1918*, New York: Weybright and Talley, 1971.
Wells, H. G., *The War that Will End War*, London: F. and C. Palmer, 1914.
Wells, H. G., *In the Fourth Year: Anticipations of a world peace*, London: Chatto and Windus, 1918.
Williams, Raymond, *The English Novel from Dickens to Lawrence*, London: Chatto and Windus, 1970.
Willson, Beckles, *In the Ypres Salient: The story of a fortnight's Canadian fighting, June 2–16, 1916*, London: Simpkin, Marshall, Hamilton, Kent, [1916].
Wohl, Robert, *The Generation of 1914*, Cambridge, Mass.: Harvard University Press, 1979.

Index

A. E. (George Russell), 30
Aegean Intelligence Service, Syria, 94
Aisne offensive, 162
Aldington, Richard, 28
Allerton, Mark, *The Girl on the Green*, 43
Alston Rivers, 20
American Expeditionary Forces, 162
Amery, L. S., 186
Arnim, Elizabeth von, 192
Arts Theatre, London, 59
Askew, Alice and Claude, *The Telephone Girl*, 172–3
Athens, 94
Attorney General, 206
Authors
  biographical information about, 25–8
  education of, 25–6
  employment of, 26
Ayscough, John
  Jacqueline, 167
  The Tideway, 161

Baldwin, Stanley, 108, 109
Balzac, Honoré de, 52, 91
Banks, W. Dare
  James, 38
Barbusse, Henri
  Le Feu, 164
Barrett, Frank, 19
Barrie, Sir James, 109, 161, 204
Bartram, George
  The Last English, 40
Baskerville
  Beatrice, Love and Sacrifice, 170

BBC, 93
Beaverbrook, Lord, 204, 205, 206
Beerbohm, Max, 37–8, 93
Belloc, Hilaire, 31
Benn, Ernest, 191
Bennett, Arnold 15, 18, 19, 27, 30, 79, 81, 84, 96, 166, 202
  Books And Persons, 204
  From the Log of the 'Velsa', 204
  Liberty!, 203
  The Lion's Share, 204
  The Old Wives' Tale, 34
  Over There, 203
  The Pretty Lady, 175, 203–13, 165
  Self and Self-Management, 204
  The Title, 204–5
  War Journal 1914–1918, 203
Bennett, Marguerite, 204
Benson, A. C., 204
Benson, Edward W.
  Initiation, 38
Benson, E. F.
  Dodo the Second, 19, 21, 42–3
  Up and Down, 168
Benson, R. H., 204
Bentley, E. C.
  Trent's Last Case, 19
Beresford, George C., 139
  God's Counterpoint, 172
Besant, Walter, 15
Best-sellers
  1914, 34
  1914–1918, 22–3
Bethmann-Hollweg, Theobald von, 182

241

Index

Binns, Ottwell
   A Sin of Silence, 173
Birkenhead, Lord, 206
Birmingham, George, A.
   The Island Mystery, 166–7
   The Red Hand of Ulster, 21
Bismarck, Otto von, 183
Blackwell, Basil, 183
Blast, 146
Blue Guides, 12
Blunden, Edmund, 156
Bodley Head, 20
Boer War, 44
Book costs and prices, 13–16, 164–5
Bookman, The (London), 18
Bookseller, The, 33
Boothby, Guy, 18
Boot's, 12, 93
Bordeaux, Henry
   Footprints beneath the Snow, 21
Bowen, Marjorie
   The Burning Glass, 173
Braddon, M. E., 18
Bridges, Robert, 17, 204
Bridson, D. G., 149
Briggs, Asa, 126
British Expeditionary Force, 155–7
British Weekly, 18
Broadstairs, 177
Brontë, Charlotte, 4, 6
   Jane Eyre, 4
Broster, D. K.
   Sir Isumbras at the Ford, 172
Broughton, Rhoda
   Concerning a Vow, 39
Brown, Curtis, 15
Browning, Elizabeth B., 92
Bryce, Viscount James, 12
Buchan, John, 28, 109
   Francis and Riversdale, 183
   Greenmantle, 175, 184–90
   These for Remembrance, 183
   The Thirty-Nine Steps, 175, 177–81, 184, 189
Buchan, Susan, 184
Buckrose, J. E.
   The Silent Legion, 172
Burke, Thomas, 17–18
   Limehouse Nights, 17
   Night in Town, 17–18
Burroughs, Edgar, R., 83
   The Return of Tarzan, 172
Bütow, Kurt, 192

Cable, W. Boyd
   By Blow and Kiss, 21
Caine, Hall, 19, 49
Caldwell, Erskine
   Cambridge Bibliography of English Literature, 25
Tobacco Road, 17
Cambridge Modern History, 44
Cameron, Gilbert, 16, 96
   Old Mole, 41
   Round the Corner, 34
   The Stucco House, 170
Capes, Bernard
   Story of Fifine, 42
   Where England Sets Her Feet, 171
Carlyle, Thomas
   Sartor Resartus, 139
Cassell, 191, 204, 206
Cassell's Pocket Library, 138
Catholic Federation, 206
Catholic Trust Society, 206
Century Magazine, 204
Champion, Jessie
   The Foolishness of Lilian, 172
Chapman and Hall, 14
Chatto and Windus, 80, 147
Chekhov, Anton, 77
Chesterton, G. K., 8, 108–9, 204
Childers, Erskine, 179
Church of England, 26
Churchill, Winston, 12, 192
Clark, Barrett H., 53
Coles, Sophie
   Tabernacle, 39
Colins, Wilkie, 5, 15
Compton, Edward, 91
Compton, Fay, 91
Compton, Virginia, 91
Compton Comedy, 91
Conrad, Joseph, 18, 19, 30, 46, 132
   Chance, 34, 36–7, 117, 119
   '*Dollars*', 119
   '*Heart of Darkness*', 119
   Lord Jim, 119, 120, 189
   Nostromo, 120
   The Secret Agent, 120
   Under Western Eyes, 120
   Victory, 107, 113, *117–23*
Constantinople, 184
Contemporary, The, 137
Cooper, Lady Diana, 211
Corelli, Marie, 18, 19, 49
   Is All Well With England?, 49

Corelli (*continued*)
  With Eyes of the Sea, 49
Costa, Richard H., 195
Courtney, William L., 32
Crockett, R. S.
  Silver Sand, 40
Croker, Mrs.
  Lismoyle, 40
Cronin, A. J., 200
Crosland, T. W. H., 31
Crowley, Aleister, 160
Cruse, Amy
  After the Victorians, 19
Cunard, Nancy, 77

Daily News, 20, 82, 203
d'Anethan, Baroness Albert
  The Twin-Soul of O'Take San, 20
Dark, Sidney, 201
de Grey, Nigel, 80
de la Mare, Walter, 109
de Morgan, William
  When Ghost Meets Ghost, 21, 43
Dearmer, Mabel, 12
Deban, Richard
  That Which Hath Wings, 168
Delafield, E. M.
  The Pelicans, 169
Dell, Ethel M., 83
Dent, J. M., 79
Dickens, Charles, 7, 50
Dobson, Austin, 31
Dooley, D. J., 102
Doran, George, 206
Douglas, Elsa F., 73
Douglas, Lloyd C., 200
Douglas, Lord Alfred, 31
Douglas, Norman, 27
  Alone, 68
  Experiments, 72
  Fountains in the Sand, 72
  London Street Games, 72
  Old Calabria, 72
  'On the Darwinian hypothesis of sexual selection,' 72
  South Wind, 17, 65–77
  The Tribulations of a Patriot, 72, 73
Doyle, Sir Arthur C., 15, 26, 178–9
  The British Campaign in France and Flanders, 181, 182
Drabble, Margaret, 211
Du Maurier, George, 4
  Peter Ibbetson, 5

Trilby, 5–6
Dujardin, Edouard, 52
  La Source du fleuve chrétien, 57
Dunleavy, Janet E., 50, 53
Dunsterville, Lionel C., 139

Easton Glebe, Essex, 191, 192
Eglinton, John, 30, 50, 52, 57, 61
Egoist, The, 147, 148
Egoist Ltd., The, 147
Eliot, George, 4, 6, 8
  Adam Bede, 6
  Daniel Deronda, 4, 6
  Felix Holt, 6
  The Mill on the Floss, 6, 50
  Romola, 4
  Scenes of Clerical Life, 6
  Silas Marner, 6
Eliot, T. S., 30, 31
Encyclopaedia Britannica, 15, 95
English Review, 57, 72, 117, 125
Ervine, St John, 53
Essays and Studies by Members of the English Association, 37
Evans, Caradoc, *My People*, 17
Eveleigh Nash, 16
Everyman's Library, 19, 79

Faguet, Emile, 35
Fairfield, Letitia, 192
Farrell, Sergeant, 158
Farrow, Anthony, 53
'Femina Vie Heureuse' Committee, 109
Ferdinand, Archduke, 117
Fergusson, John, 31
Feuchtwanger, Lion
  Jew Süss, 17
Figgis, Darrell
  Jacob Elthorne, 42
Findlay Muirhead, 12
Fitzgerald, F. Scott
  This Side of Paradise, 93
FitzGibbon, Constantine, 77
Flanders, Battle of, 49
Flatau, Dorota
  Yellow English, 160, 168
Flaubert, Gustave, 119
Flecker, James E., 17
Fleming, Guy
  Over the Hills and Far Away, 172
Fletcher, J. S.
  The Amaranth Club, 167
  Heronshawe Main, 173

Ford, Stella, 129
Forster, E. M., 83
  Aspects of the Novel, 39
Forster Act of 1870, 25
Foundations, 25
France, Anatole, 35, 201
Frankau, Gilbert, 83
Frost, Robert, 31

Gallipoli, 93
Galsworthy, John, 19, 28, 84, 202
Garvice, Sir Charles
  The Woman's Way, 21, 38
G. Bell and Sons, Ltd., 21
George, Lloyd, 156, 192
George, W. L.
  A Novelist on Novels, 161
George Allen and Unwin Ltd., 17
Gibbs, George
  Madcap, 40
Gibbs, Philip, 83
Gissing, George, 17, 38, 80
Gooch, George P., 32
Gorell, Lord, 79
Gosse, Edmund, 33
Graves, Robert, 156
Gray, Thomas, 33
Greene, Graham, 77
Gregory, Lady, 30
Grey, Sir George, 22
Gross, John
  The Rise and Fall of the Man of Letters, 18
Gull, C. Ranger
  When Satan Ruled, 20

Haggard, H. Rider, 20, 178–9
  Love Eternal, 171
Haig, General Sir Douglas, 156, 181
Haldane, Lord, 182
Hannay, Canon
  The Lost Tribes, 40
Hanshew, Thomas W. and Mary E.
  The Riddle of the Purple Emperor, 173
Hardy, Thomas, 21, 30, 31, 109, 123, 161, 204
  A Changed Man, 21
  The Dynasts, 187
  The Return of the Native, 110
  Under the Greenwood Tree, 110
Harris, Frank
  Great Days, 20
Harrison, Herbert
  A Lad of Kent, 41

Harte, Bret, 15
Hayward, Rachel
  Letters from Lá-Bas, 22
Hearn, Lafcadio, 4–8
Heinemann, 21, 80
Henley, William E., 8
  'In Hospital,' 8
Herbert, Alice
  Garden Oats, 38
Herrick, Robert, 79
Highways and Byways Series, 12
Hills, Marion, *Sunrise Valley*, 41
History, books about, 22
Hitler, Adolf, 148
Hodder and Stoughton, 21, 184
Hofmannsthal, Hugo von, 127
Hogarth Press, 202
Holland, Clive
  A Madonna of the Poor, 22
Holloway, Mark, 73
Hope [Hawkins], Anthony, 83, 204
  Captain Dieppe, 174
House of Commons, 117
Housman, A. E., 12, 109
  A Shropshire Lad, 12, 17
Housman, Laurence
  The Royal Runaway, 42
Hueffer, Ford M., 28, 30, 37, 93
  The Good Soldier, 46, 107, 125–33
  Romance, 132
Hughes, Thomas
  Tom Brown's School Days, 137
Hulme, T. E. H., 31
Hume, Fergus, 19
Humphreys, Mrs
  Jill-All-Alone, 38
Hungerford, Mrs M. W., 18
Hunt, Violet, and Ford Madox Hueffer
  Zeppelin Nights, 50
Hutchinson, A. S. M., 83
Huxley, Leonard, 31
Huxley, T. H., 27
Hyatt, Stanley P.
  The Way of the Cardines, 19
Hyde, Douglas, 30

Illustrated London News, 203
Inge, Charles
  Square Pegs, 38
International Publishing Bureau, 15
Irish Literary Renaissance, 52
Ironside, Edmund, 186
Irving, Henry, 91

Index

James, Henry, 16, 18, 34, 37, 44, 46, 90, 95–6, 119, 128, 166
Jeffares, A. Norman, 50
Jerusalem, 58
Joffre, Marshal, 156
Johnson, Samuel, 32
Johnston, John H., 159
Joseph, Michael
  The Adventure of Publishing, 162
Joyce, James
  Dubliners, 46
  A Portrait of the Artist as a Young Man, 46, 147
  Ulysses, 46, 82

Kafka, Franz
  The Castle, 17
Kaye-Smith, Sheila
  Three against the World, 22
Keeling, Ben, 201
Kembles, 91
Kenner, Hugh, 151
Kennington Park, 81
Kingsley, Charles
  Alton Locke, 4
  Hereward the Wake, 4
  Hypatia, 4
  Yeast, 4
Kipling, Carrie, 158
Kipling, John, 158
Kipling, Rudyard, 4, 5, 12, 15, 179
  The Light That Failed, 5
  The Naulahka, 5
  'The Ship that Found Herself,' 188–9
  Stalky & Co., 137–40, 141
  war poems, 157–9
Kitchener, Lord, 155
Knopf, Alfred A., 147

Lane, John, 17, 20, 125, 215
Lang, Andrew, 33
Laurie, Werner, 19
Lawrence, D. H., 17, 30, 31, 35, 83, 93, 98, 102
  The Rainbow, 46
  Women in Love, 46
Le Gallienne, Richard
  Pieces of Eight, 172
Le Queux, William, 18
  Her Royal Highness, 21
  The Yellow Ribbon, 167
Leacock, Stephen
  Behind the Beyond, 20

Leavis, Mrs F. R.
  Fiction and the Reading Public, 83
Lemaître, Jules, 35
Lewis, Wyndham, 30, 31
  Men Without Art, 150
  Rude Assignment, 147, 151
  Satire and Fiction, 150
  Tarr, 107, 147–51
  The Wild Body, 150
Libraries, public, 14
Lindeman, Ralph D., 75
Linklater, Andro, 96
Lloyd's Weekly Newspaper, 203
Locke, William J.
  The Fortunate Youth, 39
  The Rough Road, 171
London Star, 119
Loos, Battle of, 181
Love of an Unknown Soldier, The, 175, 215–22
Lowndes, Mrs Belloc
  Out of the War, 168
Lyall, David
  An English Rose, 173–4
Lynd, Robert, 109
Lyon, A. Neil
  Simple Simon, 20

Macaulay, Rose
  The Making of a Bigot, 37
Machen, Arthur, 28
Machine Gun Corps, 136
MacDougall, J.
  Gillespie, 42
Mackail, J. W., 204
Mackellar, Dorothea, and Ruth Bedford
  Two's Company, 20
Mackenzie, Compton, 15, 17, 28
  Carnival, 34, 93
  The Early Life and Adventure, of Sylvia Scarlett, 91–103
  Extraordinary Women, 99
  The Four Winds of Love, 99
  Guy and Pauline, 93, 95
  Octave Five, 94
  The Passionate Elopement, 16, 92–3
  Sinister Street, 93, 94, 95, 96, 98
  Sylvia and Arthur, 94
  Sylvia and Michael, 94–5, 98, 103
  Sylvia and Philip, 94
  Thin Ice, 99
  Vestal Fire, 99

Index

Macmahon, Ella
   The Job, 39
Macmillan, 12, 16, 21
Magic Tale of Harvanger and Jolande, 38
Mallarmé, Stéphane, 52
Mann, Thomas
   Buddenbrooks, 17
   Stories of Three Decades, 17
Marne, Second Battle of the, 162
Marryat, Florence, 18
Marsden, Dora, 30
Masefield, John, 156, 204
Masterman, Charles, 107, 204
Maugham, William, 28
   Of Human Bondage, 159–60
Maupassant, Guy de, 5, 126
Maurois, André, 93
Maxse, Leopold J., 31
Maxwell, W. B.
   The Mirror and the Lamp, 169
Meixner, John A., 131
Meredith, George, 18, 108
Merrick, Leonard
   Conrad in Quest of his Youth, 161
   While Paris Laughed, 173
Merriman, Henry S., 83
Methley, Violet
   The Loadstone, 40
Methuen, 80, 138
Metropolitan Magazine, 204
Meynell, Viola
   Modern Lovers, 38
Miss Pim's Camouflage, 173
Modern Library, 67
Monro, Harold, 31
Moore, George, 205–6
   Aphrodite in Aulis, 50
   The Apostle, 57, 59
   Avowals, 51
   The Brook Kerith, 17, 49–63
   Confessions of a Young Man, 52
   Hail and Farewell, 58
   Héloise and Abelard, 50
   John, Christ, and Peter, 57
   The Lake, 50, 51
   Mike Fletcher, 56, 57
   The Passing of the Essenes, 59
   The Untilled Field, 50
Moore, George
   Uniform Edition, 59
Moore, T. Sturge, 151
Mordaunt, Elinor
   The Pendulum, 169

Morgan, Charles, 12, 16, 26
Morning Post, 20, 161
Moult, Thomas, 108
Mudie's, 12, 15
Muir, John, 30
Muir, Ward
   Observations of an Orderly, 160
Munsey's Magazine, 119
Murray, Gilbert, 204
Murray, John, 31
Murry, John M., 30–1
Musician, The, 57

Napoleon, 187
Napoleon III, 187
Nation, 137
Nazism, 149
Nelson History of the War, 181–4
Nelson's (publisher), 181
Nelson, Tommy, 183
Net Book Agreement, 15
New Age, 18, 119, 204
New Book Agreement, 15
Newbolt, Henry, 30, 204
New Statesman, 96, 203
Newton, W. Douglas
   The War Cache, 168
Nicoll, Robertson, 18
Nivelle, General, 162
Noël, Jean C., 53
Non-fiction war books, 157, 160

Ochiai, Teisaburo, 6
O'Donovan, Gerald
   Waiting, 21
Ohmann, Carol, 133
Oliver, F. S., 12
Onions, Oliver
   The New Moon, 172
Opie, Iona and Peter, 73
Oppenheim, E. Phillips, 19
   The Double Traitor, 167
Orage, A. R., 31
Orczy, Baroness
   Unto Caesar, 21
Ouida, 18
Oxenham, John
   Maid of the Mist, 22
Oxford, 93

Pall Mall, 119
Pater, Walter, 51–2
   Marius the Epicurean, 52

Index

Paternoster Row, 12
Pax Britannica, 126
Pemberton, Max
   The Man of Silver Mount, 173
Percival, Dorothy
   Footsteps, 174
periodicals, English, as reviewing media, 1900–1918, 30–2
Pinker, J. B., 15, 204
Pontesbury, Nr Shropshire, 108
Pound, Ezra, 31, 93, 147
Powys, T. F., 83
Price, Cormell, 138
Priest, Christopher, 202
Prussian Diet, 183
Public Schools, 25
Publishers' Association, 12
Publishers Circle, 163

Quarterlies, Victorian, 29
Quiller-Couch, Sir Arthur
   Studies in Literature, 161
Quinn, John, 150

Rannoch (yacht), 184
Rawson, Mrs Maud S.
   The Priceless Thing, 41
Reade, Charles, 5
Remarque, Erich M.
   All Quiet on the Western Front, 17, 164, 189
Rhodes, Kathlyn
   The Making of a Soul, 42
Richards, Grant, 12, 17, 136, 137, 161
Richardson, Dorothy M., 27
Richardson, H. M., 205
Rickard, Mrs Victor,
   The Fire of Green Boughs, 173
Rita (Mrs Desmond Humphreys), 18
Roberts, Helen
   A Free Hand, 43
Roberts, Morley
   Time and Thomas Waring, 42
Robertson, Leo, 102
Rodke, John, 126
Rohmer, Sox
   The Mystery of Dr. Fu-Manchu, 162
Royal Literary Fund, 109
Royal Marines, 93
Russian novelists, 36

Sabatini, Rafael, 79

St Petersburg, 72
Sainte-Beuve, Charles A., 35
Saintsbury, George, 6, 33, 161
Samuel, Book of, 53–4
Sandhurst, 135
Sapori, Francesco, *La Trincea*, 166
Sassoon, Siegfried, 156
Saturday Evening Post, 203
Savile Club, 139
Scapa Flow, 181
Schorer, Mark, 130
Scott, C. A. Dawson
   Wastralls, 168
Scott, Sir Walter, 108, 187
Scottish Law of Inheritance, 81–2
Seaman, Sir Owen, 204
Seccombe, Thomas, 136
Secker, Martin, 16, 17, 79, 81, 82, 93, 94
Sedgwick, Mrs
   Karen, 174
Seinfelt, Frederick W., 59
Shaw, George B., 51, 192, 202
Sherborne, 135, 138
Shropshire, 108, 109
Siddons, 91
Sidgwick, Ethel
   Jamesie, 167
Sinclair, May, 27
Sleath, Frederick
   Sniper Jackson, 169
Smith, Elder and Co., 21
Smith, W. H., 12, 15, 93, 206
Somme, Battle of the, 156–7, 162
South, Henry E.
   The Destroyers, 160
Southey, Rosamond
   The Last Bout, 172
Spectator, 21, 137
Spender, J. A., 32
Sphere, 18
'Spin,' *Short Flights with the Cloud Cavalry*, 160
Spottiswoode, Sybil
   The Test, 172
Stacpoole, Mrs de Vere
   London, 1913, 39
Stanley Paul, 20
Stationery Office, His Majesty's, 12
Stendhal, Marie Henri Beyle, 91
Stephen, Sir Leslie, 31
Stern, J. B.
   A Marrying Man, 172

Sterne, Lawrence
  A Sentimental Journey through France and Italy, 161
Stevenson, Robert Louis, 4, 5, 7–8, 17, 80, 83, 119
Strand Magazine, 204
Sunday Chronicle, 205
Swinnerton, George, 17, 18, 27
  The Elder Sister, 83
  In the Night, 79
  Night-piece, 79
  Nocturne, 79–90, 204
  On the Staircase, 38
  Shops and Houses, 174
  Young Felix, 83
  The Young Idea, 81
Synge, John M., 30

Tanabé, Ryuji, 36
Tauchnitz, B., 119
Taunton Commission, 25
Temple Classics, 79
Territorial Force, 155
Thackeray, William, 7
Thickness-Woodington, F.
  Swayneford, 168
Thomas, David A. and Joyce, 93
Thorpe Division Emergency Committee, 204
Tighe, Harry
  The Sheep Path, 172
Times, The, 28, 73, 181
Times Book Club, 15
Times Book War, 15
Times Literary Supplement, 30, 32, 34–45, 137, 161, *165–75*, 194, 205
Titanic, 117–19, 123
Tomlinson, Henry M., 27, 74
Tolstoy, Leo, 35, 50, 51
Traill, H. D.
  The New Fiction, 45–6
Tressall, Robert
  The Ragged-Trousered Philanthropists, 42
Trevelyan, G. M., 204
Trollope, Anthony, 5, 7
Turner, G. Frederic
  The Red Virgin, 40

United Services College, Westward Ho!, Devon, 137–8
Unwin, Sir Stanley, 17
  The Truth about a Publisher, 17
  The Truth about Publishing, 17

Vachell, H. A.
  Quinneys', 40
Velsa (yacht), 81, 204
Victoria, Queen, 76
von Hutten, Baroness
  The Bag of Saffron, 172
von Tirpitz, Admiral, 182
Vorticism, 149

Wadsley, Olive
  Nevertheless, 172
Wagner, Richard, 51, 59
  Jesus of Nazareth, 57
  Tristan, 51
Walpole, Hugh, 16, 28, 96, 205–6
  The Duchess of Wrexe, 34
  The Green Mirror, 161–2
Warburg, Fredric, 17
Ward, Mrs Humphry, 19, 49
  Robert Elsmere, 9
Warner, Philip L., 80
Warwick, Countess of, 192
Watt, Alexander P., 15
Waugh, Alec
  The Early Years of Alec Waugh, 135
  The Loom of Youth, 83, 107, 135–46
Waugh, Arthur, 14, 135, 136, 163–4
Waugh, Evelyn, 135
Wayfarers' Library, 20
Weaver, Harriet, S., 30
Webb, Beatrice and Sidney, 202
Webb, Henry B. L., 108
Webb, Mary, 27
  Armour Wherein He Trusted, 109
  The Golden Arrow, *107–15*
  Gone to Earth, 109
  The House in Dormer Forest, 109
  Precious Bane, 108
  Seven for a Secret, 109
Webster, Nesta H.
  The Sheep Track, 43
Wells, H. G., 15, 16, 27, 35, 49, 82, 84, 96, 204
  Mr. Britling Sees It Through, 170, 191–202, 205
  The Outline of History, 137–8, 192
  The War That Will End War, 157
  The Wife of Sir Isaac Harman, 19
  The World Set Free, 40
West, Anthony, 191–2
West, Rebecca, 109, 192, 205–6
  The Return of the Soldier, 172
Western Front, 155–6

Westminster Bridge, 81
Westminster Police Court, 73
Weston-Super-Mare, 108
Weyman, Stanley, 83
Wharton, Edith, 12, 35, 44
Whittaker, T. W., 57
Whitten, Wilfred, 30
Wilhelm II, Kaiser, 182, 192
Wilson, Edmund, 103
Wister, Owen, 12
Wodehouse, P. G.
  Piccadilly Jim, 173
Women's Movement, 117
Wood, Mrs Henry, 18
Woolf, Virginia, 32–3, 83
Worboise, Emma J., 18
World's Classics, 17

Wortley, Jack, 183
Wylie, I. A. R.
  Towards Morning, 173

Yeats, William B., 30, 51, 52, 56
Yellow Book, 17
Young, Francis, B., 17
  The Crescent Moon, 166
  The Laws of Chance, 160
Ypres, 181

Zola, Émile
  La Débacle, 187
Zweig, Arnold
  Education Before Verdun, 17
  The Case of Sergeant Grischa, 17